Advertising by Design

Advertising by Design

GENERATING AND DESIGNING CREATIVE IDEAS ACROSS MEDIA

Second edition

ROBIN LANDA

WILEY

John Wiley & Sons, Inc.

Published by John Wiley & Sons, Inc., Hoboken, New Jersey

Published simultaneously in Canada

Library of Congress Cataloging-in-Publication Data:
Landa, Robin.
  Advertising by design / Robin Landa. -- 2nd ed.
      p. cm.
  ISBN 978-0-470-36268-6 (pbk. : acid-free paper); ISBN 978-0-470-91301-7 (ebk); ISBN 978-0-470-91300-0 (ebk); ISBN 978-0-470-91299-7 (ebk)
  1. Advertising. 2. Creative ability in business. I. Title.
  HF5823.L23 2010
  659.1--dc22
                          2010004726

Printed in the United States of America

10 9 8 7 6 5 4

*TO MY PRECIOUS CREATIVITY DIVA, MY DAUGHTER,
HAYLEY, AND TO MY STUDENTS AND FORMER STUDENTS.*

*"LET US BE GRATEFUL TO PEOPLE WHO MAKE US HAPPY;
THEY ARE THE CHARMING GARDENERS WHO MAKE OUR
SOULS BLOSSOM."—MARCEL PROUST*

CONTENTS

PREFACE

NEW TO THIS EDITION

The second edition of *Advertising by Design* has been greatly expanded, reflecting the suggestions of professors from esteemed institutions and ad agency creative directors. It remains the most comprehensive text on creative concept generation and designing for advertising, and it includes a number of features that make it an effective tool for instructors, students, or any reader interested in the creative side of advertising. In *Advertising by Design*, the approach to generating and designing creative integrated-media advertising for brands, organizations, and causes encompasses brand building through engagement, community building, added value, and entertainment.

This new edition of *Advertising by Design*

> *Teaches the fundamental conceptual development, design, and copywriting abilities that students need to start creating ads*

> *Guides students to think clearly and conceptually*

> *Stimulates creative thinking through brainstorming tools and exercises*

> *Integrates conceptualization, visualization, and composition*

> *Includes substantive content on visualizing and composing ideas, including information on designing with typography*

> *Utilizes illustrations to inspire critical and creative thinking*

> *Incorporates diagrams to help explain design thinking*

It offers as well the following essentials and enhancements:

> *A thorough guide to conceptualizing and designing for print, interactive applications, branded utilities, television, social media, branded content and entertainment, branded alliances, outdoor and digital out-of-home media, mobile media, and motion, ambient, and unconventional media*

> *Tools to stimulate creative thinking, tools for brainstorming, and creativity exercises to prompt and support conceptualization*

> *Methods for idea generation*

> *An extensive chapter on visualization, including approaches, methods, and media for visualization of design ideas and understanding images*

> *A comprehensive chapter on composition—covering a wide range of theories and points of view as well as media (composing for print, screen, and motion)*

> *In-depth information covering the five steps of the design process*

> *Integrated media ad campaigns*

> *Storytelling in advertising*

> *Creative approaches—the most comprehensive examination of model frameworks found in any one volume*

> *New interviews*

> *Showcases*

> *Case studies*

> *A glossary*

> *Numerous exercises*

> *New illustrations and examples*

FEATURES

> *Clear explanation of designing for major advertising applications*

> *Comprehensive examination of visualization and composition theories and methodologies*

> *Explanation of media*

> *Designing with type*

> *Writing headlines and taglines*

> *Creative approaches*

> *Historical framework that places discussed theories into a broader context*

> *Bulleted lists and sidebars to assist comprehension*

> *Exercises to jump-start critical and creative thinking as well as visualization*

> *State-of-the-profession overview of advertising*

> *Essays by designers, creative directors, and writers*

> *Showcases*

> *Timeless examples and illustrations*

> *Exercises, projects (for classroom or personal use and portfolio building), and other online supplements*

From the Field

The most highly regarded design professionals today provide insights and examples in stimulating features, *for example:*

> **Case Studies:** *"Youth Reckless Driving Prevention" (Chapter 1); "Behind the Scenes: MoMA | Tim Burton Exhibition" (Chapter 2); "Digital, 'Swaggerize Me'" (Chapter 13); and "Storyboard, Sony Ericsson 'Big Screen'" for mobile devices (Chapter 14)*

> **Interviews:** *Rosie Arnold, deputy executive creative director, BBH (Chapter 3); and Kevin Roberts, CEO Worldwide of Saatchi & Saatchi (Chapter 4)*

> **Showcase:** *Posters by Robynne Raye of Modern Dog Design Co. (Chapter 8)*

Resources for Instructors

Online instructor materials include:

> *11-week syllabi*

> *15-week syllabi*

> *Additional exercises and projects*

> *Additional interviews and creative showcases*

> *Powerpoints*

> *Grading rubric*

> *Web site links*

> *Test questions for every chapter*

ORGANIZATION

A historical perspective is provided online; an instructor can start there or use the history as a reference. *Part I* provides a substantial foundation of essential information, including an introduction examining the advertising profession; the steps in the design process and the creative brief; and comprehensive coverage of thinking creatively. *Part II* focuses on formulating advertising ideas, writing, and designing: understanding the brand idea; idea development; copywriting; creative approaches; typography and visualization; and composition; and storytelling.

Part III is an in-depth examination of designing for print; motion, broadcast, and broadband; integrated campaigns; storytelling; Web sites and branded utilities; mobile devices; social media; and unconventional marketing. The chapters are easily used in any order that is appropriate for the reader or that best suits the educator. Each chapter provides substantial background information about how the advertising application is used and how to design for that medium. Also included are sidebars with suggestions, tips, and important design considerations, as well as informative features such as essays, case studies, and showcases of outstanding creative professionals. Some chapters are much longer than others because of the role they play in most curricula.

This new edition covers a vast amount of information, therefore:

> *Instructors have plenty of content from which to choose;*

> *This book can be used in several courses, carrying over from semester to semester;*

> *This book is a reference and resource.*

At the end of the book, there is a glossary to help with terminology, a selected bibliography to encourage further reading, and an index.

Additional material and resources (including many exercises and projects) are available online.

The Illustrations and Quotations

Ads are created daily, and there are many places to see contemporary and historical advertising solutions—from periodicals to blogs to online galleries. In selecting illustrations for this book, I tried to choose classic examples of creative conceptual thinking and thoughtful design that would endure. Also, I chose the illustrations to represent different approaches, schools of thought, and design sensibilities.

Learning about advertising design comes from deconstructing effective examples. When you examine solutions, whether in this text or aired works, ask yourself *how* and *why* the pros did what they did. As with any creative visual communication endeavor, there are innumerable possible ideas and executions. We measure efficacy in terms of problem solving, communicating, being creative within the constraints of the communication problem, design, how the solution affects the audience in its call to action, and perhaps even how it enters popular culture.

The quotations from well-respected creative professionals are taken from a variety of sources, including: personal e-mails, interviews, conversations, books, agency Web sites, and other online sources. Some of the quotations, for example, those from Bill Bernbach, have found their way into advertising culture.

THE COVER

This edition benefited from the creative vision of many talented design students who entered our cover competition, the Wiley Student Cover Design Challenge (see http://www.facebook.com/landacontest). The winning cover submitted by design student Angel Guzman of the University of Texas at El Paso was selected from over one hundred entries. The panel of judges included professionals from Wiley's marketing, editorial, and creative services, as well as me. We also brought on board a panel of external judges:

Mark Chamberlain, vice president and associate creative director, Mullen

Drew Neisser, chief executive officer, Renegade

Robynne Raye, cofounder, principal, and designer, Modern Dog Design Co.

First Prize: Use of cover plus a $500 American Express Gift Certificate — Angel Guzman

Second Prize: $200 American Express Gift Certificate — Kevin Fenton

Third Prize: $100 American Express Gift Certificate — Shani Tucker

Congratulations to the prizewinners!

ABOUT THE AUTHOR

Robin Landa holds the title of distinguished professor in the Robert Busch School of Design at Kean University in New Jersey. She is among the teachers that the Carnegie F oundation for the Advancement of Teaching calls the "great teachers of our time." Most recently, Landa was a finalist in the *Wall Street Journal*'s Creative Leaders competition.

Robin has won many awards for design, writing, teaching, and creative leadership, including the New Jersey Authors Award, the Presidential Excellence Award in Scholarship from Kean University, the Rowan University Award for Contribution to Design Education, and honors from the National Society of Arts and Letters, the National League of Pen Women, *Creativity*, *Graphic Design USA*, and the Art Directors Club of New Jersey.

Landa is the author of twelve published books about graphic design, branding, advertising, and creativity, including *Graphic Design Solutions* (2010) and *Designing Brand Experiences* (2007). Her books have been translated into Chinese and Spanish.

She and her colleague Professor Rose Gonnella coauthored *Visual Workout Creativity Workbook* (2004). Gonella and award winning designer Steven Brower coauthored *2D: Visual Basics for Designers* (2008). Known for her expertise in creativity,

Landa penned *Thinking Creatively* (1998), and coauthored *Creative Jolt* and *Creative Jolt Inspirations* (2000) with Rose Gonnella and Denise M. Anderson. Robin's article on ethics in design, "No Exit for Designers," was featured in *Print* magazine's European Design Annual/Cold Eye column; other articles have been featured in *HOW* magazine, *Step Inside Design*, *Critique*, and *Icograda*. Robin's Amazon Shorts—"Advertising: 11 Insights from Creative Directors" and "Branding: 10 Truths Behind Successful Brands"—both reached the number-one spot on the Shorts best-seller list.

Robin has lectured at the *HOW* International Design conferences, the Graphic Artists Guild conference, the Thinking Creatively conference, the One Club Education Summit, and at events hosted by the College Art Association and The Art Directors Club of New Jersey. She has been interviewed on radio, television, in print, and on the World Wide Web on the subjects of design, creativity, and art.

In addition, working with Mike Sickinger at Lava Dome Creative (www.lavadomecreative.com), Robin is a brand strategist, designer, copywriter, and storyteller. Robin is, as well, the creative director of her own firm, robinlanda.com. She has worked closely with marketing executives and their companies and organizations to develop brand strategy, enhance corporate creativity through seminars, and develop brand stories. With the keen ability to connect the seemingly unconnected, Robin uses her research and writing to support her teaching and professional practice.

ACKNOWLEDGMENTS

According to Albert Einstein, "It is the supreme art of the teacher to awaken joy in creative expression and knowledge." All the brilliantly creative professionals whose works inhabit this second edition are now "teachers" who will awaken some reader's delight in ideas and designing. Humbly, I thank all the organizations that granted permission and the creative professionals and their noble clients who so generously granted permission to include their work.

For the new features, essays, and interviews, I thank: Rosie Arnold, BBH; Richard Binhammer, Dell; John Butler, Butler, Shine, Stern & Partners; Tom Clark, ICCTrio; Mark D'Arcy, Time Warner Inc.; Steven Fechtor, Fechtor Advertising; Mark Fitzloff, Wieden + Kennedy; Dale Herigstad, Schematic; Arto Joensuu, Nokia; Michael "Mac" McLaurin, Della Femina, Rothschild, Jeary & Partners; Drew Neisser, Renegade; Robynne Raye, Modern Dog Design Co.; Alan Robbins; Janet Estabrook Rogers, professor of visual and performing arts at Kean University; Kevin Roberts, Saatchi & Saatchi; Bill Schwab, the Gate worldwide; David Schwarz, HUSH; and Mike Lebowitz, Big Spaceship.

I am indebted to many people whose help was invaluable, including Ellyn Fisher of the Ad Council, who has always supported my book projects. Thanks also to:

Anjali Bhargava, HUSH; Beth M. Cleveland, Elm Publicity Inc.; Ashley Futak, Brickfish; Chelsea Greene, and Jo Wilby, Schematic; Mish Fletcher, Ogilvy; Shannon Heuer, Big Spaceship; Bianca Hogan, Michelin North America; Anjana Kacker, Butler, Shine, Stern & Partners; Carrie Murray, BBH London; Chemin Steele, Wieden + Kennedy; Kouhei Steele, DDB London; Sarah Tan, Saatchi & Saatchi; and Zach Tan, the Ad Council.

My sincere thanks to my esteemed colleagues in the Robert Busch School of Design at Kean University, and to Dr. Dawood Farahi, president of Kean University; Dr. Mark Lender, provost; Professor Holly Logue, dean of the College of Visual and Performing Arts; and Robert Busch, president and CEO, All-State Legal.

At John Wiley & Sons, I extend my great thanks to the wise and wonderful Margaret Cummins, senior editor, for her unwavering support and excellent insights; to marketing treasure Valerie Hartman for her great support of the Wiley Cover Competition; and to the outstanding Wiley team: Penny Makras, Amanda Miller, Kerstin Nasdeo, Lauren Poplawski, David Riedy, David Sassian, and Leslie Saxman.

I am thankful for the thoughtful comments from reviewers.

Dawn Keene, Atlanta Technical College

Art Novak, Savannah College of Art and Design

Brenda Innocenti, Kutztown University

David Koeth, Bakersfield College

Alan Rado, Columbia College Chicago

Norm Grey, Creative Circus

Edward LeShock, Radford University

Deborah Morrison, University of Oregon

Larry Stultz, Art Institute of Atlanta

Forever, I extend my sincere gratitude to my students, my former students, and my family and friends, especially Denise M. Anderson, Dr. Michael Balogh, Jill Bellinson, the Benten/Itkin family, Paula Bosco, Steven Brower, Alice Drueding, Donald Fishbein, Rose Gonnella, Andrea Harris, Frank Holahan, Mike Sickinger, and Karen Sonet Rosenthal. And finally, my loving thanks to my dear husband and tango partner, Dr. Harry Gruenspan, and our beautiful daughter, Hayley, who is the most understanding and perceptive person I know.

PART 01

THE ESSENTIALS
PURPOSE, PROCESS, AND THINKING CREATIVELY

WHAT IS ADVERTISING?

THE PURPOSE OF ADVERTISING

Have you ever stopped a friend from driving drunk?

Perhaps you were influenced by the "Friends Don't Let Friends Drive Drunk" advertising campaign. Have you ever "spoken up" to stop someone from texting while driving because you recalled a public service ad (see p. 4)? These two highly effective Ad Council campaigns prove that advertising matters.

From engaging in public service to choosing goods and services, advertising calls people to action.

Advertising is used in a free-market system to promote one brand or group over another. Most competing brands are of equal quality—that is, they are parity products or services. For example, most shampoos in the same price category (perhaps even across price categories) use similar ingredients and provide equivalent results. That said, effective advertising could persuade you that a particular brand is better or more appealing than the competition. An ad campaign for a shampoo might convince you that its use would leave your hair shinier or fuller, curlier or straighter, less frizzy, or more fragrant than any other that might appeal to you. For such advertising to affect you, it has to seem relevant to you, and it has to be presented through media channels that will reach you.

In the West (and, increasingly, globally) advertising is part of daily life and inseparable from popular culture. In many countries, advertising is the one common experience shared by a large, diverse populace. Advertising is a mass media leveler, the pop

Figure 1-1

PRINT:
"OUR VACCINE DOESN'T FIT
ALL CATS EITHER"

AGENCY: COLLE + MCVOY /
MINNEAPOLIS

Creative Director:
Annette Bertelsen

Art Director: Liz Otremba

Copywriter: Jay Walsh

Photographer: Dublin
Productions

Client: Pfizer Animal Health
© 2000

*Making an analogy to a cat
that does not fit into a pet car-
rier, this ad for feline vaccines
grabs viewers' attention with a
large, provocative photograph.*

culture vehicle—from outdoor boards to Web banners to television commercials—with which we all come into contact.

Advertising has become more ubiquitous than ever, as advertisers try to find new ways to get their message through. Advertising differentiates brands, groups, and causes, and ultimately sells products and calls people to action.

An *advertisement* (or "ad") is a specific message constructed to inform, persuade, promote, provoke, or motivate people on behalf of a brand or group. (Here, "group" designates both commercial concerns and government agencies and nonprofit organizations.) An advertising campaign is a series of coordinated ads, based on an overarching strategy, connected by look and feel, voice, tone, style, imagery, and tagline, where each individual ad in the campaign can also stand on its own. An integrated ad campaign involves various media and might include broadcast, print, interactive, and other screen-based, out of home, and unconventional media.

Advertising Comes in Many Forms

Public service advertising is advertising that seeks to further the common good. According to the Advertising Council, an American public service advertising organization (www.adcouncil.org): "The objectives of [public service] ads are education and awareness of significant social issues, in an effort to change the public's attitudes and behaviors and stimulate positive social change."

Commonly referred to as PSAs, public service advertisements are created by advertising agencies around the world in service of a great variety of social causes. For example, according to the Ad Council, the "Youth Reckless Driving Prevention" PSA campaign "targets young adults between the ages of 15 and 21, and encourages them to speak when riding in a car with a reckless driver. The message is simple: 'If your friend is driving recklessly, say something.'"

In most countries, PSAs are considered a service to the community, and therefore the media does not charge to run them on

CASE STUDY

Campaign Sponsor: State
consumer protection agencies
and attorneys general offices

Campaign Web site:
www.SpeakUpOrElse.com

PSA Campaign:
The Ad Council

Volunteer Agency:
Y&R / New York

Creative Team
  Chief Creative Officers: Scott
    Vitrone and Ian Reichenthal
  Associate Creative Director:
    Neil Heymann
  Senior Copywriter:
    Brandon Henderson
  Senior Art Director:
    Dan Treichel
  Copywriter: Anthony Falvo
  Art Director: Roy Torres
  Intern / Copywriter:
    Ciaran Parsley
  Intern / Art Director: Purvi
    Naik

Account Management and
Brand Planning
  Shelley Diamond, President,
    Y&R New York
  Trish Mello, Vice President,
    Account Director
  Caleb Lubarsky, Account
    Supervisor
  Tessa Cosenza, Account
    Executive
  Belle Frank, Executive Vice
    President, Director of
    Strategy and Research

Production
  *Executive Director of Content
    Production:* Lora Schulson
  Content Producer:
    Tennille Loevenguth
  Radio Producer:
    George Croom
  Art Producer:
    Maggy Lynch Hartley
  Print Producers: Luigi Lubrano
    and Jack Hughes
  VML Interactive and Account
    Management / Production:
    Seth Galena
  Account Supervisor:
    Seth Galena

Youth Reckless Driving Prevention

Background: For more than two decades, car crashes have been the number-one killer of teens. Reckless driving among America's youth is a serious problem and it has deadly consequences. Young drivers are more likely to speed, run red lights, make illegal turns, and die in an SUV [sport utility vehicle] rollover. That is why the Youth Reckless Driving Prevention campaign is so critical. With the message, "If your friend is driving recklessly, say something," the campaign aims to encourage teen passengers to "speak up" when they are in a car with a friend who is driving recklessly and they do not feel safe.

Campaign Objectives: To reduce the number of injuries and deaths among teen drivers and passengers in reckless driving related accidents.

To educate teens on how to be safer drivers by focusing on safe speeds, avoiding distractions, and wearing seat belts.

To help teens understand the dangers associated with driving SUVs, which can have a higher risk of rollover. Care in handling, tire maintenance, and loading must be exercised.

Target Audience: Male and female teen passengers, ages 15 to 21, who ride with friends who drive recklessly.

Did You Know? Car crashes are the leading cause of death for 15- to 21-year-olds.

Crash rates increase drastically for 16- and 17-year old drivers with every additional passenger in the car.

During 2006, a teen died in a traffic crash an average of once every hour on weekends and nearly once every two hours during the week.

Of all drivers involved in fatal crashes, 13 percent were between the ages of 15 and 20 years.

A survey of 1,000 16- and 17-year-old drivers found that 61 percent of teens admit to risky driving habits. Of that 61 percent, 46 percent text and 51 percent talk on cell phones while driving.

—The Advertising Council

television, radio, or in print. To have more control over PSA placement, however, some nonprofit organizations and government agencies have begun to purchase advertising time and space, to supplement the donated placements.

Cause advertising, though initiated by commercial concerns, seeks to raise funds for nonprofit organizations or raise awareness on a social issue and runs in paid media sites. It is generally affiliated with a corporation and used in part to promote a corporation's public image or brand, unlike public service advertising, which has no commercial affiliation.

Commercial advertising promotes brands and commodities by informing consumers; it is also used to promote individuals, groups, corporations, manufacturers. Commercial advertising takes many forms, from single print advertisements to campaigns in any media to sponsorships to branded utilities.

Within the commercial category, subcategories are *business to business* (B2B), which

is from one company to another, and *trade advertising, which is* consumer-product advertising intended not for the consumer but for the various entities and people who influence consumers (for example, health-care professionals) or advertising aimed at a specific trade or profession (for example, a publisher's ad aimed at potential authors; see figures 1-1 and 1-2).

Consumer advertising and promotion are directed toward the general public and comprise almost all the ads shown in this book, as in figures 1-3 and 1-4.

Advertising takes many forms. From the earliest days of radio and television, there have been commercial sponsorships of broadcast programming. For example, a sponsor (that is, a company or brand) would subsidize a radio or television program, thereby gaining an outlet for its advertisements. Such sponsorship also built a positive association of the brand or product with popular programs. The brand name might also be prominently featured in the program name, as with the *Texaco Star Theater,* which began as a radio

› Figure 1-2

POSTER: "GIRLS"

AGENCY:
MUSTOES / LONDON

Creative Directors: Alan Morrice and Paul Diver

Art DIrector: Dean Hunt

Copywriter: Simon Hipwell

Client: Penguin Books

The obvious approach would have been to develop a trade campaign targeted at authors and agents. However, we believed that this wouldn't give Penguin the step change required. Instead, we decided to create a campaign that looked and felt like a major consumer campaign.
—Mustoes

Figure 1-3

TEVA TOUCHSCREEN KIOSK

AGENCY:
PLANET PROPAGANDA /
MADISON, WISCONSIN

Interactive Director: Ben Hirby

Creative Director: Dana Lytle

Designer: Zack Schulze

Developer: Marcus Trapp

Copywriter: Andy Brawner

Client: Teva

© Planet Propaganda

Teva Touchscreen Kiosk features multimedia content about Teva products, collections, events, athletes, and culture.

"We've always been big fans of Teva's authenticity, originality, and performance heritage," says Michael Murray, Planet Propaganda's senior brand manager. "Creating the content and interface required us to draw on literally all of Planet's different specialties, across design, motion, interactive, and strategy. We jumped at the chance to help tell Teva's story in such an innovative way."

Source: www.dexigner.com/design_news/
planet-propaganda-hired-by-teva.html.

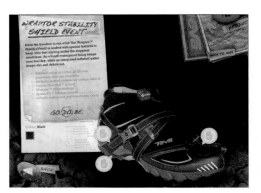

program in the 1930s and moved to television in the 1940s, and *Philco Television Playhouse*, which ran from 1948 to 1955. Soap operas are another example of brand-sponsored programs; for example, the production of CBS's *As the World Turns* was sponsored by Procter & Gamble.

By associating itself with good television entertainment, brands acquired the cachet of the programming. Product placement, in which brands are embedded into television or Web programs, banks on the same cachet, hoping the viewer associates the brand with the characters on the show. Branded entertainment involves content marketing, vehicles for brands for and across digital TV, Web TV,

gaming, mobile apps, social networks, and motion pictures. For example, "Bud.TV" from Anheuser-Busch Inc. and "Web Therapy" is "brought to you" by Lexus. For Grey Goose and Sundance, @Radical Media produced "The Iconoclasts" series, which is a sophisticated, branded entertainment.

Realizing that the tools to create and share graphic or audiovisual messages are increasingly available to the average person, some brands have turned to soliciting consumer-generated content by sponsoring contests. For example, Doritos brand snack food started an impressive conversation with consumers through a strategy of cocreation, sponsoring contests for amateur filmmakers

Figure 1-4

PRINT:
"BOO" AND "PUMPKIN"

AGENCY:
BUTLER, SHINE, STERN & PARTNERS / SAUSALITO, CALIFORNIA

Client: MINI USA

© MINI USA & BSSP

Advertising Media

Conventional Media

> Broadcast

> Television

  > Major network

  > Independent station

  > Cable

> Radio

  > Network

  > Satellite

  > Local

> Print

  > Magazines
    > National
    > Statewide

  > Newspapers
    > National
    > Statewide
    > Local

  > Direct mail

Screen-Based Media And Applications

> Web sites and micro Web sites

> Platforms and other branded utilities

> Web films

> Web and interactive content and entertainment

> Webisodes (short audio or video presentations or broadband pro-gramming, used to promote a brand or group, preview music, or present any type of information)

> Web commercials

> Mobile advertising

> Mobile applications (or apps)

> Mobile content entertainment

> Social networking applications

> Video sharing Web sites

> Photo sharing Web sites

> Widgets

> Video e-mail

> Banners and floaters

> Blogs (from web logs)

> Vlogs (video blogs)

> MoBlogs (mobile blogs)

> Online guerrilla or marketing that goes viral

> Ads embedded in video and online games

> Digital presentations

> Digital outdoor

> Digital signs

Support media

> Out of home

> Outdoor (bill)boards

> Transit

> Posters

In-store

> Kiosks

> Installations

> Live-feed boards

Unconventional

> Ambient

> Unconventional or guerrilla media (advertising in unpaid media that ambushes people in public or private environments)

Sponsorship and Branded Entertainment

> Event sponsorship

> Exhibit sponsorship

> Site sponsorship

> Television program sponsorship

> Product placement in television programs, music videos, films, books, ads, or products embedded in video games

> Any branded entertainment

Miscellaneous

> Branded utility

> Premiums and other incentives (giveaways)

> Calendars

> Logo apparel

> Novelties, such as pens, mugs, etc.

to create commercials. (For this kind of advertising to work, brands must recognize and accept that the public has enormous sway over a brand's content anyway—through blogging, reviewing, parody videos, take-offs, and more.)

In-game advertising—whether product placement, live billboard feeds, or ads embedded into games—is often well received by appropriately targeted gamer audiences. Research indicates that young male gamers think product placement enhances the reality of the content and game experience.

A *branded utility* is a product created by a brand or sponsor that is ostensibly useful to the consumer and generally (but not always) offered free of charge. The product (or branded utility) should provide a useful and pleasant experience for the consumer. The tradition of branded utilities dates back to the well-respected Michelin guides and continues today in a variety of forms, from books to Web sites to mobile phone applications. Nike+ is a branded utility, for example, that offers something useful—a training system that lets runners easily track and share their running data—to a global community operating 24/7. A result of a strategic alliance between Nike and Apple, Nike+ is now a proprietary utility.

Drew Neisser, president and CEO of Renegade, advocates "marketing as service." In their ideal form, branded utilities provide something useful to people for free. Bowne's Compliance Configurator (figure 1-5a) is an example of such a utility. (For more on branded utilities, see page 52.)

Widgets are another form of branded utility. They are essentially microapplications, built upon a Web service. Widgets usually have a very specific purpose and are simple products made to be widely and easily disseminated. Examples include photo slideshows, video players, news readers, concert updates, and more. Environmental branded utilities are useful services that become part of the common environment, such as sponsored spaces—for example, clean bathrooms in Times Square (sponsored by Charmin) or self-service laundries at European music

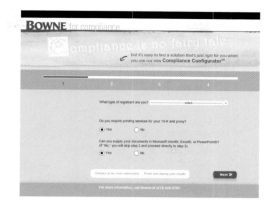

festivals (sponsored by Wrangler). These may even include sponsored activities, such as those created by Renegade for Panasonic's "Share the Air" Dew Action Sports Tour, which offered athlete autograph signings, instant-win games, and camera loans. A Web site can be a branded utility, too—for example, Babycenter.com offers information for parents from Johnson and Johnson.

The creation of branded utilities requires expertise that many ad agencies and/or their clients alone do not have; this often leads to brands becoming media owners and to the development of strategic alliances, such as the one between Nokia, Sony BMG, and Universal Music for the "Nokia Comes with Music" download service or the alliance between Google, Adidas, and Samsung for miCoach.com, an interactive personal coaching and training system.

Brand fans abound on social networking sites. People view brand videos on YouTube and share them with friends. Sharing links to

Figure 1-5

BOWNE "PERFECT FIT" CAMPAIGN

AGENCY: RENEGADE / NEW YORK

Executive Creative Director: Drew Neisser

Creative DIrector: Jeff Vinick

Art Director: Andrew Betlyon

Compliance Configurator Postcard: Bowne—Fairy Tale campaign

The Challenge: *To generate interest in and sales of Bowne's various tax-compliance solutions.*

Target Insight: *Bowne's customers and prospects aren't quite sure which combination of compliance solutions best matches their filing and financial needs.*

The Program: *For the oldest continuously operating company in the United States, Renegade turned to classic fairy tales to tell Bowne's story as a provider of solutions that fit "just right." The heart of the campaign is an online compliance configurator that quickly and easily identifies the best compliance solution for each prospect. Traffic was driven to the configurator through highly targeted print advertising, e-mail, and direct mail.*

The Result: *The "Fairy Tale" campaign exceeded expectations on all measures, including site traffic, lead generation, and sales conversion.*
—Renegade

SHOWCASE

"GOTTA LOVE IT" BY TOM CLARK

Tom Clark is senior vice president, creative director of copy, and cofounder of ICCTrio, a pharmaceutical advertising agency in Parsippany, New Jersey. Tom is also an adjunct professor of advertising in the Robert Busch School of Design at Kean University, Union, New Jersey.

It's True: You gotta love what you do. Here's an example of CGL (customer generated love). See how personal passion for a brand fuels more persuasive communications and tremendous overall personal satisfaction. My love for the New York Mets began in 1969, twenty years ahead of my love for my family. When I got an opportunity to bring my loves together for the Mets' "15 Seconds of Fame" TV commercial contest, I jumped at the chance.

The Brief: Mention the brand's tagline, "Your Season Has Come." Encourage ticket sales through Mets.com. Winning spot to be broadcast during Mets games on SNY-TV, and the winners to be honored in an on-field ceremony at the storied Shea Stadium.

Inspired by another love, Kevin Costner's *Field of Dreams,* I storyboarded a slice-of-life spot: Dad tells daughter about different heroes from every Mets era. She asks to attend a game. They run off to purchase tickets. On the evening of the shoot, Hannah, Ellie, and I arrived at the soggy local field. Thankfully, the baseball gods were with us. The rain stopped as sparkling sunbeams cut through the clouds. I never climbed a backstop before. We edited the spot that night, and FedExed it the next day.

Two days later, Hannah called me at my office. "We won, Dad! We won!" Soon, my mom and dad were calling: "We saw your commercial tonight!"

Cut to my family standing on the field at Shea, as our prize-winning commercial filled the scoreboard. Afterwards, with the crowd showing its appreciation, I pointed to Hannah and called out to all-star David Wright, who was warming up on the sidelines. He nodded, saying: "Hey look, Carlos, we've got the star of the commercial right here!"

Moral: Put everything you have into your brand's work. It's the path to building memorable advertising—and some memorable family moments. God willing.

—Tom Clark

▸ *TV: "TEAM OF DREAMS": 15 (FIFTEEN SECONDS)*

AGENCY: FGC—FAN-GENERATED CONTENT FOR THE NEW YORK METS "15 SECONDS OF FAME" CONTEST

Creative Directors: Tom Clark, Daun Clark, Hannah Clark, and Ellie Clark

humorous micro–Web sites is commonplace. Using mobile devices to send photos of oneself enjoying a branded experience is not unusual. Millions of free branded applications (apps) have been downloaded. Offering deals to brand fans on FaceBook and Twitter further endears a brand to such fans.

Some formats—such as sponsorships, branded utilities, events, micro–Web sites, and maybe even television commercials—are practical vehicles for ad messages. Whether these ad forms stay, change, or go, one thing will be constant: *Advertising designers and art directors will need to be creative thinkers who can design. Always.*

WHO CREATES ADVERTISING?

In an advertising agency, a conventional creative team is a duo comprised of an art director and a copywriter. This model was Bill Bernbach's brainchild. Bernbach, of Doyle Dane Bernbach (DDB), paired writers with art directors; his vision, along with that of his creative teams, produced seminal work (see figure 1-6) during advertising's "Creative Revolution," of the 1950s and 1960s.

A creative director or associate creative director—who makes the final creative decisions about the concept, approach, copywriting, and art direction—supervises the creative team before the work is presented to the client. Some agencies prefer interdisciplinary creative teams or brand teams with several additional members, which might include an account manager, an information technology (IT) expert, an interactive designer, and a marketing expert, among others. Depending upon the kind of project, there may be several creative leads, including perhaps a creative, technology, user-experience, or account lead.

Teams generate ideas. Once an idea is chosen, the art director is responsible for the art direction (the overall look and feel, the visual style, and the selection of photographer or illustrator) and the visualization and design, and the copywriter is responsible for the writing. When a creative team works well, the division of labor might overlap. Any good art director should be able to write copy, and any good copywriter should be able to think visually.

Figure 1-6

PRINT: "THINK SMALL" (1960)

AGENCY: DDB / NEW YORK

Creative Director: Bill Bernbach

Client: Volkswagen

DDB's visual style set a new creative standard in the 1960s.

Advertising is collaborative. Besides the traditional creative team of art director and copywriter, advertising depends upon other professionals, including strategic planners, account and marketing managers, programmers, and interactive designers or agencies. When dealing with screen-based media, there are also unconventional marketing agencies, media planners, commercial directors, producers, production and postproduction agencies, talent (actor, musicians, photographers, and illustrators), casting directors, and location scouts, among others.

Traditionally, advertising agencies created advertising and controlled the advertising for brands. Now technology (iMovie, digital video cameras, Pro Tools, and other such tools) makes it possible for regular people—customers, consumers, anyone—to create, both economically and practically, in ways previously available only to advertising professionals. Brand companies and agencies are handing over content-making to the public, ceding some control but trying to engage people as brand-makers. Technology has shifted much of a brand's power to consumers. The more people work with a brand, the more those people will use as well as feel loyal to that brand.

The Ad Agency

An advertising agency is a business that provides clients with creative, marketing, and other business services related to planning, creating, producing, and placing advertisements. In the late 1980s many prominent advertising agencies merged into conglomerates. Today there are several major conglomerates, such as the Omnicom Group, Interpublic Group, WPP Group, Havas, Publicis Groupe, and Dentsu, among others. Of course, there are many independent agencies throughout the world. An independent agency is a single agency owned and operated by individuals and not part of a conglomerate.

TYPES OF AGENCIES

Full-service agencies offer a broad range of business and creative services related to the advertising process, including planning, creative ideation and design, production, implementation, and placement. Some full-service agencies also handle marketing communication, such as public relations, promotional design, interactive advertising, and direct marketing, or are in partnerships with companies that provide those services. Clients choose full-service agencies because these organizations are able to handle any aspect of a client's marketing needs.

Independent agencies are privately owned. They are usually small, and they often attract clients who prefer to work directly with the principals of an agency.

Interactive agencies focus on screen media. In the past, these media specialists worked with other agencies that served as the creative leads. Now, many interactive agencies are the lead agencies for brands.

Some companies prefer to produce part or all of their advertising, branding, direct marketing, and promotional design themselves. Such companies own and operate their own in-house advertising agencies.

ETHICS

Advertising and ethics can coexist. Certainly, public service advertising helps society and is the advertising profession's greatest contribution to the general good, one that cannot be denied or overstated. Consumer advertising also can be held to ethical standards. When clients and agency professionals are aware of what is unethical and keep to standards of fair practice and social responsibility, then we can have ethical advertising. There is no exit from social responsibility—everyone is accountable. As John Butler, creative director of Butler, Shine and Stern

& Partners, Sausalito, California, reminds us: "We are given a voice, and we have to be responsible in how we use that voice."

What is unethical is almost easier to identify than what is ethical. Here is an obvious list of do's:

> *Treat the audience with respect; respect people's religion, race, gender, age, and ethnicity.*

> *Be truthful.*

> *Be responsible.*

Beyond self-policing there are watchdog groups, such as Adbusters, Mediawatch-UK (www.mediawatchuk.org.uk), Commercial Alert, the Advertising Standards Authority, and Guerrilla Girls, as well as individual critics such as Jean Kilbourne, whose video *Still Killing Us Softly* (1987) is important viewing, and collectives such as Men Organized Against Sexism and Institutionalized Stereotypes (OASIS), which produced the video and slide show *Stale Roles and Tight Buns*

(1988). The "First Things First Manifesto," originally written in 1964 and updated by Adbusters and six design magazines in 2000, is still important reading.

Advertising Women of New York (AWNY) aids in ensuring ethical behavior with an award program—The Good, the Bad, and the Ugly—that examines good as well as bad images of women in advertising. Professional groups, such as D&AD in England and the One Club, AIGA, and the Art Directors Club in New York, also aid the profession. Of course, there are government agencies that regulate advertising. And consumer advocates and consumers often take the lead against unethical behavior.

All students, novices, and professionals should be aware of criticisms so that advertising can be made more ethical. It is far better to be overly concerned about respecting one's audience and aware of how veiled stereotyped thinking can be than to be unconscious of such matters.

02

THE PROJECT PROCESS

SIX PHASES

OVERVIEW > STRATEGY > IDEAS > DESIGN > PRODUCTION > IMPLEMENTATION

Creative thinking is needed through all the phases of an advertising project. Creative solutions are produced by a keen and imaginative mind or by a team of keen, imaginative minds. A model developed by Benjamin Bloom, called "Bloom's Taxonomy," categorizes thinking skills; we will use it here to represent the developmental phases of a project. Bloom's Taxonomy is as follows:

> *Knowledge*

> *Comprehension*

> *Application*

> *Analysis*

> *Synthesis*

> *Evaluation*

During *Phase 1*, we gain knowledge—we gather information. In *Phase 2*, we comprehend—we grasp the meaning of the material we have gathered, gaining insights. And we apply, making use of the material in new, more immediate contexts. During *Phase 3*, the traditional conceptual design stage, we analyze, examining our material in search of an idea. And, we synthesize, combining different ideas and influences, bringing parts together to form a new whole. In *Phases 4, 5 and 6*, we evaluate, considering and scrutinizing in order to judge the value of our ideas, first conceptually, in relation to our initial goals, and then practically, as designed, produced, and implemented.

Phase 1: Overview

Orientation is Phase 1 of a project. It includes the initial meeting with a client; a briefing on the assignment; the internal planning meeting; a definition of the client's goals and requirements; learning about the client's business or organization, product, service, or group; determining the audience; and analyzing the competition. It also involves material gathering, meetings, setting the design and production schedule, and sometimes market research.

Usually, this type of planning does not involve junior art directors and copywriters; junior art directors will be briefed by their creative director (CD) or associate creative director (ACD). However, junior art directors should understand how the design process works at every level and stage. The orientation might be conducted by several individuals: the client, the client's team, an account manager or a team from your own agency, your CD or ACD, or any individual who serves as the liaison with a client.

During this phase, key issues are addressed:

> *Project goals and objectives*

> *Client's business goals*

> *Role of the project in the client's broader plan*

> *Identification of the audience*

> *Competitive analysis*

> *Budget*

> *Schedule and deadline*

> *Other parameters*

It is important to learn as much as possible about the brand or group:

> *What makes this brand or group (organization, company, any entity) unique?*

> *What are the functional and the emotional benefits of the brand or group?*

> *How does the brand or group compare to the competition? Is the brand or group a category or industry leader? In second place? A newcomer?*

INFORMATION GATHERING

Learning about your client's business (general industry or sector and particular business, product, service, or organization) is paramount. Being a creative professional in advertising necessitates learning about each product, service, or cause under assignment. In a midsize or large agency, the account manager and client provide information to you. Most smart creatives do some digging themselves. The Internet, of course, has made information more accessible than ever. Develop an understanding of how best to conduct research, specifically where to look for and gather information.

People use a variety of information-gathering tools, from sticky notes to index cards to notebooks to digital storage devices to digital assistants such as a widgets (interactive tools that provide services such as showing the user desktop notes). Some take advantage of Web 2.0 capabilities by using social bookmarking Web sites, such as http://del.icio.us.com, that allow online storage and access of bookmarks from any computer.

Listen carefully to the information the client offers; the client is expert about his or her business. Listen to what he or she says about the problem, audience, and marketplace— and thoughtfully examine the information provided. By paying careful attention to what the client says about the brand or group *and* about the competition, you might gain useful insights.

A critical component is learning about the audience—the targeted, specified group of people at whom you are aiming your message, design, and solution. The audience is the main group who would purchase this product, utilize this information or service, or patronize this entity or brand. Demonstrating an insight into their audience's desire for easy and free access to fashion and beauty expertise, Schematic's "Shop *Vogue* TV" strengthens the bond between *Vogue*, their

Figure 2-1

BROADBAND CHANNEL: "SHOP VOGUE.TV"

AGENCY: SCHEMATIC

Creative Lead / Art Director: Ian Cunningham

Technology Lead / Solutions Architect: Paul Newman

CondeNet was looking for a highly interactive and stylish new way to entice advertisers to Vogue magazine. The result: ShopVogue.TV, a glamorous and entertaining broadband channel that allows readers of Vogue to shop online quickly and easily for the products featured in the magazine's print ads.

The first edition of ShopVogue.TV generated 727 ad pages for CondeNet (as opposed to 620 the previous year)—a significant bump in incremental revenue.

Schematic turned ShopVogue.TV into a fashion destination, establishing the site as a central home for Vogue editorial content that was currently being distributed in disparate locations. Visitors can also watch runway video, fashion ads and shows created by Vogue, and [they can] submit photos of their personal fashion statements to a user-generated section of the site. By allowing easy, and free, access to fashion and beauty expertise, the site allows Vogue—and its advertisers—to strengthen and leverage their bond with their desired audience.

The standout feature of the site is the inclusion of price and store location (and, where possible, a "Buy Now" function) for each of the items featured in the Vogue print ads. This makes shopping simple and attractive, and [it] creates an immediacy that encourages shoppers or casual visitors to become purchasers.

ShopVogue.TV has garnered extensive, and extremely favorable, media attention around the world, including a feature in the New York Times. The momentum carried through to the Spring 2008 release.

—Schematic

advertisers, and their desired audience (see figure 2-1).

Phase 2: Strategy

Once you and your team or studio have completed Phase 1, the next focus is strategy. After much reflection on the data and material you have gathered, you develop the direction your solution(s) will take. In this phase, you examine, assess, discover, and plan; you are not conceptualizing or designing. Strategy is the conceptual underpinning of any visual communication, unifying every visual and verbal application within a program of applications. Essentially, advertising strategy is considering the brand's or group's positioning and aiming your advertising application (the type of design problem) in the marketplace to achieve differentiation, relevance, and resonance. Moreover, the strategy is a conceptual plan that provides guidelines—for both client and creative professionals—for all visual communication applications.

Figure 2-2

OUTDOOR BOARD: "EAT MOR"

AGENCY: THE RICHARDS GROUP / DALLAS

Creative Director: Doug Rucker

Art Director: David Ring

Copywriter: Gail Barlow

Client: Chick-fil-A

Why are we advertising? To position the Chick-fil-A chicken sandwich as the best alternative to other fast-food sandwiches and to remind people how much they like them.

Whom are we talking to? Adults, ages 18–49, who are infrequent users or nonusers of Chick-fil-A. They are primarily women, college graduates, and in white-collar jobs. They associate chicken with a healthy lifestyle and believe that quality food is better for you and worth the money.

What do they currently think? "Unless I'm in the mall, I just don't think of a Chick-fil-A. I guess they're pretty good, but I haven't been there in a long time."

What would we like them to think? "I'd rather have a chicken sandwich than a hamburger. And Chick-fil-A makes the best one."

What is the single most persuasive idea we can convey? Every other sandwich is second-rate.

Why should they believe it? Chick-fil-A is simple and wholesome and doesn't take itself too seriously.

Are there any creative guidelines?
-The Richards Group

THE CREATIVE BRIEF

A *creative brief* is a strategic plan—a kind of map—that both the client and the design firm or advertising agency agree upon, a written document outlining and strategizing a design project—it is also called a *design brief* or a *creative work plan*. (Strategy, and strategy statements, can be determined outside a design brief or within a brief.) Most briefs are made up of questions and answers—a handy format to fully delineate the assignment, the objectives of the project, the design context, and the audience. The answers to questions posed in a brief are usually based on predesign (or preliminary) market research; information gathered about the product, service or group, and audience; and the budget. The brief becomes the strategic plan for implementing objectives and a written standard against which creative solutions can be measured. The client and creative professionals can go back to the brief for guidance, or designers can use it to support their concepts or solutions. A thoughtful, clear brief can foster focused, critical thinking and lead to creative concept formulation. I have heard creative directors say that they have rewritten briefs so they provide clearer guidance for ideation.

Who constructs the creative brief?

Newer models for strategic planning include designers and art directors in brief construction. Assembling from the outset an integrated team (including client, planners, account managers, designers, copywriters, producers, information technology [IT] professionals, architects, interior designers, and industrial designers, among others) is more progressive, leading to broader strategic thinking, multiple perspectives, and greater collaboration. With new and emerging media, an integrated team is critical to strategic planning.

In small studios and agencies, junior art directors and designers might have the opportunity to work on a brief; in medium and larger studios and agencies, juniors are not likely to be part of design-brief development. Everyone on the team, both marketing and creative professionals, should intimately understand the assignment, brand or group, and audience.

Sample Creative Briefs

Briefs may take different forms. (See also the brief for Chick-fil-A, figure 2-2.)

Sample Creative Brief #1

> *Project Title*

> > *Define the challenge*

> > *Determine the key audience*

> > *Describe our current understanding of the brand or group*

> > *Identify the brand essence*

> > *Determine the strategy*

> > *Ascertain the best methods of execution*

> *Media*

> *Parameters:*
> > *Deadlines*
> > *Budget*

Sample Creative Brief #2

Who are we talking to? (See figure 2-3 for an example of a target audience.)

What is the single most important message we want to communicate?

Why should people believe this?

What tone of voice should we use?

What do we want people to think or feel after experiencing the advertising?

What are the requirements?

Is there a best media channel for this message?

Sample Creative Brief #3

> *Client or brand*

> *Product category*

> *Unique selling proposition (USP): benefit unique to the advertised brand*

> *Long-term position*

> *Communication strategy*

> *Brand personality*

> *Target audience*

> *Buying and usage habits*

> *Values, attitudes, and lifestyles*

> *Competition*

> *Support*

Sample Creative Brief #4

Position: What differentiating idea would be both relevant to our target audience and challinging to their current thinking concerning the brand or group?

Connection: What social or emotional association does our target audience have with this idea?

Conjecture: How can we best inform our conjecture to solve this communication problem?

Insight: What about the brand could help us start a dialogue between the brand and our consumers, among our target audience and/or within pop culture?

Each type of creative studio—interactive studio, ad agency, or unconventional agency—handles the brief differently, if it is used at all. A brief can be written collaboratively by the client and design firm or ad agency, or the client gives it to the design firm or ad agency. The design brief can be initiated by the client's marketing team or by the design firm or ad agency's account team, creative director, or design director. The brief may include input from the creative team, strategic planners, research or media departments in the design firm or agency, or any related media unit.

In an advertising agency, the agency account manager—the usual liaison between the creatives and client—gives the creative brief to the creative team.

CLIENT REVIEW DURING PHASE 2

During certain phases of the process, the client reviews, offers input, and approves decisions made thus far. Asking a client to review and sign off on what has been discussed and determined can help avoid misunderstandings down the road.

Phase 3: Ideas

For many students and novices, idea generation is the most challenging stage in the process. Creative advertising requires the communication of a meaningful message to an audience through an idea, expressed through the visual design and copy. Formulating an idea necessitates research, analysis, interpretation, inference, and reflective and creative thinking. For any assignment, an agency must generate several viable concepts to present to their client. (See also pp. 66–93.) For the *Harvard Business Review*, Hadrian's Wall, an advertising firm, formulated an idea that could demonstrate the benefit of reading engrossing articles in a dynamic business journal (figure 2-4). Not only does the design serve to catch the viewer's attention with its atypical appearance, but its form and content

Sample Detailed Creative Brief

Question 1: What is our challenge?

Every project has a goal and desired outcome(s). Succinct answers to these questions will aid concept generation.

Question 2: Who is the target audience?

Identifying the people who comprise the core audience is essential to formulating insights, strategies, and, then, relevant ideas. Many factors and criteria are evaluated when defining the core audience, for example, a demographic, psychographic, or behavioral profile. *Demographic* refers to the selected population characteristics. Some common variables include age, sex or gender, income, education, home ownership, marital status, race, and religion. Psychographic profiles are attributes relating to personality, attitudes, interests, values, and lifestyles. Behavioral variables refer to things such as brand loyalty or the frequency of product use, interests, or activities. Understanding the target's culture or community is necessary. Even language is constrained by culture; what might connect to an audience in the United States might not to an audience in England, though the language is shared.

Question 3: What does the audience currently think about the brand or group?

People's perceptions of a brand or group are critical to understanding how you can influence their opinions or start a conversation with them. Also, perceptions fluctuate.

Question 4: What would we like the target to think and feel?

Determine a clear reaction you want the audience to have. The answer to this question should reflect the goals of the assignment as well as take into account the audience's current perceptions (relates to Question 3).

Question 5: Which facts, evidence, or thoughts will assist in this change of thinking? How can we support our proposition?

Provide facts and information that will enable people to change their beliefs and opinions. Support the claims in the advertising message.

Question 6: What is the brand essence?

The brand essence should be maintained in the advertising. Each brand or group should have a well-defined essence that allows for positioning (in the marketplace or realm the entity has in the minds of the target audience and against the competition).

Question 7: What is the key emotion that will build a relationship with the core audience?

Identify an emotion that people will feel when connecting with the brand or group. Establishing the right emotional connection with people creates deep relationships, builds brand communities, and fosters loyalty.

Question 8: What media will best facilitate our goal?

Consider media where the people you want to reach spend the most time. When searching for answers to this question, consider media in creative ways. Determine the manner in which your viewers relate to each different medium. Budget can also have a great effect on the selection of media.

Question 9: What are the most critical elements? What is the budget?

Determine visual and text elements required for each application. Elements can include requisite visuals, color palette, typeface(s), logo, tagline, sign-off, tone of voice, main text or copy, features, rules or regulations, promotions, values, expiration dates, 800 numbers, Web site addresses, and games. Again, budget will affect many of your decisions, including media, paper selection or substrates for print, and colors for print.

The number of required elements will vary depending on the nature and scope of the project. For example, a logo and Web address may be the only elements required for an outdoor billboard; for a Web site, there will be a long list of required components.

Determine which elements are most important in establishing visual and verbal identity and personality in a consistent and relevant manner.

Question 10: What is the single most important takeaway?

Determine the single most important thought. What do you want the audience to remember, to take away with them? Some people prefer to answer this question first. By answering it nearly last, the answers from the previous nine questions might provide insight into the answer for this question.

Question 11: What do we want the audience to do?

Define the call to action: What do you want the viewer or visitor to do? You might want the audience to: purchase the brand, donate to a cause, get a medical exam, call an 800 number or helpline, visit the Web site, complete a survey, click through, share a video or link, donate blood, or something else.

director or creative director, he or she may wish to see your ideas at each visual stage—from thumbnails through comps—for comment or approval. (A client sees a more refined comprehensive [comp] representation of the design concept.)

If a rough is not working, go back over your thumbnail sketches, generate more ideas, or try a new visualization method. It is important to generate several workable design ideas at the outset so that you have alternate solutions. Most clients prefer to select from among at least three different concepts and executions.

STEP 3: COMPREHENSIVES

A comprehensive, referred to as a *comp*, is a detailed representation of a design concept thoughtfully visualized and composed, a very close representation of how the piece will look when produced. Comps usually look like a printed or finished piece; though they have not yet been produced, they fully represent your solution to the problem before it goes public, before it is printed or viewed on screen or in any other media.

In the comprehensive, type, illustrations, photographs, and layout are rendered closely enough to the finished design application to convey an accurate impression of the final piece. Every line of type should be adjusted, all the letterspacing considered. A final comp must be well crafted.

For screen-based applications, design and technical development happen simultaneously. Visual explorations and design happen at the same time as prototypes. Testing happens at various stages, and a good amount of testing is required when new models of on-screen thinking are employed. Testers tend to be put off by new models, requiring exposure to newer models again to test preferences.

CLIENT REVIEW DURING PHASE 4

Rarely do clients throw up their arms in wild approval and say, "That's great! Let's produce this." More often than not, clients request changes and refinements. During this phase, the designer evaluates, refines, and secures approval from the client.

Very often, the comp is used as a visual agreement of the solution between the designer and client and as a guide, or blueprint, for the printer. If you are creating an application for print, it is important to remind the client that the paper stock will most likely change the appearance of the printed piece.

Phase 5: Production

For a graphic design student, executing a print solution means printing one's solution on a home printer. Students who know how to create motion graphics or interactive design have a better understanding of the demands of producing digital solutions.

In a professional setting, various digital solutions involve interaction models, user testing, detailed wireframes, functional specifications, development activities, quality assurance, and exit criteria (once testing is complete).

Implementing one's design solution takes a variety of forms depending on the type of application and whether the application is print, screen-based, or environmental. Production necessitates working closely with other professionals, including interactive experts, Web producers, technology directors, developers, media directors, media-activation leads, code developers, other IT professionals, and perhaps psychologists and social anthropologists.

Phase 6: Implementation

In this final phase, solutions are deployed and put into effect. After a design assignment has ended, some clients and designers find debriefing useful. This involves reviewing the solution and its consequences.

It is exceptionally useful to debrief, that is, to examine your finished assignment to figure out what went wrong and what went right.

CASE STUDY

Case Study: Behind the Scenes: MoMA | Tim Burton Exhibition / Big Spaceship, Brooklyn

Long before *Beetlejuice* and *Edward Scissorhands*, Tim Burton was busy drawing, painting, sketching and building his carefully crafted world. When the Museum of Modern Art launched a major retrospective exploring the artist's work, they approached Big Spaceship to reveal the exhibition in an interactive setting. Longtime fans of Mr. Burton, they created an environment that draws inspiration from the artist.

While concepting, the agency put together three design directions. The first focused on the abstract elements of Burton's work, extending them into a digital atmosphere. Their use of color was minimal. They instead concentrated on striped and checkered patterns to create movement.

For the second, they chose to play off of the artist's drawings and illustrations and his use of contrasting colors, lights and darks, shadows and extreme angles.

In the third approach—the one Big Spaceship ended up pursuing—they employed a practice that Tim Burton is known for: stop-motion animation. For this hands-on approach, they created three model staircases with foam board and covered them in Spackle. They then conducted a number of stop-motion tests, in the end moving the models around a stationary camera.

—Big Spaceship

SHOWCASE

BILL SCHWAB: THE GATE WORLDWIDE

Bill Schwab is creative director at the Gate Worldwide
in New York. Bill has worked
as art director and creative
director at Fallon McElligott,
BBDO, Ammirati & Puris, Chiat
Day, and the Gate Worldwide.
He coauthored the best-
selling business book *Death
to All Sacred Cows* (New York:
Hyperion, 2007) and has
designed and art directed
two volumes of the One Show
Annual series.

Additionally, Bill serves on the
advertising faculty of the Pratt
Institute, Brooklyn, New York.
His work has been recognized
repeatedly with awards in
Communication Arts, the One
Show, the Effies, *Graphis*,
and Cannes.

What is the role of storytelling in your work?

Anyone worth knowing is attracted to stories,
aren't they? And some of the most powerful
stories are told with imagery: the cave paintings of Lascaux, the Sistine Chapel, Picasso's
Guernica to name a few. So being a kid who
always had either a drawing pencil or a book
in my hand, I was predestined to find myself
in a business that creates imagery for the purpose of communicating a particular message.

**The best adverting works by attracting
people to the benefit of a product or service with a story.**

I've been fortunate to work with terrific writers, who had the ability to create an entire
story in a sentence. As a junior art director, I found that intimidating, but I learned
quickly that you could do the same thing with
imagery. Great illustrators, photographers,
filmmakers, and art directors are constantly offering us new examples of visual storytelling.

**If you were to give a workshop in advertis-
ing, what topics would you stress?**

If you were my student in this workshop, I
would want you to learn to craft two critical
elements to successful advertising: the *idea*
and the *engagement*.

The most important thing about a good idea
is articulating it to yourself. When I teach my
advertising class, I always ask my students to
evaluate the validity of an idea by articulating it in a single sentence and then playing it
back against the strategy.

Once you have developed an idea, you need
to deliver it in an engaging way.

An interesting way to look at the ads we all
do is to think of them like people we meet at
a party. Picture the types in your mind: "the
loud and repetitive," "the tasteless innuen-
do," "the self-absorbed and self-important."
Now picture the kind of person you would

want to get to know. When you make your
ads in this way, you are far more likely to create effective and original advertising.

**How do you collaborate with others on
a project?**

I approach collaboration in different ways
depending on what stage the project is in. In
the beginning, I tend to listen and ask general and what-if questions. I want to learn
everything I can about the consumer I'm
advertising to, so I talk to anyone who can
offer me an insight.

A good client knows a heck of a lot, so I like to
draw them into the process as soon as possible.

After the ideas are approved, you look for
the best possible people to collaborate in the
execution. The right people think in terms of
adding to the idea—it's never no, it's where
does that lead us? I worked on a project recently where the challenge we gave ourselves
was always [to] respond by saying, "keep going." It was wonderful to see what happened.

You know you are working with the right
people when you talk about how you see
something and they respond by saying
"that's great, what about this . . ."

How would you define a big idea?

There's the physical sensation for one thing.
If you've ever watched a big-league player
at bat when a pitcher grooves a fastball, you
know what I'm talking about. A big idea is like
the story of Paul on the road to Damascus,
it's a bright shining light that knocks you off
your horse and makes everything clear.

Because big ideas reveal their potential in a
flash, you can literally see everything fall into
place. A big idea grows outward, absorbing
smaller ideas and creating whole families
of supporting ideas. It works across media
and multiple types of executions and leaves
conventional advertising campaigns behind

by becoming news, commentary, comedy and watercooler conversation.

When you create a big idea, you can see it literally leapfrogging, seemingly on its own, through the very media where you've placed your advertising.

Any good idea grows out of and illuminates a brand; big ideas cause consumers to see the brand from a whole different perspective. Big ideas move brands beyond function to status and can make even nonessential service brands indispensable parts of our lives.

Big ideas, like clouds and angels, exist and function on a higher plain.

What do you look for in a junior book (portfolio)?

I don't care about the work that mimics current award show books as much as work that tells me someone has an active mind and an inherent curiosity. People that are intelligent and curious, polite and articulate generally have interesting lives and make work that is interesting as well. I look for a thinker, not an imitator.

What's the best piece of advice you can offer an aspiring creative?

Open your eyes! New stories and ways of telling them are all around us, sometimes in seemingly mundane environments. Think of it, a simple arced line curving upward on a page can make people feel hopeful.

Whenever possible, be a witness to the miracle that occurs when the presentation of a visual image sets off a reaction from a viewer. When you can combine a series of far more complex images, sound, voices, and music, wow, what amazing things you can do.

Be there when it happens and take notes, because using that power to illuminate your ideas is what it's all about.

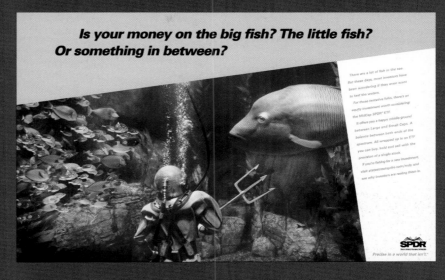

PRINT: "BIG FISH," "METEOR," AND "WAGON TRAIN"

AGENCY: THE GATE WORLDWIDE / NEW YORK

Writer: David Bernstein

Art Director: Bill Schwab

Producer: Jean Wolff

Photographer: Tom Nagy

Client: SSGA

YOUR IDEA WAS SO MUCH BETTER ON PAPER

By Bill Schwab

Why is it that so many great ideas die on a piece of paper? They "look" great, they "sound" great, and then something terrible happens. I suggest that the next time an idea turns out just the way you imagined, or better yet, way better than you imagined, first thank the great people you worked with, and second, reconstruct the events that led to that success and try to learn from them.

You'll be teaching yourself to listen to what other people have to say and allowing them to make your ideas better.

Knowing what made an idea come together well once has made me be more receptive to letting it happen again. And again.

What follows are three examples from my career where small things happened that really brought ideas off the paper and started them on the path of becoming a great execution.

I was working at Fallon McElligott with Bill Westbrook. We were developing the first commercial in a new ad campaign. The idea for the concept came from imagining how the Wright brothers might have felt about air travel if they had had a particularly bad day filled with delays on their way to their historic flight at Kitty Hawk. The strategy involved a commitment by United Airlines to deliver the best possible air travel experience for their customers.

We had a headline for a potential ad—"If Orville and Wilbur had to go through what you do just to fly, they'd have stayed in the bicycle business." And I thought I remembered seeing pictures of their bicycle store in a certain book I had.

I didn't find that picture in the book. What I did find were pictures of early gliders, like the one the Wright brothers built. A few pages later, I found a vision of how our idea could work, beyond words on paper, in a very odd picture.

In the photo, a group of nicely dressed people were walking away from camera into a barren landscape. They were leaving an event and returning home.

Suddenly the glider sitting on the sand and the people walking away through the hills connected. Because I went looking for a picture in a book that I didn't find, a way of executing the idea that was on paper came together.

Now we would film not the Wright brothers, but the Wright brothers' plane, sitting on the sand waiting for them. People would come to see the "event" but due to unforeseen delays, the brothers would never make an appearance, and the people would get bored and tired and go home.

Later when we showed the photos to director Tony Scott, he suggested we shoot with old lenses, and use film stock that would be as close to shooting a hundred-year-old movie as we could get. As Tony began to draw his storyboards, all the parts fell into place. It was going to be a film from that day when the Wright brothers were going to fly.

The other possible ways of depicting our idea—the "real life" approach—scenes of people scurrying to the airport—ensuing mayhem—happy resolution, or title cards revealing one brilliant headline after another, or beautifully shot scenes with a clever counterpoint of contemporary music—were washed away.

The pictures had helped us imagine how a different kind of execution could work.

Our idea might have been successful without finding that photo in a book. But finding the photo was the key to our process of creating this concept.

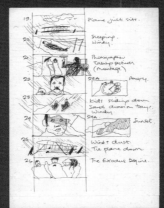

UAL STILL FRAMES / DIRECTOR'S STORYBOARD: "KITTY HAWK"

AGENCY: FALLON MCELLIGOTT / MINNEAPOLIS

Writers: Bill Westbrook, Joe Lovering

Art Director: Bill Schwab

Producer: Betsy Barnum Hicks

Director: Tony Scott, RSA

Director of Photography: Dan Mindel

Editor: Barry Stillwell

Client: UAL

TV: "DOG'S BURIED TREASURE"

AGENCY: THE GATE WORLDWIDE / NEW YORK

Writer: David Bernstein

Art Director: Bill Schwab

Producer: Bob Samuel

Directors: Tom and Charlie Guard, Smuggler

Director of Photography: Joost Van Gelder

Editor and Post: Chuck Willis, Absolute Post and the Mill

Music: Big Foote

Client: SSGA

Another project went from paper to execution in a very different way.

The commercial concepts we were developing illustrated the benefit of precision investing, and we did this by creating two involving little films about a dog and a tiny Swiss village.

The dog commercial was a story about a boy who struggles to find precisely the "right thing"—his "buried treasure" —for his girl. Like Disney's *Lady and the Tramp* it would be a love story with dogs playing the roles of humans. We planned to have the entire story take place in a backyard. In the end, we would reveal that the dog had dug hundreds of holes, all his "buried treasures," in the process of finding precisely the right thing for his love. Our client approved the concepts, but asked if we could "push the idea further."

I remembered a scene in Godard's *Breathless* where Jean Paul Belmondo is trying to impress Jean Seberg as she is selling newspapers on the Champs-Elysees. He tries so hard to impress Seberg; she pretends not to care. So we added the idea into the treatment as a way of avoiding an overly sentimental take on the concept. A suggestion was made that we change the story to have the boy dog search in other places for his treasure. In a city not unlike Paris, our little dog races around like Antoine Doinel in Truffaut's *400 Blows*. The girl dog moved from the backyard to an apartment not unlike Seberg's.

When our directing team, Tom and Charlie Guard, read the reference to *Breathless* in our treatment, other New Wave references came pouring out. The film references helped us re-imagine what the concept could be.

Continuing the New Wave vibe, it's shot in grainy B&W. Our editor used jump cuts, and even has the girl dog look directly into the camera, à la Anna Karina in *Band of Outsiders*.

The way of executing the story began to lead us to more interesting territory, eventually including *North by Northwest* and *Amores Perros* as well.

But the core idea always had its own personality.

Although *Breathless* uses hard driving jazz, our story still retained a powerful sense of sweetness. So when it came time for music, it seemed something like Louis Armstrong singing "Le vie en rose." The directors had a charming recording of a woman singing a sweet little song with a less than perfect voice. We took this input to a composer and got a wonderfully charming track. It fit perfectly with our story, which ends, unlike many New Wave films, with the boy happy and the girl satisfied with his gift.

You can't always rely on films to create a direction, however. Sometimes you just have to pick up a pencil and let your story flow from your imagination to the pictures you draw.

Our "Clocktower" commercial was done exactly this way.

When you are illustrating a concept board, you'll find yourself asking a lot of questions. What would a village look like? Where would it be? What are things that depend on time to run effectively? How dramatic would it be if they stopped working?

Answer as many of these questions as you can in a board and a written treatment. The more thoughtful you are in this process, the more questions you ask, the more interesting the answers become and the better the finished piece will be.

In the case of our story of the village, we wanted to show that the people ran their lives around time. So the setting of the story needed to be a perfect Swiss village. I imagined a village like Geppetto's town in *Pinocchio* or the scenes photographed in *The Sound of Music* or *The Great Escape.* I remembered trips to Italy, Germany, and Austria and composited those images in my drawings.

Not only did the village need to look perfect, so did the villagers. When I was drawing my board, I looked at photos of Tyrolean life from the 1930s. We decided to get the right faces by casting as many local people as possible. During this process, the look of the wardrobe began to take shape.

Our village is run by a precise clocktower. What does that look like? Miles of stairs leading up and up. How to draw that? I looked at Piranesi's etchings, M. C. Escher's prints of people ascending stairways, Merlin's castle tower classroom in *The Sword and the Stone.* We found the tallest clocktower in the Tyrol for our commercial.

Eventually our hero is confronted with the massive nonworking clock—what to do? When I drew the storyboard, it seemed like an old-fashioned kickstart would make the clock move. At our casting session in Milan we tried a number of things; finally we asked one actor to just hit the clock with his fist and react with surprise and relief. It worked in the casting as well as the commercial.

Probably because the village itself reminded me of a wonderful toy train layout my uncle used to set up at Christmas time, I wanted to have a train in the storyboard. It became a very important part of the concept because the train could not move until the clock tower was restarted. And then after it was fixed, the conductor adjusts his watch to keep the train "on time."

Nothing great—except a miracle—happens without the effort of many people. I've been fortunate to work on these projects with many talented partners. So my last word of advice is the same as my first. Whenever you start creating your next great idea, make sure it includes working with the best people you can.

Thanks for the title, Bob.

SSGA ART DIRECTOR'S STORYBOARD AND TV: "CLOCKTOWER"

AGENCY: THE GATE WORLDWIDE / NEW YORK

Writer: David Bernstein

Art Director: Bill Schwab

Producer: Bob Samuel

Directors: Tom and Charlie Guard, Smuggler

Director of Photography: Joost Van Gelder

Editor and Post: Chuck Willis, Absolute Post and the Mill

Music: Big Foote

Client: SSGA

SSGA "CLOCK TOWER"
:30   the gate

OPEN ON A SWISS STATIONMASTER STOPPING A TRAIN FROM LEAVING THE STATION.

SFX: SCREECHING BRAKES

CUT TO THE TOWN CLOCK. IT'S STUCK AT *A MINUTE TO 3:00.*

CUT TO WORKER RUNNING UP STEPS OF CLOCK TOWER.

SFX: RUNNING FEET

CUT TO CLASSROOM WHERE THE KIDS AND TEACHER STARE OUT THE WINDOW AT THE CLOCK TOWER.

SSGA "CLOCK TOWER"
:30   the gate

CUT BACK TO WORKER RUNNING UP MORE STEPS OF CLOCK TOWER.

SFX: FOOTSTEPS AND PANTING

CUT TO A FARMER STARING AT THE CLOCK TOWER WHILE A COW WAITS TO BE MILKED.

CUT BACK TO WORKER KICKING THE GEARS OF THE CLOCK.

THE GEARS START TO TURN AGAIN.

SFX: LOUD KICK AND GRINDING OF GEARS

CUT TO CLOCK HITTING 3:00.

SFX: 3 BONGS, LOUD CHEERS

VO: Some things in life need to be precise.

SSGA "CLOCK TOWER"
:30   the gate

CUT TO KIDS RUNNING OUT OF CLASS.

SFX: SCREAMING HAPPY KIDS

VO: Investing is one of them.

CUT TO COW BEING MILKED.

That's why State Street created SPDR.

CUT TO TRAIN LEAVING STATION.

A family of ETFs that are so precise...

CUT TO STATIONMASTER AS HE WINDS HIS POCKET WATCH BACK A MINUTE AND PUTS IN POCKET.

...you could set a clock to them.

SSGA "CLOCK TOWER"
:30   the gate

CUT TO MDY TICKER SYMBOL, SPDR LOGO AND TAG.

VO: SPDR. Precise in a world that isn't.

MDY
BY
SPDR
Precise in a world that isn't.

How to Facilitate a Group Brainstorming Session

> *Define the problem clearly and succinctly.*

> *Determine criteria.*

> *Appoint two people: (1) a good note taker and (2) an effective facilitator who will be responsible for running the session. (Useful tools include oversized notepads and a marker board or an interactive whiteboard screen. Or the session might be recorded in its entirety.) Notes should be evaluated at the conclusion of the session.*

> *Include participants with different expertise. Encourage all participants to contribute freely.*

> *Stay focused on the problem under discussion.*

> *Do not judge any contributed ideas during the session. Creativity should not be stifled, no matter how harebrained an idea might seem in the moment.*

> *Schedule a second round of brainstorming that will build on ideas suggested in the first.*

Average Time: 30–45 minutes per session

At the conclusion of the session, ideas are evaluated. According to creativity expert Edward de Bono, ideas should be evaluated for usefulness, for whether they merit further exploration, and for originality.

An effective idea-generating tool, brainstorming:

> *Encourages creative thinking,*

> *Generates many ideas,*

> *Provides an opportunity for collaboration.*

"What is it that is going on here?" and "Under what circumstances do we think things are real?"

Frames can be thought of as conceptual structures that determine meaning—the meaning of an argument or the meaning of a situation. Take a school, for example. The frame elements of a school would include: teachers, dry erase boards, erasers, books, a library, desks and chairs, and so on. Going further, a scenario in a school would tell us what happens in a frame, which might include a teacher reading from a book in front of a class of children or a child writing at her desk.

If a child were to instruct the teachers seated in student chairs, that scenario would break the frame—it would not fit the frame common to us. Frames offer meaning in context, and they help us understand our world and quickly assess what is going on in it.

We can use a frame to examine a brand or group, looking for insights on which to base an advertising idea.

HOW TO FRAME A SCENARIO

1. Determine the scenario: What happens in this frame?

2. What is the setting? What are the conditions?

3. Who are the people or groups?

4. What is their point of view around this specific experience?

5. What are their goals?

6. What are their assumptions? What are their perceptions?

7. Are there conflicts? Is there cooperation?

8. What are the outcomes?

CHANGING THE FRAME

When brainstorming to generate ideas, frames might inhibit creative thinking, since they are based on common expectations derived from shared experience. During brainstorming, once you identify a frame, a *change of frame* can be very useful.

Changing a frame allows you to explore possibilities, to imagine what a brand or organization could be beyond its current personality or how it is commonly perceived. Here you set aside preconceived notions and explore alternatives.

THE AS-IF FRAME

George Kelly, American psychologist and author of *The Psychology of Personal Constructs* (1955), argued that there are an infinite number of ways to construe the world, to interpret an event. Hans Vaihinger, German philosopher, in *The Philosophy of "As If"* (1924) stresses people's reliance on "pragmatic fictions" to navigate an irrational world. Also relevant is Jeremy Bentham's *Theory of Fictions* (1932). Since reality is not definitively given, we construct ways to understand the world, ignoring contradictions, proceeding "as if" our constructs are real. For example, scientists conduct experiments based on theories, which are not certainties.

If you were to entertain a different construction of an event, you could behave "as if" that construction were real, thus exploring possibilities within that frame. If you were to approach a problem with an as-if frame, if you were to construe the world differently, you might gain a fresh perspective or a transformative perspective; for example, you might behave as if you had a wizard's powers or act as if you couldn't understand your native language.

Meaning depends on context; by changing the context, you can imagine a different meaning. Basically, entertaining the as-if experiment allows for novel possibilities.

Figure 3-1

PRINT:
"STOLEN HANDBAG I"
"STOLEN HANDBAG II"

AGENCY:
LEO BURNETT / DENMARK

Creative Director:
Charlie Fisher

Art Director: Nete Borup

Copywriter: Thomas Fabricius

Client: Best Behavior

© February 2001

REVERSAL

Seeing a situation, brand, organization, product, service, or behavior from a different perspective *(reversal)* can help stimulate ideas.

You can use reversal to reframe a problem to stimulate ideas or to see it from a different viewpoint, or reversal may help you to see different ways to *define* the problem. For example, in figure 3-1, reversal is used to show the desirability of a handbag brand, in that the thief steals the bag while leaving the contents behind.

How to use reversal

> *Select a topic such as gaming, running, or dieting.*

> *Select an aspect (elements, characteristics, components, principles) of that topic or the entire topic, and then reverse it. For example, when dieting one can eat whatever one likes. When running, one must do it lying down.*

> *Any level of absurdity is welcome. Consider opposite perspectives, look at a situation or activity sideways, backwards, or from outside in.*

Osborn's Checklist

In the mid-1960s, American artist Richard Serra began experimenting with nontraditional sculptural materials including fiberglass, neon, vulcanized rubber, and lead. He combined his examination of these materials and their properties with an interest in the physical process of making sculpture. Serra enacted an action verb on a material; for example, a work could be the result of enacting "to lift" on discarded rubber. He compiled a list of verbs (to roll, to crease, to curve), and then enacted them on the materials he had collected in his studio.

It struck me that instead of thinking what a sculpture is going to be and how you're going to do it compositionally, what if you just enacted those verbs in relation to a material, and didn't worry about the results?[3]
—Richard Serra

Before Serra's sculptural experimentations, Alex Osborn of BBDO created an inspired checklist technique as a tool to transform an existent idea or thing. Arguably, this could be the only tool you ever need to foster creative thinking. In short, Osborn's Checklist comprised a list of action verbs:

> *Adapt*

> *Modify*

> *Magnify*

> *Minify*

> *Substitute*

> *Rearrange*

> *Reverse*

Mapping

A *mind map* is a visual representation, diagram, or presentation of the various ways words, terms, images, thoughts, or ideas can be related to one another. A useful tool in understanding relationships and organizing thoughts, it leads to idea generation. Mapping is a brainstorming and visual diagramming tool that is used to develop an idea or lead to an idea; it is also called word mapping, idea mapping, mind mapping, word clustering, and spider diagramming. It can be used to visualize, structure, and classify ideas and as an aid in study, organization, problem solving, and decision making. The resulting visual map is a diagram used to represent thoughts, words, information, tasks, or images in a specific diagrammatic arrangement. There is a central key word or thought, and all other words or thoughts or visuals stem from and are linked to that word or thought, in a radius around that central focal point. It has been said that mapping is a visualizing technique dating to ancient Greece.

---

3. Richard Serra, Museum of Modern Art, New York; www.moma.org.

TYPES OF MIND MAPS

Mapping is a useful tool for the writing process, design process, brainstorming process, or simply for thinking something through. You can approach mapping in two basic ways.

Automatic mapping relies heavily on the surrealist strategy of spontaneous free association, trying to avoid conscious choices and allowing associations to flow freely.

Deliberate mapping, although not totally controlled, relies more on the natural growth of associations, revealing the way your mind instinctively organizes or makes associations.

You can reorganize or revise what you have mapped based on new information, on a deeper understanding derived from the first go-round, or on something that occurred to you while mapping. You can articulate a range of connections or see links among items on the map. The resulting mind map is a tangible representation of associations that may reveal thinking or lead to an idea. You can rearrange items to create a new beginning (central word or image, or primary item), reordering subtopics (secondary items), sub-subtopics (tertiary items), and so on.

HOW TO CREATE A MIND MAP

Mapping software is available that offers templates, notes, labels, cross-linking, and more. However, since the nature of the drawing process maximizes spontaneous mapping, doing it by hand offers more outcomes. Drawing your own map is likely to increase personalization and to encourage a natural flow of thoughts. A mind map can be created in the following manner:

> *Position an extra-large sheet of paper in landscape position.*

> *Draw a primary visual or write a key word, topic, or theme at the center of the page; this is your starting point.*

> *Starting with the central word or image, draw branches (using lines, arrows, or any type of branch) out in all directions, making as many associations as*

possible. (Don't be judgmental; just write or draw freely.)

Each subtopic should branch from the major central topic. Then, each sub-subtopic or image should branch out from the subtopic, branching out on and on. Seek relationships, and generate branches among as many items as possible. Feel free to repeat items and/or cross-link items.

Spontaneous mapping draws upon the unconscious. Write or draw as quickly as possible, without deliberating or editing. This type of mapping promotes nonlinear thinking. Interestingly, it can be the most unforeseen item or possibility that becomes a key to idea generation. (You can always go back into the map to make adjustments later.)

Deliberate mapping utilizes long and careful thinking. As a complement, you could consider note taking—writing down some explanatory notes near the items or branches so that, later, when you reexamine the map, you can more easily recall exactly what you were thinking.

Graphic Organizer

A *graphic organizer* is a visual aid used to illustrate the relationships among facts or ideas, similar in purpose to a mind map. It is a visual rather than narrative way to display information, making it easier to see previously unrealized and significant connections (diagram 3-2). Usually, a graphic organizer is a segmented structural configuration with blank areas to be filled with related ideas and information, which can be *written* (words) or *drawn* (pictures).

There are differently structured organizers for different purposes (diagram 3-3), including the following:

> **Spider Map:** *used to describe a central idea and its supports (how they function, their characteristics); a thing (e.g., a product, such as shampoo); a service (such as cancer screenings or roofing); a process (such as grinding glass for lenses or learning to read); a concept*

Diagram 3-2

Graphic organizer

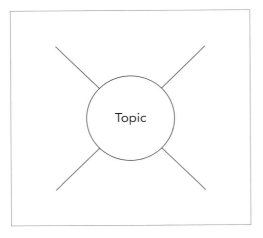

(bravery); or a proposition (education should be available to every citizen).

> *Series of events chain: used to delineate the consecutive steps in a process or a step-by-step method of doing something and how they lead to one another (such as how to bake bread); the stages of something (such as the cycle of a disease); a sequence of events (such as how dropping out of school leads to difficulties).*

> *Time line: used to represent significant events, chronology, or ages (e.g., the incarnations of Betty Crocker).*

> *Cycle: used to illustrate a sequence of events that are repeated to demonstrate relationships, key events in the cycle, perpetuation (e.g., growth cycles, laundry cycles, etc.).*

> *Continuum scale: a low-to-high scale range, used to illustrate the degrees of something (noise), degrees of value (agreement to disagreement), or ratings (popularity).*

> *Compare/contrast matrix: used to point out likenesses and differences between things, such as between two objects (think kettle and drum), between processes (think constructing a building and designing a page), between ideas, places, candidates, etc.*

> *Tree structure: used to illustrate the relationship of subordinate levels or categories stemming from a central element in a hierarchy (e.g., types of tools or levels of government).*

> *Problem and solution ladder: a top-down diagram used to represent a problem (at the top of the ladder), attempted solutions on the next rung(s), and the end result (the last rung).*

Attribute Listing

By focusing on the attributes of an object, person, place, character, topic or theme, product, or service, you can find a characteristic that might lead to an idea. *Attribute listing* is a method for analyzing and separating data through observing and identifying various qualities that might have otherwise been overlooked; basically, it is a diagrammed list of attributes. It works deconstructively, breaking down information into smaller parts that are then examined individually.

It can be useful to first break the object down into constituent parts and examine the attributes of each part. For example, if the item under examination is a laptop computer, you could break it down into the screen, keyboard, and motherboard. Or if the topic in question is a tax preparation service, you could break it down into the online operation, the brick-and-mortar storefront, the name, the staff, the environment, their proprietary preparation process, and so on.

THE PROCESS OF ATTRIBUTE LISTING

> *Select an object, person, place, character, topic or theme, product, or service for examination.*

> *List the physical or functional attributes (parts, characteristics, properties, qualities, or design elements) of the object under examination.*

> *List as many attributes as you possibly can.*

Diagram 3-3

Various graphic organizers

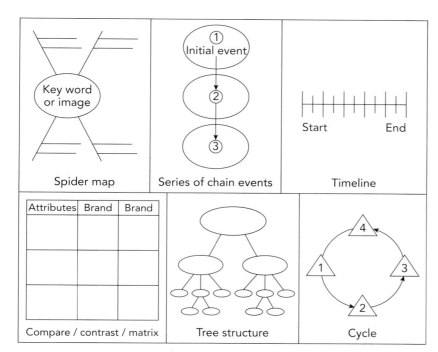

Spider map

Series of chain events

Timeline

Compare / contrast / matrix

Tree structure

Cycle

Problem	
Who:	
What:	
Why:	
How:	
Where:	

Attempted solution	Results
1.	
2.	
3.	
4.	

End results

Problem-solution ladder

SHOWCASE

INTERVIEW WITH ROSIE ARNOLD
DEPUTY EXECUTIVE CREATIVE DIRECTOR, BBH / LONDON
http://www.bartleboglehegarty.com

Rosie Arnold started moonlighting at a tiny creative hot shop called Bartle Bogle Hegarty (BBH) in 1983 while studying at Central Saint Martins College of Art & Design, London. She has been there ever since. Always motivated by the opportunity to do mold-breaking creative work among like-minded people, she has had no reason to move.

She spent the formative years of her career working closely with John Hegarty, learning the trade. While at BBH, Rosie has been responsible for some of the agency's most iconic work: Pretty Polly and Levi's in the 1980s; the *Independent*, TAG Heuer, and Levi's in the 1990s; and Axe (Lynx) and Robinsons in the 2000s.

Her work has collected many industry awards, including six Cannes Gold, six D&AD Pencils, and three Campaign Golds. For the last ten years she has spent most of her time as creative director on the Axe account where she has nurtured many other hugely well regarded pieces of work. The brand has become one of the most famous advertisers globally and one of Unilever's major brand successes.

Rosie's talent for producing outstanding ideas in traditional media such as TV and print is well documented. In 2007 she rose to a new challenge in a whole new area. BBH had been developing its digital offerings as clients needed their "above the line" (TV, radio, print, etc.) ideas to work online. Rosie was the creative director responsible for pitching for Unilever's European digital account. The work she and her team developed won the pitch and went live in January 2007. The "Get in There" digital campaign used mobile phones to get boys out from behind their computer games and back into the mating game. The campaign picked up a gold at D&AD in May 2008 and a silver at Cannes. Rosie has subsequently been named as one of *Revolution* magazine's most influential players in the digital advertising game.

In September 2007 Rosie took a three-month sabbatical and went back to art school; this time to the Royal College of Art to pursue a personal art project.

On her return to BBH, she was one of the three creative directors appointed to the U.K. Management Board, and in July 2008 she was appointed deputy executive creative director. She is, sadly, one of just a few women running creative departments in advertising agencies in the United Kingdom.

Rosie regularly appears in the press and is featured in a Channel 4 documentary, called *From the Top*, on life as an advertising creative. She is on the executive committee of D&AD and was chairman of the D&AD print awards in 2008. She was chairman of the print jury for the 2008 Big Awards (*Campaign* magazine's annual advertising awards).

Rosie has managed to combine her successful career with raising her two boys and three stepdaughters and learning to fence. She says of her multitasking role: "It feels a bit like being Ginger Rogers. You're expected to do everything that Fred does just backwards and in heels!"

You studied graphic design. Why did you choose advertising as a profession?

I loved the ideas most of all and wanted control of the whole piece of design. It seemed to me, as a graphic designer, you often only handled the type or only the illustration, and I loved thinking of the idea and designing the type (but I didn't have the photography or illustration skills) and having control of the whole piece.

You joined BBH in 1983 and have been one of the agency's most consistent creative stars. To what do you attribute your longevity at one agency, your rise and great success?

BBH is a great place to work. They have consistently believed in the primacy of the idea, and clients come to the agency because of the creative quality. I am totally motivated by doing great work, being surrounded by extremely talented and like-minded people, and BBH has always offered that...plus it's a great place to work with lovely people.

Can you talk a bit about your role as deputy executive creative director?

It is all still quite new. I oversee more brands than before and most of a global nature. I don't really get the chance to do my own work, but I guide and help teams, which is very rewarding. I also have an overview—a broad view on the direction I think the work should take and the idea of building a platform that will last years—and a direction the creative team should follow, which is a major responsibility but fun.

If you were to give a speed workshop in creative advertising, what are the top points you would stress?

Find the single thing you need to say. Find a fresh way of saying that. Question the best media solution (TV? Poster? Banner?)

Figure 3-2

*PRINT: "SHRINK TO FIT"
"FOOT" & "DOG"*

AGENCY: BBH / LONDON

Creative Director:
John Hegarty

Art Director: Rosie Arnold

Copywriter: Will Awdry

Client: Levis

You've said sometimes you accept your first thoughts on something but that's not always good enough, and you have to push yourself beyond that. How do you push your thinking? What's the best way to zag when everyone else is zigging?

First thoughts can be very useful, as they often are the most direct for the public—but they are often so obvious, they don't really tickle people. It is often the marriage of the first thought with a twist that works...it's just that twist that takes so long to come up with! I push myself by questioning if it feels familiar and imagining how I would react to the work if I came across it while judging an awards scheme, or what the papers would say. I am pretty hard on myself, which can be stressful.

Figure 3-3

TV: "IDEAL WOMAN"

AGENCY: BBH / LONDON

Creative Director:
Rosie Arnold

Art Director: Rosie Arnold

Copywriter: Shawn Preston

Director: Paul Goldman

Client: Lynx

I've heard a story about you sticking to your guns while presenting a Levi's campaign. You went up against your boss and won. What is your advice to creatives about selling others on their ideas or defending work?

First thing is to make sure you really really believe in the idea or person you want to use. You need to understand where your audience will be coming from and think about any problems or concerns they might have before you start to sell or defend. I think the best way to convince people is to be convinced yourself and try . . . [to] bring the idea to life as well as possible.

Your Lynx "Pulse" commercial created a media sensation and resulted in a number-one recording in Europe. What type of creative thinking allows an ad's content to cross over into pop culture and become part of the pop culture lexicon?

If you find a human insight, it crosses boundaries. In fact, I am always looking for the insight that unlocks the problem, and then I try to find a fresh way of bringing that to life.

Many of your TV spots involve storytelling, for example, "Lynx Getting Dressed." (See figure 3-4.) What role does storytelling play in advertising?

I think it is the most emotive way to get across an idea. It involves the viewer [and] inspires and entertains.

Would you kindly predict the future of advertising over the next decade?

Wow! Successful brands continue to advertise throughout economic turmoil. Disney was created and advertised in the Great Depression. So I don't think there will be a decline in advertising. However, consumers have greater opportunities to edit out advertising—they can choose when to watch programs without the ads! Therefore, we have to be more inventive about how and where to talk to people, and we have to be so good that people actively seek us out. Look at the popular appeal Cadbury's "Gorilla" recently had on YouTube.

Since you joined BBH straight from art school, what advice can you offer aspiring creatives looking for entry-level positions?

Work hard on getting a really good book [portfolio] together. You have no client constraints [when you are a student], so it is the opportune time to show what you are made of. Don't feel you have to be too conventional; there is, increasingly, no such thing as a set ad. Come up with original thinking, and be clear about who is the art director and who is the writer. We want people who have craft skills. It is no longer good enough to just have ideas; you need to be able to show us you can art direct or write.

As one of only a couple female executive creative directors in London, what advice would you offer to future generations of women in advertising?

Stand up for your ideas. I think women tend to be more amenable, but you need to push an idea through as you see it. That does not mean you have to become a man, but find ways of persuading people why your idea works in the way you see it.

What are the most important characteristics and skills a junior art director should possess?

Being good at having ideas and a restless curiosity, passion, and love of art design and all things visual. The most tricky to define is also having an "eye."

Figure 3-4

TV: "GETTING DRESSED"
AGENCY: BBH / LONDON

Creative Director:
Rosie Arnold

Art Director/ Copywriter:
Nick Gill

Director: Ringan Ledwidge

Client: Lynx

PART 02

FORMULATING AN ADVERTISING IDEA
WRITING AND DESIGNING

04

THE BRAND IDEA

Technology is an enabler, it makes stuff possible faster. That's all. Technology facilitates, it doesn't replace the human imagination.
—Kevin Roberts, CEO Worldwide of Saatchi & Saatchi

THE BIG IDEA

Imagine life without the Internet, without mobile phones or personal computers. Now imagine what the next ten years will bring, imagine how ideas will be transmitted. Can you predict the impact of the next wave of technology? Can you predict how fragmented the media landscape will become? The one sure thing is that critical and creative thinking will be necessary. Ideas, ideas. Ideas matter—no matter what the technology used. We have to generate ideas and content that people will seek out, that pulls people in across media. When so many people stay continually connected throughout the day by mobile phone or computer, each person decides which advertising messages they care to receive and where to hear or view them. The ideas we generate will have to use media to build relationships and dialogue with people, allowing two-way conversations, offering utilities, with the understanding that each advertising message is an invited guest who can be tossed out at any moment if he or she does not bring something useful to the table. In fact, the more likely scenario is that people will have their own individual digital mechanism to receive the kind of information they want, whether on the mobile phone, family television or computer screen, granting permission to select brands. The time of pushing advertising at people is over.

That is why it is critical to understand how a strategy and idea can work across media and how to start a conversation with people. To simply place an ad conceived for print in mobile media is not enough. One must understand what each medium can do and do well and what people want on that platform or device.

THE BRAND IDEA

In an overcrowded, competitive marketplace, relevant and engaging branding can ensure efficacy for a quality product, service, group, individual, or commodity. Not only does branding identify and distinguish, it builds *equity* (the value of the brand or group).

Just think of the strength of Nokia, the American Red Cross, Coca-Cola, Toyota, or (RED) if you have any doubts about how crucial effective branding is to success. Certainly, factors other than branding contribute to a brand's success, including the quality of its product or service, public perception and enthusiasm, relevance to people's lives, the time period and culture, and the communities and/ or celebrities who adopt it. The branding idea is based on several factors:

> *The nature of the brand or group*

> *The goals of differentiation and distinction*

> *A strategic brand personality*

> *The target audience*

> *What is important to the target audience*

> *Positioning*

Over twenty-five years ago, marketing guru Jack Trout coined the term "positioning." In *Positioning: The Battle for Your Mind* (1981), Al Reis and Jack Trout wrote that a company must create a "position" in the prospect's mind, a position that takes into account both the brand's (or group's) strengths and weaknesses as well as those of its competitors.

Before advertising comes a core branding idea—the idea that imbues a brand or group with character that differentiates it and builds a relationship with the audience. Branding is the creation of a comprehensive, strategic, and unique program for a brand or group, with an eye toward building a relationship with people based on how they experience— interact and use—the brand or group. Rather than approaching individual marketing and advertising applications as isolated design solutions, branding encapsulates a strategic imperative, to make every application contribute to the entire effort—to the brand story—and therefore to a person's experience with the brand.

Very few products, services, or groups are unique; most are parity products, that is, they offer qualities and functions similar or identical to those of their competitors. Branding and advertising differentiates these parity products, services, and groups in a crowded marketplace.

We can think of a brand construct as a developed personality—a strategic concept incorporating a positioning platform based on the product or group with insights into the brand and the prospective audience. It is both an armature and a point of departure for differentiating and connecting with the audience. It also helps you determine if your concept is "on brand" (in step with the brand or group's core identity and positioning) or "off brand" (not in sync with the brand or group's core identity). Advertising that is off brand is a potential marketing hazard.

Construct Indicators

Whether brand strategy is determined before an advertising agency comes on board or developed with agency collaboration, the following must be identified for the brand, group, or individual:

Attribute: a defining property or characteristic.

Functional benefit: the practical or useful

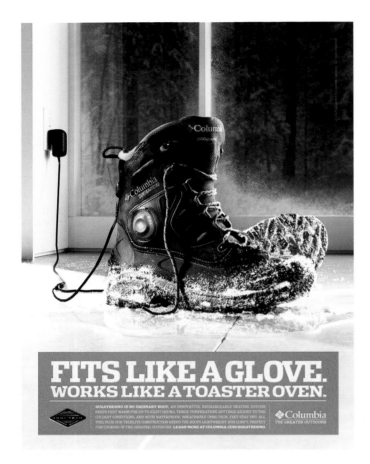

Figure 4-1

characteristics of a product or service; for example, in figure 4-1, "Shirt," a print ad in a campaign for Columbia, lets you know that this "Water-Resistant Powers Vertical" shirt will keep you dry.

Emotional benefit: an intangible asset based on feelings, not on a functional characteristic of a product or service. It is a response that may derive from personal significance or reward and the desire to feel good. Emotional benefits are not based on a tangible characteristic of a product or service but rather on subjective experience; for example, for the 2008 holiday season, OfficeMax launched the third edition of its world-famous holiday eGreeting site with new features for spreading holiday cheer at www.ElfYourself.com (see figure 4-2).

Value: in the end, what a person wants from a product, service, or group.

At times, benefits are multidimensional, as in the Drunk Driving Prevention efforts through the Ad Council. According to the Ad Council, "Research . . . indicates that 62 percent of Americans exposed to the now-iconic Friends Don't Let Friends Drive Drunk campaign have personally intervened to stop someone from driving drunk, no doubt saving countless lives." What's in it for a friend to stop a friend from driving drunk? Is the person altruistic? Would someone feel good about himself or herself if he or she prevented a drunk driver from getting behind the wheel? Certainly, this type of intervention provides a functional benefit for the driver, the driver's family, and others on the road.

▸ Figure 4-2

THEME: "ELFYOURSELF"

Web Site: ElfYourself.com

Placement / Airing:
Web, print, in stores

AGENCIES: JIBJAB (2008);
EVB / SAN FRANCISCO
AND TOY / NEW YORK
(2006–2007)

Client: OfficeMax

"ElfYourself" is an annual holiday campaign from OfficeMax that began in 2006 and returns each holiday season at ElfYourself.com. Each season, consumers are invited to upload up to five digital photos, attach them to elf characters, select a dance theme—disco, country, classic, or charleston—and hit play ready to be entertained by hilarious dancing elves. Customized ElfYourself videos can be sent to friends and family as a holiday/eCard, embedded into social media sites via "QuickPost" options, or added to Facebook profiles through an ElfYourself Facebook application. In 2008, ElfYourself enabled users to take their elves offline (for a small fee) by downloading custom videos to their desktops or creating custom photos gifts including ornaments, mouse pads, playing cards, or coffee mugs.

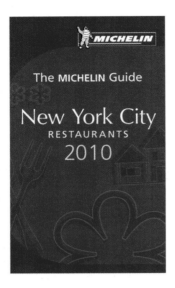

Brand Idea Guide

Implicit in each construct must be the following markers, which are indicators for effective promotion and potential growth.

DIFFERENTIATION

What differentiates a brand is how it is characterized, its visual and verbal identity as expressed in each media unit and through every point of contact. Simply stated, differentiation is what distinguishes one brand from the rest.

OWNERSHIP

The advertising man studies the consumer. He tries to place himself in the position of the buyer. His success largely depends on doing that to the exclusion of everything else.
—Claude Hopkins, from
Scientific Advertising

Part of what differentiates a brand or group is "owning" a selling point, benefit, attitude, or any characteristic that contributes to a distinct construct. In 1923 Claude Hopkins, in *Scientific Advertising*, explained the notion: Claiming ownership of a quality, even though others in your category have the same quality, establishes the brand in the audience's mind as the primary possessor of that quality.

RELEVANCE

The brand idea is based on an insight into the audience that makes the brand relevant to them. It must exemplify something—tangible or intangible—that people find compellingly relevant to their lives.

BRANDED UTILITY: USEFULNESS

One way to make a brand relevant is to provide something useful—to appeal to people and earn their attention—based in their special interests or needs.

It's where the brand creates a commitment to a relationship. It's where the brand creates something useful to you, something that's a utility in your life. The consumer will feel more confident with the relationship if the brand will continue to be part of your life.

Branding has been about cultural relevance— what we're saying is that it's not so much about relevance as usefulness. . . . Brand messages need to be in a useful format. Branded utility can cover social events, software, maybe even free printing from Kodak.
—Benjamin Palmer, the Barbarian Group

Rory Sutherland, vice chairman of Ogilvy Group UK, believes that brands will resonate with consumers if they fulfill one of three Old World roles: courtier (trusted advisor), court jester (entertainer), or courtesan (pleaser).

Branded utilities encompass a variety of applications, from print to mobile and from Web sites to environmental installations. Introduced over a century ago, the Michelin Guide is an excellent example of a branded utility, a pocket-size book containing useful information (figure 4-3). According to Michelin, "When the Michelin Guide was first introduced, it set out to encourage people to drive, and along the way, enjoy the journey." The first edition of the guide was published in 1900, for the Paris Universal Exhibition.

Other successful branded utilities include the Samsung Mobile Charging Stations in airports and the Charmin Restrooms. During the fall-winter holiday season, the Charmin Restrooms in New York City provide residents and tourists with twenty clean, fully staffed ADA-compliant restrooms as well as stroller parking, seating, and family photo opportunities. Although a broadcast television spot reaches many more people, a clean, available bathroom and baby-changing station in the middle of Times Square may leave users with a much more enduring, and endearing, brand experience.

At airports, the Samsung Mobile Charging Stations offer travelers the convenience of free recharging of their mobile phones, laptops, and other personal electronic devices. "The Samsung Mobile Charging Stations are an easy way to reduce some of the stress that can

CASE STUDY

Renegade

HSBC "BankCab" Program

The Challenge: Make HSBC's position as "the World's Local Bank" tangible to New Yorkers.

Target Insight: Savvy New Yorkers pride themselves on their local knowledge.

The Program: The BankCab program brings to life HSBC's brand position as the World's Local Bank. An iconic Checker cab is the cornerstone of the program, driving the streets of New York five days a week, offering free rides to HSBC customers. To further demonstrate HSBC's local knowledge, we orchestrated an exhaustive search for the most knowledgeable cabbie in the city. Culminating with a major press event, the BankCabbie coronation was covered by TV (ABC, NBC, Fox, WB, NY1, Nippon, Telemundo), radio (880AM, WOR/710AM), newspapers (*Daily News*), AP, and several online pubs. To put HSBC's local knowledge into the hands of all New Yorkers, we created the HSBC BankCabbie guides. Written by Ed Levine, a local food critic, and designed to look like checkbooks, they identified the best of the best in each NY neighborhood. Over 100,000 copies of the guides were distributed by street teams dressed in BankCabbie attire. An HSBC BankCab micro site supports all aspects of the program and is designed to encourage visitors to expand their relationship with HSBC.

The Results: The HSBC BankCab program, in its sixth year of continuous operation, generated over 20 million PR impressions during the launch event. Customers exposed to the program were five times more likely to recommend HSBC to a friend.

—Renegade

AGENCY: RENEGADE / NEW YORK

RENEGADE.COM

Executive Creative Director: Drew Neisser

Creative Director: Fanny Krivoy

Associate Creative Director: Alan Irikura

›

Figure 4-4

WEB VIDEO PLAYER: SILVERLIGHT PLAYER FOR NBC OLYMPICS

AGENCY: SCHEMATIC

Creative Lead / Creative Director: Ian Cunningham

Technology Lead / Tech Director: Paul Abrelat

© Schematic, Inc.

The Situation: *2,200 hours of live, interactive video; 3,000 hours of on-demand video; 20 simultaneous live video streams. Multiple camera options. Massive traffic spikes. Metadata overlays. Video rewind/replay. Enhanced play-back mode. Picture-in-picture functionality. Social networking capability.*

These are just some of the things that NBC required of its Silverlight-powered 2008 Summer Olympics video player—a player that had to perform perfectly under the intense media scrutiny that adheres to everything associated with the Olympics. Microsoft and partner Schematic welcomed this high-profile opportunity to demonstrate to the world just what Silverlight can do.

Our Contribution: *Built by Schematic in close coordination with NBC and Microsoft, NBC's Olympic video player brought digital convergence to the Beijing games, making streamlined, customizable video the centerpiece of the Web experience. The attention to superior user experience began with the player's adaptive streaming, which dynamically adjusted the bit rate based on a user's connection speed and hardware, thus providing the best possible viewing experience for each individual member of the audience.*

The NBC Olympics player provided access to every moment of video of every event at the Beijing games; value-added features provided both context and control for users. The standard version of the player enabled users to view on-demand and related video as well as athlete bios, sport-specific information, and trivia. The enhanced video player provided near HD quality video, picture-in-picture capability; it also used Silverlight's transparency capabilities so users could simultaneously navigate through menus while watching an event onscreen. Users could also track the action and navigate via a continuous stream of broadcasters' live expert commentary and play-by-play links. "Share" capability allowed people to send their favorite Olympic moments to their friends. Perhaps the standout feature was the "Live Video Control Room," which allowed viewers to select videos, configure the display and watch as many as four live video streams simultaneously.

The Impact: *During the 17 days of the 2008 Olympics Games in Beijing, NBCOlympics.com, powered by Silverlight, had more than 50 million unique visitors, resulting in 1.3 billion page views, 70 million video streams and 600 million minutes of video watched, increasing the average time on the site (from 3 minutes to 27 minutes) and Silverlight market penetration in the U.S. by more than 30 percent. Broadcasters in France (France Televisions SA), the Netherlands (NOS), Russia (Sportbox.ru), and Italy (RAI) also chose Silverlight to deliver Olympics coverage online. In addition, leading companies such as CBS College Sports, Blockbuster Inc., Hard Rock Cafe International Inc., Yahoo! Japan, AOL LLC, Toyota Motor Corp., HSN Inc., and Tencent Inc. are building their next-generation experiences using Silverlight. According to Microsoft, as of October 2008, one in four consumers worldwide have access to a computer with Silverlight installed; in some countries, Silverlight enjoys 50 percent and growing market penetration.*

—Schematic

come with traveling for business travelers and vacationers alike," says Bill Ogle, chief marketing officer of Samsung Mobile. "The charging stations are easy to find and simple to use."

Another successful branded utility was the Silverlight player for the NBC 2008 Summer Olympics coverage (figure 4-4). Schematic harnessed the features of Silverlight "to provide a truly interactive, hi-def experience that puts the viewer in control of the content," says Steve Sklepowich, group product manager, Silverlight media, Microsoft Corporation.

STORYTELLING

Storytelling reveals meaning without committing the error of defining it.
—Hannah Arendt

People are engaged by compelling narratives. If a brand or group has a story to tell, then it will be more dimensional. Through the branding, advertising, and every point of contact, people learn the brand story.

What took Dove from being a bar of beauty soap to a powerful brand is their brand story: they "challenge beauty stereotypes and help women feel more positive about their own individual beauty." If the story gets it right, hits a nerve, then the brand moves from being a product or service to becoming an influencer with a set of values.

Several brand experts emphasize the importance of communicating the underlying brand philosophy through strategy, positioning, and construct, through each concept executed in each media unit, referring collectively to the practice as "storytelling." Figure 4-5, "Videogame" for Coca-Cola, is a brilliant example of storytelling with an emotional benefit. Not only does this television spot tell a highly engaging story, but it also tells the greater story of the brand.

Henry Jenkins, director of the Massachusetts Institute of Technology (MIT) comparative media studies program, coined the term "transmedia storytelling," referring to a "process where integral elements of a fiction get dispersed systematically across multiple delivery channels for the purpose of creating a unified and coordinated entertainment experience. Ideally, each medium makes it own unique contribution to the unfolding of the story."[1]

Related to storytelling is theme. A theme is a distinct conceptual or pictorial, topic-based element that might be derived from nature, society, politics, or religion—freedom, poverty, or empowerment, for example. Variations on a theme also can work as a platform for idea generation.

UNITY

Unity is imposed across media, permitting a consistent brand voice and tone in all verbal and visual communication, with necessary and appropriate variations for interest and media variables.

COMMON EXPERIENCE

A brand or group allows people to connect through common experiences, whether through a social networking site, a community-building Web site, a passed-on link or interconnected functionality, discussion through a broadcast commercial, or simply through membership in a brand community.

Branding Construct Approaches

"Anybody who is honest about consumer behavior knows that often what we buy is not simply some thing but some idea that is embodied by that thing," writes Rob Walker, referring specifically to clothing company Lululemon's "yoga-inspired athletic apparel."[2]

Dan Ariely, professor of behavioral economics at Duke University, and Michael Norton, assistant professor of marketing at Harvard Business School, call this notion "conceptual consumption."[3]

Successful brands are based on concepts. There are as many possible conceptual

1. http://www.henryjenkins.org/2007/03/transmedia_storytelling_101.html

2. Rob Walker, "Consumed: Lululemon Athletica Promotes Yoga as a Lifestyle Brand," *New York Times Magazine*, 21 July 2009.

3. *Annual Review of Psychology* 60 (2009): 475–99

Figure 4-5

TV: "VIDEOGAME"

Format: :60 (sixty seconds)

AGENCY: WIEDEN + KENNEDY (W+K) / PORTLAND

Client: Coca-Cola

Creative Directors: Hal Curtis and Mark Fitzloff

Copywriter: Sheena Brady

Art Director: Shannon McGlothlin

Account Team: Lee Davis and Kirsten Hartill

Producer: Niki Polyocan

Agency Executive Producer: Ben Grylewicz

Production Company: Nexus
   Director: Smith & Foulkes
   Executive Producer:
     Julia Parfitt
   Producer: Kara McCombe

Sound Design
   Executive Producer:
     Michelle Curran
   Sound Designer:
     Chris Smith
   Producer: Carol Dunn

The hero of a gritty, car-racing videogame has a change of heart after drinking a Coke. Instead of hijacking cars and stealing purses, he decides to give a little love.
   —Wieden + Kennedy

SHOWCASE

INTERVIEW WITH KEVIN ROBERTS

Kevin Roberts is CEO Worldwide of Saatchi & Saatchi, one of the world's leading creative organizations. Principal clients include Procter & Gamble, Toyota, General Mills, JC Penney, and Novartis. Since his leadership began in 1997, Saatchi & Saatchi has achieved record creative and financial performance. Kevin Roberts has authored several books and is best known for his creation of Lovemarks, an idea that has transformed the conventions of brand marketing. His book *Lovemarks: The Future Beyond Brands* (2004) has been published in eighteen languages. He is honorary professor at the University of Auckland Business School, New Zealand, and honorary professor of creative leadership at Lancaster University, United Kingdom, and holds honorary doctorates from a number of universities worldwide. Kevin is business ambassador for the New Zealand–United States Council, a member of the board of directors of Telecom New Zealand, the chairman of USA Rugby, and a trustee of the Turn Your Life Around Trust in West Auckland.

Q: What are lovemarks?

Lovemarks are super-evolved brands that have become irresistible, that attract premium margins, preference, and share because they are constituted firstly around emotional connections. The owners and producers of the products are passionate and empathetic. Lovemarks can also be places, people, and experiences. At the heart of Lovemarks are three elements: mystery, sensuality, and intimacy.

Q: Would you give us an example of Saatchi's lovemark thinking?

Our transformation of JC Penney from a middle of the road American retailer to a desired and attractive destination for American housewives is an example. JC Penney sought us because of an idea, and have allowed us to create magical work for them that has produced stellar results in terms of sales, retention, and overall results in a bitingly tough retail market. Twice they have won "best in world" retail awards for our work with them. The role of business is to make the world a better place.

Q: What are the five ideas you believe in?

Nothing is impossible.

One team one dream.

Think with your heart.

Be an inspirational player.

Never give the customer what she wants; give her what she never dreamed possible.

Q: Would you tell us about the World Changing Ideas program?

This was a program created by Bob Isherwood and Richard Myers, creative leaders of our company, to identify, encourage, profile, and reward the world's most innovative ideas that would make the world a better place. The award brought together many of the world's best innovators to judge the entries. Bob has retired from the company but (a) his inspiration lives on and (b) we are doing it differently now. At the last worldwide creative board meeting there was a networked piggy bank at the center of the table; it had an electronic coin counter and a wi-fi connection to a Web site. Go figure. We can produce ideas ourselves that might transform categories as important as saving.

Q: What is your role as the global leader of Saatchi & Saatchi?

My number-one job is to inspire our people and our clients. We're in the emotional connections business, so I need to lead from [the] front as an emotional conduit. The number-two job is to sustain the enterprise by exceeding financial goals, delighting and inspiring our people toward peak performance and client creativity. And job number three is to nurture a place where world-changing ideas take root and flourish.

Q: At Saatchi & Saatchi, where do your ideas come from?

From the culture. From everyone. The founders of the company had some pretty huge ideas, and some beliefs for getting to them. Simple things like "Nothing Is Impossible." Give this to six thousand people and turn them loose and you have ideas coming from everywhere.

Q: How do you recognize the difference between a good idea and a great one?

A great idea has to be original, new, never done before, and instinctively amazing. You can't define "instinctively amazing" but I trained for thirty years to sense what sells, and experience gets you closest to the visceral moment. So experience, having

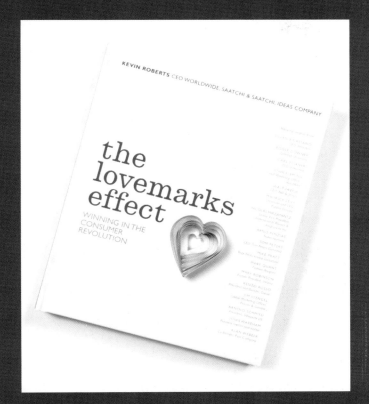

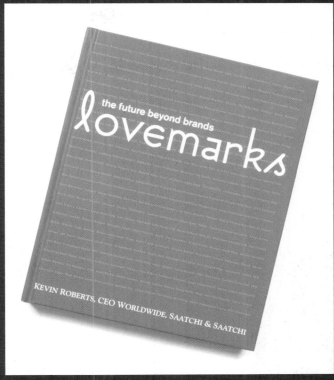

▸ *THE LOVEMARKS EFFECT* (2006)

Kevin Roberts

▸ *LOVEMARKS: THE FUTURE BEYOND BRANDS* (2004)

Kevin Roberts

▸ *PRINT: "CANNERY ROW"*

AGENCY: SAATCHI &
SAATCHI / MALAYSIA

Executive Creative Director:
Adrian Miller

Art Directors: Karen Wong
and Richard Coping

Copywriter:
Ramanjit Singh Gulati

Client Servicing: Tina Tong

Photographer:
Lim Sok Lin, Studio DL

Retoucher:
Simon Ong, Studio DL

Client: Penguin Books

Headline: Be prepared with Ariel

PRINT: "SPAGHETTI"

AGENCY: SAATCHI &
SAATCHI / GUANGZHOU

Executive Creative Director:
Ng Fan

Creative Director:
Wendy Chan

Chief Creative Officers:
Edmund Choe and
Andy Greenaway

Copywriter: Au Kin Cheong

Art Directors: Ng Fan,
Wendy Chan, Liu Zhong Qing,
and Ye Zhi Guang

Photographer: Gao Shi Yuan

Account Management:
Ann Jingco, Sherry Tan,
and Pully Chau

Advertisers:
Ruediger Koppelmann,
Farrell Wang, and Jerry Liu

Retoucher: James Chan

Product: Ariel

Client: Proctor & Gamble

seen a lot of stuff, having had stuff that has
bombed, these are effective experiences for
both recognizing a great idea and for encouraging people who have also an eye, a heart,
and a mind, for a great idea.

**Q: Do all great ideas have something in
common? If so what is it?**

All communication ideas are ultimately
about language: a revelation, a word, a
phrase, a visual image or symbol, a construction, an information design—whatever,
there is always language at the center of an
idea. There is a phrase "surprising with the
obvious" that well describes a great idea,
though in these tough times sometimes "the
obvious is surprising."

**Q: Why is love such an important factor in
creating ideas that build strong, long-lasting
relationships between brands and people?**

Love is the strongest emotion. You can't ask
for love. It has to be given. Therefore a relationship is implicit.

Q: How can a brand return that love?

By being honest, ethical, true; by improving
lives; and by joining in the fun.

Q: Can any brand be loved? Why?

Ask the people who love them.

Q: What other emotions are important?

Many of our emotions are negative: fear,
disgust, rage. But I'm from the school that
believes people are inherently good, so I
root for emotions like altruism and generos-
ity and always hope for the best.

**Q: What role (if any) does logic play in
building these relationships?**

About 20 percent. Neurologist Donald
Calne—people are 80 percent emotional,
20 percent rational. Reason leads to conclu-
sions. Emotion leads to action.

**Q: Does the concept of love differ in differ-
ent parts of the world? Why or why not?**

Love is a universal concept; it exists everywhere in every person in the same way. This
is one of the wonderful discoveries about
Lovemarks. We have people from 215-plus
countries who have contributed, and they
exhibit the same emotional desires, the same
wishes for their families. Love can differ po-
litically, but that's not the business we are in.

Q: Can creative ideas build brand-customer relationships and exist on a purely emotional level? Why/why not?

You have to first fulfill all the respect elements—performance, trust, sustainability. If you don't have your act together, people simply won't love you. If you're great in the looks department but lousy in performance, you'll never find true love. Love has to be operationalized, like everything.

Q: How do technology and innovation affect creative thinking?

Technology is an enabler; it makes stuff possible faster. That's all. Technology facilitates—it doesn't replace the human imagination.

AGENCY: SAATCHI & SAATCHI / LOS ANGELES

Executive Creative Director: Mike McKay

Creative Director: Andrew Christou

Integrated Design Creative Director: Ryan Jacobs

Associate Creative Director / Art Director: Sean Farrell

Art Director: Tito Melega

Copywriter: Simon Mainwaring

Senior Producer: Jennifer Pearse

Production Coordinator: David Weaver

Director of Integrated Production / Multimedia: Tanya LeSieur

Account Director: Marisstella Marinkovic

Production Company: The Sweet Shop

Executive Producers: Stephen Dickstein and Susan Rued Anderson

Director: Mr. Hide

Edit: Bikini Edit / Avi Oron

Telecine: Co3 / Dave Hussey

Special Effects: Perceptual Engineering / Fin Design / Brickyard

Music
   Artist: Petra Haden / Licensed Track: "Let Your Love Flow"
   Sound Design: Human
   Mix: LIME / Rohan Young

Client: **Toyota Prius**

05

THE BIG IDEA

An effective ad is driven by the underlying concept. An *advertising idea*—or *concept*—is the creative reasoning behind a solution. The concept determines the resulting message: what you say and how you design. Though your concept or idea may be broad, it is foundational. Essentially, the idea drives your design decisions—how you create, why you select imagery and typefaces or lettering, and the reasoning behind your color palette selection. The idea sets the framework for all your design decisions. An ad idea is visually and verbally expressed through the creation, selection, combination, manipulation, and arrangement of visual and verbal elements and the written copy. A big idea is a solid, creative, on-brand idea that is large enough and flexible enough to be used effectively across media for a period of time.

IDEA KICKOFF: THE SIX ESSENTIAL QUESTIONS

Almost certainly, when you first learned to write compositions, you followed three general stages: (a) *prewriting* (or brainstorming), (b) *writing*, and (c) *revising* and *editing*.

During the first stage, you most likely were taught to ask six essential questions intended to help you flesh out your thinking. These same questions are used for conceptualization in advertising design. Rudyard Kipling immortalized these questions, referring to them as the "six honest serving men" that taught him all he knew, in a short poem embedded in "The Elephant's Child." This essential set of questions can help solve

Figure 5-1

TV: "TIPS"

AGENCY: WIEDEN + KENNEDY / PORTLAND, OREGON

Client: CareerBuilder.com

Format: :60/:30 (60 seconds/ 30 seconds)

Executive Creative Directors:
Mark Fitzloff with Susan Hoffman

Creative Directors: Jason Bagley with Danielle Flagg

Copywriter: Eric Kallman

Art Director: Craig Allen

Account Team:
Maggie Entwistle, Tamera Geddes, and Taryn Lange

Agency Producer: Sarah Shapiro

Production Company: MJZ

Director: Tom Kuntz

Executive Producers: David Zander and Jeff Scruton

Producer: Scott Kaplan

Editor: Gavin Cutler

Postproduction: Mackenzie Cutler

Audio Postproduction: POP Sound, Mitch Dorf

Director of Photography: Bryan Newman

Effects Method: Studios Robert Moggach

Color Correction: Company 3, Stefan Sonnenfeld

Titles / Graphics: Method Studios

Talent
   Animatronic Animals: Stan Winston
   Sound Design: Stimmung
     Sound Designer: Gus Koven
     Producer: Kelly Fuller

The Brief: Create advertising that actually helps people Start Building.
   We believe that advertising that is not only fun and memorable, but also useful, would be the ultimate expression of the Start Building line, the perfect extension of the CareerBuilder.com spirit, and could make looking for a new job feel a little less daunting.
   Synopsis of TV spot: It can be hard to know when you need a new job. This spot gives the viewer a number of warning signs they should watch out for so they'll know when it's time for them to move on.
   —Wieden + Kennedy

Exercise: Aspiration as One's Identity

Inscribe the shape of a T-shirt on a page.

Determine your most passionate aspiration, one that identifies you, or how you identify yourself—for example, "I want to dance" or "I am an artist."

Visualize and design that line of copy on the T-shirt.

problems and trigger ideas. In fact, they are the basis of a creative brief. Before using any of the creativity tools in this chapter, or any others, for that matter, always answer these questions first to the best of your ability and based on your research.

> *Who?*

> *What?*

> *Where?*

> *When?*

> *Why?*

> *How?*

Rather than proceeding directly to the conceptual development stages, our study benefits greatly from a discussion of the process of finding insights and the use of a visual brief collage board.

Looking for Insight

Finding a relevant insight into how people think, what they need or desire, and how they act, termed a *consumer insight,* is paramount for idea generation. That consumer insight should be coupled with an insight into the brand, according to Lisa Fortini-Campbell, advertising expert and professor in the Medill School of Journalism at Northwestern University, Chicago. In her book, *Hitting the Sweet Spot: How Consumer Insights Can Inspire Better Marketing and Advertising* (2001), Fortini-Campbell argues that by combining consumer and *brand* insight, one can attain an advertising "sweet spot"—the most

effective place to hit the audience with your marketing messages. For example, for Career Builder, they realized just how daunting looking for a new job could be and how their brand could help (see figure 5-1).

In his book *Juicing the Orange: How to Turn Creativity into a Powerful Business Advantage,* Pat Fallon calls an insight an "essential truth" as well as an "emotional truth." After finding that emotional truth, generate an idea that makes it *actionable*, make it a way to connect with the audience.

Seeking a Consumer Insight

According to Sigmund Freud, the father of psychoanalysis and one of the most influential thinkers of the twentieth century, all people have an unconscious mind in which "potent sexual and aggressive drives, and defenses against them, struggle for supremacy."[1]

What drives us is critical to finding an insight.

According to Abraham Maslow, one of the founders of humanistic psychology, we have a hierarchy of needs that influence our behavior. Maslow arranged these needs into a hierarchical pyramid. At the bottom of the pyramid are the basic (or physiological) needs, such as air, water, food, sex, sleep, etc. As you ascend the pyramid, physiological needs are followed by safety, love, and then esteem. Finally, at the pinnacle, we find self-actualization, which is defined as "the desire to become more and more what one is, to become everything that one is capable of becoming."[2]

Maslow also maintained that self-actualizing people have "peak experiences," such as love, understanding, happiness, or rapture, that allow us to feel part of the world; this allows us to feel more aware.

In his book *The Culture Code* (2006), Clotaire Rapaille claims to have figured out the hidden desires of American consumers. Rapaille finds "reptilian" (referring to the region of the brain that includes the brain stem and the cerebellum, called reptilian because of its similarity to the reptile brain) hot buttons

1. Quoted in Peter Gay, *Freud: A Life for Our Times* (New York: W. W. Norton & Company, 1998), 46.

2. A. H. Maslow, "A Theory of Human Motivation," *Psychological Review* 50: 370–96.

that compel us to buy. Humans are driven by unconscious needs and impulses:

The Culture Code is the unconscious meaning we apply to any given thing—a car, a type of food, a relationship, even a country—via the culture in which we are raised. . . . The combination of the experience and its accompanying emotion create something known widely (and coined as such by Konrad Lorenz) as an imprint. Once an imprint occurs, it strongly conditions our thought processes and shapes our future actions. Each imprint helps make us more of who we are. The combination of these imprints defines us. (p. 5)

In *Spent: Sex, Evolution, and Consumer Behavior* (2009), Geoffrey Miller, an evolutionary psychologist, examines why we buy and why we make the choices we do. He contends that we are motivated by primal desires: "We've known since Darwin that animals are basically machines for survival and reproduction; now we also know that animals achieve much of their survival and reproductive success through self-advertisement, self-marketing and self-promotion" (p. 90).

The passages from Freud, Maslow, Rapaille, and Miller discuss human nature. What about nurture (to which nature is often contrasted)? The totality of environmental factors affecting our nature is called nurture; so, from this perspective, the context in which we live makes us who we are. How we are nurtured plays a significant role in how we make choices and in our behavior. The *context* of your family, culture, community, values, friends, aspirations, basic drives, cognitive abilities, defenses, habits, all factor into why you would respond to advertising, donate to a specific charity, purchase one detergent over another, and so on. From a moderate viewpoint, it is the interaction between genes and environment that shape our behavior. Basically, all are factors that influence why you buy one brand of shampoo over another, or why you respond to a particular public service message.

Bill Schwab, creative director of the Gate Worldwide, points out: "There are two important things to know before positioning a brand or product. Consumers see a product as an extension of themselves. Purchasing decisions are often motivated by a desire for self expression."

Seeking an Insight into the Brand or Group

SIX PHASES OF THE PROJECT PROCESS

OVERVIEW > STRATEGY > IDEAS > DESIGN > PRODUCTION > IMPLEMENTATION

During the first two phases of the advertising process, an *insight* might be identified and defined in the *creative brief* (see Chapter 2). Careful listening to the client or account manager might also point toward an insight. Predesign research, too, might help you to identify an insight. If you have not been able to identify or define a function through the abovementioned methods, or if you are working alone, you may need to conduct your own research, especially research that considers the user's point of view.

Do you ever walk into a business establishment and think, "Boy, if I owned this place, I would handle things differently!" Have you ever thought, "This juice carton should be easier to open" or "This charity really seems to help a lot of people in a significant way." That type of commentary points to the advantage of seeing a product, service, or group "from the user's point of view," and that can lead to an insight into the advantages a brand (or a group) has over other brands (or groups).

A thorough appraisal of the product, service, or group you are advertising will help find a brand insight. Complete the following tasks before beginning the process of ideation. Your responses might overlap, but that will help point out features:

> *Delineate the particular product, service, or group you are selling or promoting.*

> *Answer the fundamental question about a benefit: "What's in it for me?"*

Diagram 5-1

Tool: Fact versus opinion mapping

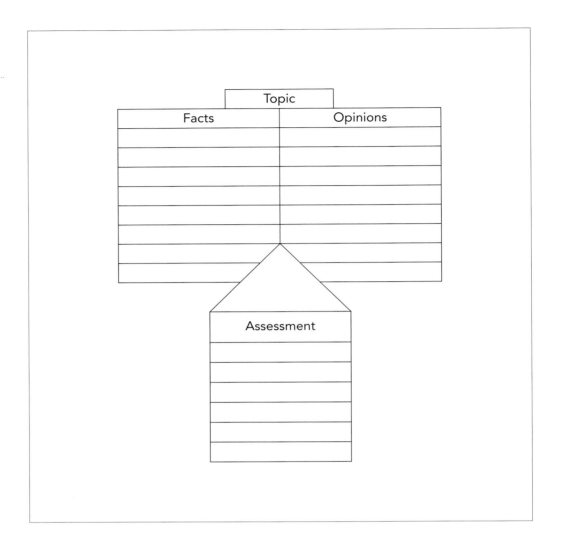

> Assess the brand or group from the consumer's point of view.

> Separate fact from opinion.

TOOL: FACT VS. OPINION

> Write your topic, brand, or group at the top of a page.

> Divide the page into two columns.

> In the left-hand column, list facts.

> In the right-hand column, list opinions.

> Add details to each column.

TOOL: FROM BENEFITS TO INSIGHT

> Identify the functional benefit(s).

> How can the benefit(s) best be explained?

> Identify any unique selling point (USP). If there is no functional USP, is there anything that this brand or group does differently from the competition that could be highlighted?

> Distinguish the emotional benefit in order to discover the relationship between the product and the consumer.

> Couple the functional and emotional benefits to find an insight.

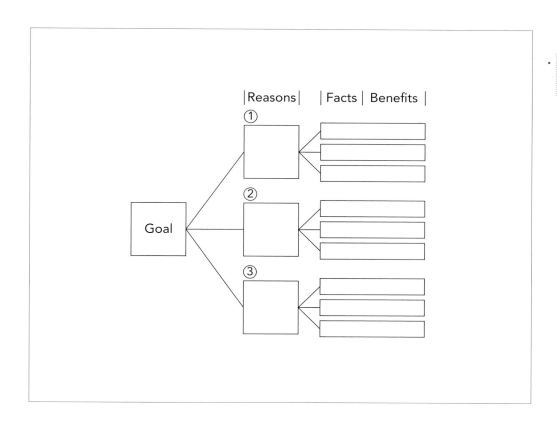

• **Diagram 5-2**

Tool: From benefits to insights

TOOL: PERSUASION MAPPING

> *In the first box, write out the goal.*

> *In the next set of three boxes, write a different reason in each.*

> *List examples and facts in the boxes that branch from the reason boxes.*

In her book, *Hitting the Sweet Spot* (2001), Fortini-Campbell offers excellent tools for finding a brand insight. Also, these *tools and strategy games* can be particularly helpful when looking for an insight into the brand or group. Using these tools (or any other aid) can be helpful in finding what specifically it is about this particular brand or group that could resonate with audiences.

Morphological method. The morphological method is based on analysis and synthesis. You analyze a problem by defining all of the important factors, which some call the parameters, as well as the options. Then you synthesize—you combine the factors and options to produce a *matrix* containing possible solutions. (See pp. 33 for more on how to use the matrix you have produced.)

Fritz Zwicky, Swiss scientist, pointed to the use of a concept called morphology, which was first adopted for scientific inquiry by Johann Wolfgang von Goethe.

Graphic organizer. This tool is a visual aid used to illustrate the relationships among facts or ideas. It provides a visual picture of information that facilitates seeing previously unrealized and perhaps significant connections. (See pp. 37–38 for more on how to use a graphic organizer.)

Deletion strategy game. Imagine the world without this product, service, commodity, or group type. Then imagine the world without this specific brand or group. For example, imagine there were no ketchup. Now imagine the world without Heinz ketchup. Once you imagine this scenario, it might be easier to understand what people like or love about the brand or group. A successful example of this strategy is found in the original "Got Milk?"

campaign created by San Francisco ad agency Goodby, Silverstein & Partners in the 1990s. During the research phase, the client—Jeff Manning, executive director of the California Milk Processor Board—suggested that people who drink milk tend to drink it with favorite foods, such as cookies and peanut butter sandwiches. When researchers asked focus group participants how they would feel if they had to go without milk to accompany their favorite snacks, such as cupcakes, for weeks, people claimed they would feel deprived. This insight led to the strategy of promoting milk as a complementary beverage to food.

Elicit the problem game. Rather than thinking of your brand or group as the solution to someone's problem, think of how to cause the problem. For example, how can we cause people to be dissatisfied with our delivery service? How can we frustrate people who are sending and receiving packages?

List different ways of causing the problem. Change the wording of your goal to cause the problem. Of course, then list ways to prevent the problem(s) from occurring. This tactic brings to light opposite viewpoints, issues that are not immediately obvious through a process of questioning. This turnaround offers a new perspective that might lead to a brand insight.

If-only game. This visioning process expands thinking, encourages a thorough exploration of possibilities and of what is desirable, pushes thinking beyond the practical and conventional, offers a new focus or direction, and uses a variety of viewpoints to elicit wishes and "to portray possible ideal futures." The if-only game "can help you break out of [an] overly constrained view of the product, service, or group, and [it] is a "way of tying values to action."[3] For example: If only my hair would bounce. I wish I could swim to work. Use action verbs in the exercise.

This is a great tool for brainstorming taglines. "If only" can help you identify some functional benefit people want from a brand or group; for example, I wish people couldn't tell that I color my hair; or, if only I could call this hotline or get tested anonymously.

Exaggeration game. This particular game uses exaggeration to help determine particular qualities of (and thereby gain insight into) the object or idea under discussion. For example: It is so good that . . . These heels are so high that . . . This is so minty that . . . This is so critical that . . . This is so life saving that . . .

Changing the frame. Here you set aside preconceived notions to explore alternatives. Changing a frame allows you to explore possibilities and to imagine what a brand or organization could be beyond its current brand personality or beyond how people perceive it. (See Chapter 3 for more on this process.)

Alternate uses. Can the product, service, or group serve a different function? Can it be used in multiple ways? Thinking of a brand or group in this way can illuminate an unknown function or benefit, or it may offer a new perspective on an old take. The morphological method also could be used here.

Visual Brief Collage Board

As defined in Chapter 2, *strategy* is the core tactical underpinning of any visual communication, unifying all planning for every visual and verbal application within a program of applications. The strategy is usually defined in the creative brief. Essentially, the strategy is how you are conceiving, creating, and positioning your brand or group and aiming your application (the type of design problem) in the marketplace to achieve differentiation, relevance, and resonance. The strategy helps define the brand's or group's personality and promise, differentiates it from the competition by defining the positioning, and codifies the brand essence. It is a conceptual plan that provides guidelines—for both client management and creative professionals—that drive all visual communication applications.

Fully understanding the strategy and the competition *before* conceptual design is critical. It is also helpful to state the strategy in one or two sentences and keep it in front of you while you develop a concept. Before commencing concept generation, a visual brief can be very useful. A *visual brief collage*

3. Grove Consultants International, "Strategic Visioning Process," in *National Endowment for the Arts: Resources,* http://www.arts.gov/resources/lessons/GROVE.HTML

board is a visualization method for representing strategic characteristics and building a visual vocabulary based on those qualities or characteristics. It is an alternative to using a narrative strategy, and it "translates" verbal strategy into a visual brief, which can become a foundation for (or a jumpstart to) your conceptual thinking. For example, Duffy & Partners first developed visual positioning collages for a brand revitalization of Fresca, the soda brand, with the goal of designing a "new visual brand language" to communicate the intrinsic characteristics of Fresca. After focus group research for Fresca, Duffy reports: "Two design directions clearly rose to the top and were fused to form one visual brief for the brand."[4]

Visual briefs offer another advantage, as they can be used as a tool with focus groups and clients. Directions for color palettes, kinds of imagery, photographic styles, and other graphic approaches can be narrowed to distill a strategic goal. Client involvement at this phase almost guarantees client satisfaction, because the client becomes part of the process early on.

An interesting example of a brand offering a branded utility is Moodstream by Getty Images, which is a "brainstorming tool" that allows one to build a creative palette drawing upon Getty's photo, video, and audio collections.

Concept-Generation Process

The generally accepted protocol for concept generation is based on the four-stage model outlined in *The Art of Thought* by Graham Wallas, English political scientist and psychologist, in 1926:

PREPARATION > INCUBATION > ILLUMINATION > VERIFICATION

In 1940, James Webb Young, a renowned copywriter at J. Walter Thompson, wrote an indispensable book, *A Technique for Producing Ideas*, in which he colorfully and articulately explains his process for producing advertising ideas based on Wallas's model. Here is how we can use Wallas's model:

Exercise: Mood Board Self-Portrait

Exercise idea contributed by Bill Schwab, creative director, The Gate Worldwide/ New York

> *Determine the color palettes, kinds of imagery, photographic styles, and other graphic approaches that best define you.*

> *Then build that visual vocabulary to best describe and define you.*

> *Visualize it as a Visual Brief Collage Board.*

STEP 1: PREPARATION

> *Examine materials and look for insights and connections. You are seeking a possible idea platform.*

Software can aid in organizing the materials you've gathered, allowing you to save queries and views, sort and select topics for modification, and more. Social bookmarking Web sites, such as http://del.icio.us.com, allow you to store your bookmarks online and to add bookmarks from any computer. Such sites can keep track of any source material and commentary you find online.

> *Write any idea or insight on an index card, in a notebook, or in a digital file.*

Develop the ability to ask the penetrating questions, make observations, and formulate an insightful and informed conjecture about what might answer the questions. Then you need to figure out if your conjecture is viable and how it stands up to evidence. Finally you have to decide whether to accept, modify, or drop the supposition(s).

First thoughts should be worked and reworked, leading to more mature thoughts.

STEP 2: INCUBATION PERIOD

Once you have examined all the materials, it is time to allow all you have learned to simmer in your mind. Taking a break from working on an assignment turns the concept generation over to your subconscious mind.

---

4. www.duffypov.com/duffy-article/27/a-new-look-for-fresca

Even when disengaged from concept generation, the brain is highly active. By allowing the problem to percolate in the back of your mind, your subconscious may do the job for you. Often, to take a break, designers turn to other arts that engage their conscious minds, stimulate emotional responses, and encourage the subconscious. Examples include reading award-winning fiction; seeing an art house film; attending a music or dance concert, theater performance, or fine art exhibit; or creating fine art (painting, sculpting, drawing, photography, ceramic arts). Some designers prefer semiconscious behaviors—like doodling, daydreaming, or folding paper into odd shapes—as a kind of constructive self-entertainment. Psychologists say such activity might be especially productive if the mind is turning over a problem.[5]

STEP 3: ILLUMINATION AND IDEA GENERATION

An idea is the creative reasoning underlying a design application, the guiding concept that determines how you design; it is the primary abstract idea. It sets the framework for all your design decisions.

Formulating a concept necessitates analysis, interpretation, inference, and reflective thinking. Generating ad ideas is the most challenging stage in the creative process. The ad idea is expressively communicated to an audience through the visual design and cooperative action between design and copy; therefore, it is essential to create clear and interesting communication.

Another important consideration during idea generation: for any assignment, an agency must generate several viable concepts to present to their client.

STEP 4: VERIFICATION: CRYSTALLIZING THE AD IDEA

Once you generate an ad idea, you need to evaluate it, testing it for functionality and creativity. Most ideas require refinement to strengthen them and to ensure they will work

in practice. This is the point in the process to keenly critique your own concepts. This step requires evaluating, assessing, and logically supporting your viewpoint.

Those who are able to generate concepts quickly or immediately are either seasoned designers or well informed about the subject and assignment. Experienced creative thinkers rely on a repository of frequently used creative thinking tools and on experience, just as a seasoned, winning football coach relies on experience, instincts, abilities, skills, and techniques.

Several steps are involved in concept generation:

> *Defining the problem*

> *Preparation: gathering and examining materials*

> *Incubation*

> *Generating and selecting ideas*

> *Assessing ideas*

THINKING CREATIVELY: MORE POINTS OF DEPARTURE FOR CONCEPTUALIZATION

For many, a concept comes unprompted—it pops up as if out of a magic lamp, as Athena sprung from Zeus's head in Greek mythology. Often, when we are relaxed and not working at idea generation—perhaps while driving, cooking, exercising, showering, or doodling—a concept comes to us. However, if incubation has not worked for you, refer to the creativity section in this chapter (pp. 68–91). In my book *Thinking Creatively*, I

---

5. Benedict Carey, "You're Bored, but Your Brain Is Tuned In," *New York Times*, 5 August 2008.

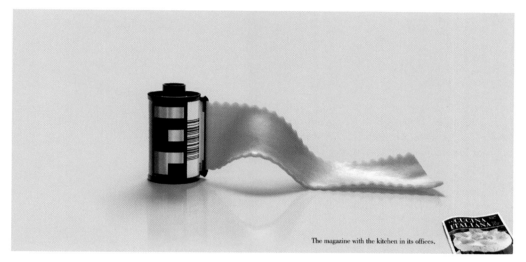

Figure 5-2

PRINT CAMPAIGN: "MINCER," "FILM," AND "TYPEWRITER"

AGENCY: D'ADDA, LORENZINI, VIGORELLI, BBDO / MILAN AND ROME

Creative Director: Stefano Campora

Art Directors: Pier Giuseppe Gonni and Vincenzo Gasbarro

Copywriters: Nicola Lampugnani and Federico Ghiso

Photographer: Fulvio Bonavia

Client: La Cucina Italiana

© October 2002, © July 2002

Merging office and film supplies with kitchen appliances distinguishes this magazine's content.

outlined points of departure, jumping-off points to ignite conceptual development. Some are visually oriented and others are more strategic; however, each can be thought of as a visual jump start or as a theoretical starter; for example, a merge can be two actual objects joined, or it can be two notions or models joined to form a new one.

Words. Legendary graphic design and ad-man George Lois advises using words to

Figure 5-3

POSTER:
"LUKOVA AT MICA"

AGENCY:
LUBA LUKOVA STUDIO

Designer / Illustrator:
Luba Lukova

Client: MICA

© Luba Lukova

Replacing the scales of the fish with a dried-up riverbed merges ideas of water, life, and death.

generate concepts. Lois believes that visual artists can think equally well in words as in visuals. Try making word lists, word associations, word maps, word mergers, or any method that will work for you.

No copy. Think in images only—in single iconic images, in cartoons—any visual that tells the whole story.

Connections. Connect ideas and images to make a point or to express a function or emotion.

Merge. Combine two related or unrelated objects or visuals together to form a unique whole.

For example, merges are used in a campaign for *La Cucina Italiana* to cleverly illustrate the idea of "the magazine with the kitchen in the offices" (figure 5-2).

Synthesis. Combine or synthesize more than two separate elements to form a new, more complex whole. For example, when esteemed designer/illustrator Luba Lukova spoke at Kean University, New Jersey, about her work, she said that her creative ideation phase includes experimenting with creative approaches, such as synthesizing a fish with a dry, cracked riverbed floor (figure 5-3).

Juxtaposition. Place two visuals side by side for contrast or comparison.

Literary and rhetorical devices. Use metaphor, simile, onomatopoeia, personification, pleonasm, metonymy, or other rhetorical device as a concept platform.

Visual analogy. Let's say you are advertising personal computers, and the brand and advertising strategy positions your brand as the fastest in a price category. What type of argument would most effectively convince someone that your computer brand is the fastest? If you simply stated your argument, the consumer would have to take your word for it. (Saying something outright usually isn't a very interesting approach.) A demonstration might work. Or you could use a visual analogy. Showing a shooting star moving at the speed of light might suggest how much faster your computer processes information than does the competition.

A visual analogy is a comparison based on similar or parallel qualities. For example, a motorcycle and a jet are both types of transportation, and we may infer that they are parallel in their ability to rapidly accelerate. We use visual analogies "to clarify, to make it easier to understand," says Richard Nochimson, professor of English at Yeshiva University, New York City. Figure 5-4 depicts a one-button shirt as analogous to the functional benefits of a single-button video player: it can be programmed easily, with only one button.

Figure 5-4

PRINT: "BUTTON"

AGENCY: SAATCHI & SAATCHI / MADRID

Executive Creative Director: César Garcia

Creative Directors: Miguel Roig and Oksy

Art Director: Amabel Minchan

Copywriter: José Luis Alberola

Photographers: Nahuel Berger and Gonzalo Puertas

Client: Sony España
© December 2000

Figure 5-5

PRINT: "RABISCOS"

AGENCY: TBWA / BRAZIL

Creative Director:
João Linneu de Paula

Illustrator: Erevan Chakarian

Client: Diveo Wireless
Internet© 2001–2002,
TBWA / Worldwide

*These metaphors for slow-
ness are linearly depicted to
express complication. The
copy reads: "Diveo Wireless
Internet for business. More
speed. Less complication."*

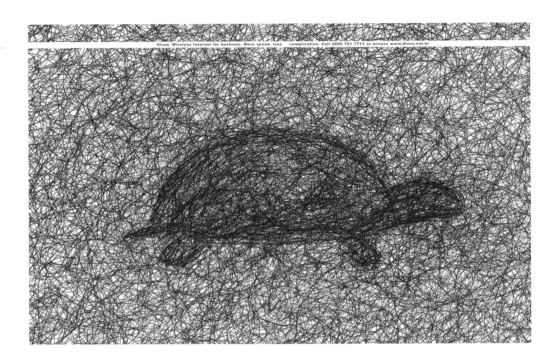

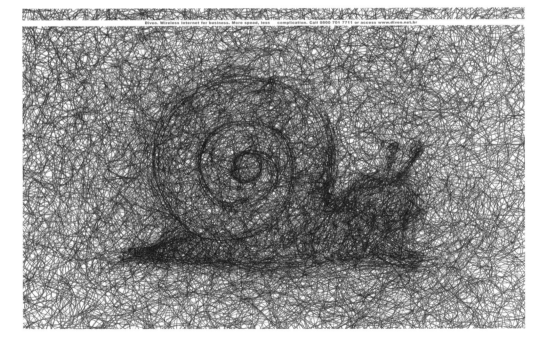

Figure 5-6

PRINT:
"I FEEL LIKE A FISH"

AGENCY: THE KAPLAN
THALER GROUP, LTD. /
NEW YORK

CEO and Chief Creative
Officer: Linda Kaplan Thaler

Creative Directors: Jack
Cardone and Michael Grieco

Art Director: Marco Cignini

Client: Childhood Asthma,
Environmental Protection
Agency, and the Ad Council

Using a simile written by a
child who suffers from asthma
heightens the emotional level
of the communication with the
hope of inspiring the audience.

"I FEEL LIKE A FISH WITH NO WATER."

–JACOB, AGE 5
DESCRIBING ASTHMA

You know how to react to their asthma attacks. Here's how to prevent them.

1-866-NO-ATTACKS | EVEN ONE ATTACK IS ONE TOO MANY.

For more information log onto www.noattacks.org or call your doctor.

 EPA

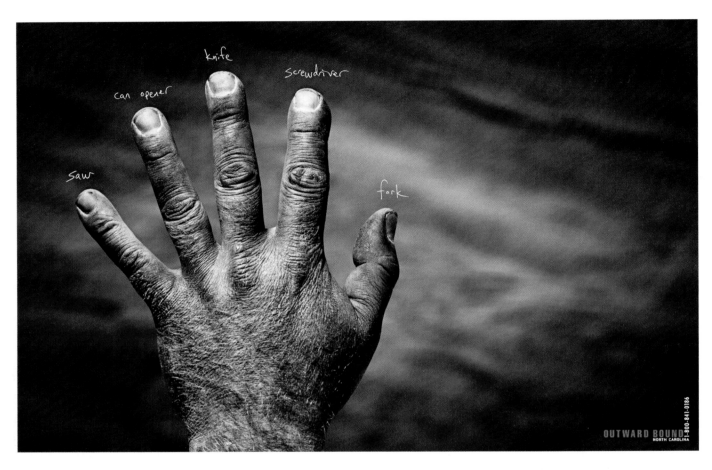

Figure 5-7

PRINT : "ROPE" AND "HAND"

AGENCY: LOEFFLER KETCHUM MOUNTJOY / CHARLOTTE, NORTH CAROLINA

Creative Director: Jim Mountjoy

Art Director: Doug Pedersen

Copywriter: Curtis Smith

Photographer: Jim Arndt

Client: Outward Bound

Combining the use of metaphors with a natural look highlights the emotional benefits of Outward Bound.

Visual Metaphor

In advertising, everything from the cliché of a dewy rose to designate moisture-rich skin to the indelicacy of a toilet bowl to suggest foul breath is employed. In ads by TBWA / Brazil for wireless Internet access, metaphors express the idea that other brands are slow and complicated (figure 5-5).

When you use one thing to identify another, especially an attribute of that thing, that is a metaphor—for example, fire is a metaphor for hot sauce in particular contexts. Substituting one kind of object for another asserts a like-ness or similarity between them. In language, a comparison between things is a simile—for example, "My love is like a rose." A metaphor would read "My love is a rose." To call at-tention to the plight of children with asthma,

a public service advertisement (PSA) uses a simile to describe and communicate to others the extreme struggle children with asthma experience in trying to breathe (figure 5-6).

Metaphors can serve another purpose: they can act as a more attractive representation of an idea when the actual product or service might be off-putting.

Visual metaphors can invite the reader to work a little bit, to interact with the ad; the reader is engaged by thinking. If the visual metaphor is interesting, on strategy, and accessible (but not clichéd), the reader is more likely to notice the ad, be engaged, and interact, as in figure 5-7.

Life experience. Entertainers who study the human comedy, such as Bill Cosby, Ellen

▶ Figure 5-8

*PRINT CAMPAIGN:
"YELLOW PAGES"
AND "MOUSE PAD"*

AGENCY: RETHINK
ADVERTISING /
VANCOUVER, BRITISH
COLUMBIA

Art Director: Ian Grais

Copywriters: Chris Staples
and Andy Linardatos

Photographer: Hans Sipma

Studio Artist / Typographer:
Brent Mulligan

Client: Ayotte

DeGeneres, and Jerry Seinfeld, base their observational comedy on everyday occurrences—ones that happen right under our noses. We relate to their humor because we can remember similar experiences. These are the little events and moments that make up an individual life—the disappointment over a fallen ice cream cone, wanting more than one bag of peanuts on an airplane, filling in a sentence for your spouse, or even waiting in line to get a table at a restaurant.

Drawing upon life experience may be one of the richest techniques for finding ideas. There is nothing funnier or more interesting than the actual way people do what they do. Ideas can be based on the ordinary things we do: how we eat a sandwich cookie, how we tug at our underwear, how we squirt mustard. Paul Renner, of Arnold Worldwide / New York, bases many of his ideas on his own life experience as well as his observations of others. A campaign for Ayotte custom drums amusingly illustrates what the people who were holding out for this brand will do while waiting—drumming on anything and everything (figure 5-8).

Musing on anything from relationships to basketball may generate an idea. In the process of examining how we interact, function, and behave in various situations, you may find a way to sell a brand or promote awareness for a social cause. Being an ardent observer of human behavior, animal behavior, interpersonal dynamics, and other life mysteries can definitely yield ideas to which people might relate. Basing ideas on personal life experience or observing others can help make your ads relevant to the lives of others.

In advertising, when you draw upon common experiences—funny, sad, bittersweet—people usually relate to them. The response from people should be something like: "Yep, that's how it is!" An ad can make an experience a communal event, making us feel that we've all participated. Their reality is our reality, and we feel a kinship with the brand or cause being advertised.

Change perspective or eccentric points of view. Looking at things—at life—from odd angles, both literally and conceptually, can be

a great point of departure for ideation.

Look at things differently—from below, above, askew, and at an extreme angle.

Look at things as if you were:

A fly, with compound eyes

An alien from another planet

A child

Inside

A one-thousand-year-old person

Look at things from odd views or angles (figure 5-9):

From a giraffe's perspective

As if you had a partial view

As if you were looking from behind a ceiling fan

As if you had multiple simultaneous vantage points

From upside down

Look at things through:

Water

Fog

Frosted or tinted glass

Smoke

The problem is the solution. At times there are products with features that may be perceived as disadvantageous. For example, in the 1960s, when the Volkswagen Beetle appeared on the American market, small, atypically shaped cars were viewed negatively. The cars of leading American brands were large, graceful, and grand. The now-famous ads created by Bill Bernbach and his creative team at Doyle Dane Bernbach (DDB) changed our thinking about car size by creatively convincing us to "think small" (figure 5-10).

For years, in various ad approaches, Listerine's medicine-like taste was presented as a positive attribute. The ads claim its taste is part and parcel of Listerine's efficacy in killing germs.

Figure 5-9

PRINT:
"ADVANCED AEROBATIC
FLIGHT TRAINING"

AGENCY: HUNT ADKINS /
MINNEAPOLIS

Creative Director and
Copywriter: Doug Adkins

Art Directors:
Mike Fetrow and Mike Murray

Client:
Aerobatic Flight Program

A darned good reason. When you give the consumer a reasonable rationale, the consumer's reaction might be, "That makes sense! I should use that brand for that particular reason."

Providing a rationale for a functional benefit can turn consumers into believers. For example, keeping your body parts is a good reason to get checkups or to conduct breast or testicular self-examinations, as seen in messages from the Canadian Cancer Society (see figure 5-11). PSAs often offer us good reasons to take up certain behaviors and stop others.

Figure 5-10

PRINT:
"THINK SMALL" (1960)

AGENCY: DDB / NEW YORK

Creative Director:
Bill Bernbach

Client: Volkswagen

DDB's visual style set a new creative standard in the 1960s.

What's worse than
getting kicked in the balls?

Getting kicked in the ball.

Testicular cancer is the number one cancer among young men. To learn more visit www.bc.cancer.ca.

Every guy in class has
already checked them out.

You should too.

Learn how to self-examine your breasts. Visit www.bc.cancer.ca.

Figure 5-11

PRINT:
"TESTICLE" AND "BREASTS"

AGENCY: RETHINK
ADVERTISING / VANCOUVER,
BRITISH COLUMBIA

Art Director: Martin Kann

Copywriter: Andy Linardatos

Photographer: Robert Kenney

Studio Artist and
Typographer: Jonathan Cesar

Client:
Canadian Cancer Society

This point of departure is used for specific brands as well as for commodities, such as meat, plastic, and oranges. For example, plastics manufacturers, in their TV spots, make a case for the functional benefits of plastics, listing the many advantageous uses of plastic. These spots counter the criticism of plastic by environmental advocates. In everyday life, we come up against all kinds of obstacles that many products, services, and organizations help us overcome. Dishwashers clean our dishes. Sunblocks protect skin. Food banks collect food and distribute it to the needy. There are actual reasons to use products or services or to aid causes, and

that is what reasonable rationale–based ads bank on. You are giving the consumer indisputable reasons to need your client's brand or to support your client's cause.

Drive home the point about the necessity of checkups, but do it with humor.

Here are some good reasons made famous in advertising:

> When you can't brush, chew Wrigley's Extra sugar-free gum. You just ate, and brushing your teeth is impossible, but you want fresh breath and clean teeth, so chew Extra instead. That is a real-life

Figure 5-12

PRINT:
"WHEN YOU CAN'T BRUSH"

AGENCY: DDB / SYDNEY,
AUSTRALIA

Art Director: David O'Sullivan

Copywriter: Michael Lee

Photographer:
Julian Wolkenstein

Client: The Wrigley Company

© 2002 DDB Sydney / The Wrigley Company

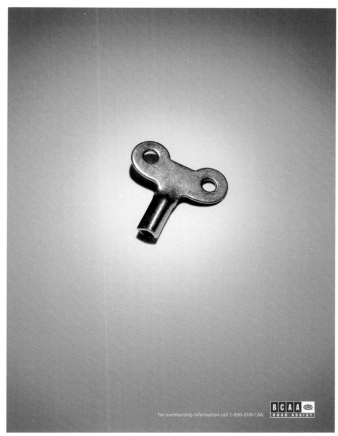

problem with a proposed solution—and a darned good reason to chew Extra (figure 5-12).

> *You deserve a break today. The ad claim is offering a practical reason to believe it is okay to view McDonald's, the fast-food chain restaurant, as a dinner restaurant alternative and giving you permission to make life somewhat easier for yourself. It is a good argument based on the reality of a working parent.*

> *It is abundantly clear that you need roadside assistance—it is 53,000 steps to the next city, or you might have to use your kid's roller skates to get back to town for assistance. Now there is an incentive to subscribe to membership with the British Columbia Automobile Association (BCAA) (figure 5-13).*

Unexpected comparison and contrast. Comparing your current boyfriend to your former boyfriend can get you into hot water. Comparisons can be mean-spirited and often uninteresting. For example, at the end of the twentieth century we witnessed fast-food chain wars (McDonald's fried burgers vs. Burger King's broiled burgers) and cola wars (Coke vs. Pepsi).

Any way you look at it, taste is a personal thing. Ask yourself why you prefer one flavor to another. Comparing foods or beverages based on taste is not a strong premise.

On the other hand, comparing a product or service to something different from it—a feeling, a sensation, or another type of experience—can be a strong premise for an advertisement; it has the potential to be extremely effective and memorable. We

> Figure 5-13

PRINT:
"53,000 STEPS" AND "KEY"

AGENCY: RETHINK ADVERTISING / VANCOUVER, BRITISH COLUMBIA

Art Directors:
Ian Grais and Andrew Samuel

Copywriter: Ian Grais

Photographer:
Dave Robertson

Studio Artist / Typographer:
Brent Mulligan

Client: British Columbia Automobile Association

Figure 5-14

AGENCY:
LEO BURNETT / PARIS

Creative Directors: Christophe
Coffre and Nicolas Taubes

Art Director: Pascal Hirsch

Copywriters: Axel Orliac and
Laurent Dravet

Photographer:
Frank Goldbrown

Client: Heinz Ketchup

In a clever reversal of quantities, this ad suggests that one would rather eat a plateful of ketchup than a traditional main course.

Figure 5-15

PRINT:
"STOLEN HANDBAG I" AND
"STOLEN HANDBAG II"

AGENCY: LEO BURNETT /
DENMARK

Creative Director:
Charlie Fisher

Art Director: Nete Borup

Copywriter: Thomas Fabricius

Client: Best Behavior
© February 2001

The tough new Polo. VW

Figure 5-16

PRINT: "BIG TRUCK"

AGENCY:
BMP DDB / LONDON

Photographer:
Gary Simpson

Agent: Vue

Client: Volkswagen New Polo

Exaggeration—so tough, a monster truck can't squash it.

associate the product with the desirable experience. This point of departure is similar to an analogy, but it speaks more to how something might feel or taste. If I bite into a York Peppermint Pattie, I'll feel the sensation of skiing down a snowy mountain or of standing under a cool waterfall.

Exaggeration. Ketchup so good, you use more ketchup than food, as in figure 5-14. A car is so sturdy, even a monster truck can't crush it.

Making an overstatement or enlarging the truth beyond bounds can express just how terrific, tasty, fast, creamy, rich, low-calorie, easy-to-use, or edgy a product is. Overemphasizing a product's quality drives home a selling point quickly. The Best Behavior brand of designer handbags is so desirable that a thief wouldn't even want the contents of the handbag; she'd take the handbag and throw the contents away (see figure 5-15). Of course, the exaggeration has to be understood as an exaggeration.

When using exaggeration to make a point, as shown in two print ads for Volkswagen (see figures 5-16 and 5-17), the exaggeration must be so extreme that we don't believe the actual events depicted in the ads, but we get the point: This product is so good that . . . .

This point of departure can be used in so

many different ways that it is almost inexhaustible.

Motivation and inspiration. Many audiences love motivational speakers, motivational preachers, motivational self-help books, motivational talk show hosts—and motivational advertising.

Figure 5-17

PRINT: "WEDDING"

AGENCY:
BMP DDB / LONDON

Photographer: Paul Reas

Agent: John Wyatt Clarke

Client: Volkswagen

The price of a Volkswagen is so low that the photographer misses the wedding shot to focus on the car ad.

THE MAN ON THE LEFT
IS 75 TIMES MORE LIKELY TO BE STOPPED
BY THE POLICE WHILE DRIVING THAN
THE MAN ON THE RIGHT.

It happens every day on America's highways. Police stop drivers based on their skin color rather than for the way they are driving. For example, in Florida 80% of those stopped and searched were black and Hispanic, while they constituted only 5% of all drivers. These humiliating and illegal searches are violations of the Constitution and must be fought. Help us defend your rights. Support the ACLU.

a m e r i c a n   c i v i l   l i b e r t i e s   u n i o n
125 Broad Street, 18th Floor, NY, NY 10004 www.aclu.org

Figure 5-18

PRINT:
"THE MAN ON THE LEFT"

AGENCY:
DEVITO/VERDI / NEW YORK

Creative Director, Art Director, and Copywriter: Sal DeVito

Client: American Civil Liberties Union

People want the ads to act like an inner voice, pushing them to do something.

The ad becomes our motivational coach.

Just the facts, Ma'am. Shocking, interesting, or little-known facts can be the basis of an idea. This is where good research can be very helpful. Using facts is informative. Facts also can be presented and interpreted in a variety of ways.

Using a shocking comparison—Dr. Martin Luther King Jr. and Charles Manson—in conjunction with a statistic, makes the ad, "The Man on the Left," produced for the American Civil Liberties Union (ACLU), an extremely gripping message (see figure 5-18). Visualizing this message as a handbill nailed to walls heightens the drama of the call to support the ACLU.

Reading facts, we learn something, and we can be enlightened, as with the train and bus wraps—an unconventional format—that use facts to discourage people from smoking, created for the Illinois Department of Public Health by Hadrian's Wall (figure 5-19). The newly learned fact will, advertisers hope, compel us to change behaviors, support a cause, act, or buy a brand.

There are many more ways to develop ideas, including the following:

Association: Use an image or feeling that people will associate with the product, service, or group.

Symbol: Employ an object or image to represent or stand for another thing, thought, idea, or feeling.

Borrow from fine art: Examine surrealist works, trompe l'oeil paintings, illusionist paintings, or other works of art.

Deconstruct graphic design and illustration: Examine works by esteemed graphic designers and illustrators.

Borrow from playwrights and film directors: Use absurdity, play with time, etc.

"Just do it"—get out there and go for it, run, jump! Some women found the Nike ads with this slogan so compelling that they tore them out of magazines and hung them on their walls. "Be all that you can be," a different ad campaign said, and when a recruit enlists, the U.S. Army makes sure she excels.

This springboard for idea generation is rooted in self-help; the ad idea becomes the stimulus for people to achieve, giving people that push to go after their personal best.

› Figure 5-19

*BUS AND TRAIN WRAPS:
"HEARSE" AND "LUNGS"*

AGENCY: HADRIAN'S WALL
/ CHICAGO

Creative Director: Kevin Lynch

Art Director: Mollie Wilke

Copywriter: Greg Christensen

Photographers: Oman and
American Lung Association

Client: Illinois Department of
Public Health

LET'S END THIS DISCUSSION OF IDEA GENERATION WITH A QUESTION

How do you make the conversation bigger?

The Nike Chalkbot, in figure 5-20, makes the conversation bigger through participation. Wieden + Kennedy remarks, "Chalking the roads is a Tour de France tradition. Spectators write messages of encouragement to their favorite riders. Outside of the Tour, LiveStrong and the Lance Armstrong Foundation have embraced the idea of using the roads as a huge canvas, encouraging people to chalk messages of hope in the fight against cancer. The Nike Chalkbot was a way to take this positive message even further. By sending a message to the Chalkbot through SMS (short message service), Web banners, Twitter or WearYellow.com, people around the world were able to make their mark in yellow."

A good or even great idea is at the heart of any effective campaign, especially those that resonate, that enter popular culture, that change the conversation, that create brand sirens and advocates and loyalists, and that build communities. The question "What's in it for me?" is at the heart of bigger ideas—bigger ideas that incorporate utilities, platforms that people will use over and over again for a long time, experiences that people incorporate into their lives.

Figure 5-20

*PROJECT: CHALKBOT +
CHALKBOT FILMS*

Client: Nike LiveStrong

Web Site: www.wearyellow.com

AGENCY: WIEDEN + KENNEDY /
PORTLAND, OREGON

Executive Creative Directors:
Mark Fitzloff and Susan Hoffman

Creative Directors:
Tyler Whisnand and Danielle Flagg

Art Director: James Moslander

Copywriter: Marco Kaye

Interactive Art Director:
Adam Heathcott

Executive Interactive Producer:
Marcelino J. Alvarez

Interactive Producers: Jeremy Lind
and Marcelino J. Alvarez

Studio Manager: Sarah Starr

Retouching: Peter Lindman

Studio Designers (Vinyl Wrap):
Rehanah Spence and Rob Mumford

Development Partners
   *Vision and Interface Software
      Engineer:* David Evans
      (Deeplocal Inc.)
   Project Lead and Designer:
      Nathan Martin (Deeplocal Inc.)
   *Systems Engineer and
      Mechanical Engineer:* Greg
      Baltus (Standard Robot)
   *Electrical Engineer and Software
      Engineer:* Mark Sibenac
      (Forth Computer)
   Hydraulic Engineer: Scott
      Tomasic (Hydraulic Services)
   Senior Electrical Technician:
      Jim Ketterer
   Lead Fabricator: Aaron Brechbill
      (Brechbuilt Design)

Chalkbot Films
   Postproduction: Joint Editorial
   Executive Producer:
      Patty Brebner
   Editor: Justin Lowe
   Videography: Marcelino J.
      Alvarez, Adam Heathcott,
      and James Stranahan
      (Legion-Media)
   Producer: Marcelino J. Alvarez

ad, Mustoes's case study explains: "We needed to find something that would reflect the prestige of the event, but also tapped into its accessibility. . . . By focusing on the people that attend the event we could bring to life why the event had been so successful

for such a long time—it was part of the fabric of British life and the British summer."

In any of these modes, the visual and line complete each other in communicating the whole ad message.

Figure 6-5

PRINT: "NOT A COMPLICATED PROCESS"

AGENCY:
MATTHEWS | EVANS | ALBERTAZZI / SAN DIEGO

Art Director and Photographer: Dana Neibert

Copywriter: John Risser

Client: The San Diego Lawn Bowling Club

© 2002 Matthews | Evans | Albertazzi

The historical-looking sepia-colored tone, type, and graphic elements and the interesting angles of photography are complemented by witty copy.

STOP.
SQUAT.
AND ROLL.

GETTING INTO LAWN BOWLING IS NOT A COMPLICATED PROCESS. YOU SIGN UP. YOU PLAY. YOU SMILE. CALL THE SAN DIEGO LAWN BOWLING CLUB AT 619.423.9286 TO FIND OUT HOW YOU GET STARTED.

Visual or Words: Which Should Dominate?

Copy-driven? Or visual-driven? Art directors, naturally, would testify to the power of visuals. Copywriters, certainly, would argue that words are powerful tools.

Visual-driven ads are those in which the visual carries the weight of the ad message or in which there is no copy other than the sign-off; the visual captures the viewer's attention first. Copy-driven ads convey the advertising message primarily through the words, and there may be no visual other than the design of the typography and the logo or product shot in the sign-off—the copy captures the viewer's attention first. For example, a campaign by DeVito/Verdi for New York Metro is copy driven (figure 6-7); the wry copy carries the message. In a dramatic campaign for the Multiple Sclerosis Society, the ads are visually driven (figure 6-8). Of course, in many of these ads, the copy and visual support one another—there is a synergistic relationship between them, and they work entirely cooperatively to convey the ad message.

To best determine a creative approach you could ask a few questions: Does this audience prefer to read or look at pictures? Are the words interesting enough for people to read them? Is the visual compelling enough to stop people, to grab their attention?

If the ad will be used internationally, it is wiser to be more visual than verbal. Are there other useful ways to think of the words as part of the ad message?

How Many Words Are Too Many?

If a headline is interesting, I'll read it. In its all-copy ad for Mystic Lake, Hunt Adkins knows its audience well, and the humor makes the ad appealing (figure 6-9).

Being concise is critical. My mother used to call it "short and sweet." My colleague Professor Alan Robbins advises students to delete what can be deleted while still retaining meaning.

Figure 6-6

PRINT: "SPORT OF KINGS"

AGENCY: MUSTOES / LONDON

Creative Director: John Merriman

Art Director: John Merriman

Copywriter: John Merriman

Illustrator: Matt Cook

Client: Epsom Derby

The copy following the line, the "Sport of Kings," was "designed as an integral part of the ad, using a distinctive calligraphy-style font; it read as a who's who of people who would, could, and have attended the Derby. This wasn't a name-dropping list, but a list of the types of people who participate in this great day out— from dog food tasters to pole dancers, vicars to milkmen."
—Mustoes

Figure 6-7

PRINT CAMPAIGN: "RACHEL, ROSS, MONICA, AND CHANDLER" AND "BECAUSE A ONE NIGHT STAND REQUIRES TWO PEOPLE"

AGENCY: DEVITO/VERDI / NEW YORK

Creative Director: Sal DeVito

Art Directors: Anthony DeCarolis and Brad Emmett

Copywriters: Pierre Lipton and Erik Fahrenkopf

Client: New York Metro

The acidic wit of the copy is perfect for a New York audience that prides itself on sophisticated humor. This agency is known for its razor-sharp wit. The tagline in this campaign reads: "Nightlife. It's a big city. You could use a little help."

Though there are effective lines comprised of two words, such as "Got milk?", a short headline can be challenging for a novice writer.

Also, the length of the headline should be appropriate to the format. A large number of words on a billboard would not work, whereas a few choice words can be extremely effective. As designer Carlos Segura, of Segura Inc., Chicago, suggests, "Put your work in context."

CONVENTIONS

The classic advertising formula is a visual plus a line, and most advertising still employs this formula. When reaching an international or heterogeneous audience, many rely on a visual to communicate the message. Visuals tend to be more universally understood.

Conversely, when addressing a particular market segment, copy-driven ads—where the words carry the main message—can communicate very clearly.

WRITING CREATIVELY

The secret of all effective originality in advertising is not the creation of new and tricky words and pictures, but one of putting familiar words and pictures into new relationships.
—Leo Burnett

Copy has to sound fresh and not predictable. It also has to sound as though you are engaging in a natural conversation with the reader.

What is creative about "Give a damn," the National Urban League's former claim? It embodies an idea, it calls us to act in a meaningful way, it is emotional, and it is dramatic yet informal. The beauty of a line such as

▸ Figure 6-8

PRINT: "PARALYSIS" AND "INCONTINENCE"

AGENCY: SAATCHI & SAATCHI / LONDON

Creative Director: Dave Droga

Client: Multiple Sclerosis Society

Using switches coupled with dramatic visuals, these PSAs explain how someone afflicted with MS never knows which part of her or his body will shut down, and they urge us to donate toward finding a cure.

**YOU DON'T NEED DUMB LUCK.
MILDLY STUPID LUCK WILL DO.**

Mystic Lake Casino

Figure 6-9

PRODUCT RELAUNCH: RELAUNCH FOR CASINO UNDER NEW IDENTITY

AGENCY: HUNT ADKINS / MINNEAPOLIS

Creative Director and Copywriter: Doug Adkins

Associate Creative Director and Art Director: Steve Mitchell

Client: Mystic Lake

Hunt Adkins differentiated Mystic Lake from other casinos with a jocular campaign. Doug Adkins says: "Humor is the best tool we have to get past people's well-earned cynicism for one brief moment, giving us an opportunity to share our message with them."

"Hey, you never know" is that it is both true and very natural to the vernacular.

What's creative about "Got milk?" Well, Jeff Goodby could have written "Do you have any milk?" or "Got any milk?" Both of these say "Got milk?" but neither says it memorably. The casualness of the line adds to the credibility.

Say It in the Line—Don't Rely on the Body Copy

Most people don't bother to read body copy. People who are engaged by the line and visual may go on to the body copy. People who are seeking information, such as consumers searching for stereo equipment or someone looking for advice in a public service ad, will be interested enough to read the body copy. However, it's sensible not to rely on the body copy to transmit the principal message. The line plus visual should communicate the primary message, and the body copy supports that message and adds to it. Often, it helps to write the body copy first; that process may generate a line.

TAGLINE AS MESSAGE

The tagline is the catchphrase that conveys the brand or group's benefit or spirit and expresses an umbrella theme or strategy for a campaign or a series of campaigns; it also is called a *claim, end line, slogan,* or *strap line.* Two great examples are "Friends don't let friends drive drunk" (U.S. Department of Transportation) and "Don't leave home without it" (American Express).

If for any reason the ad concept is not fully communicated, the tagline can clarify or round out the communication, advises Gregg Wasiak, creative director, the Concept Farm, New York.

Once you come up with the idea for the tagline, the entire campaign should embody the same spirit, as in Work's campaign for Crestar Bank (figure 6-10). Cabell Harris of Work says about the Crestar campaign

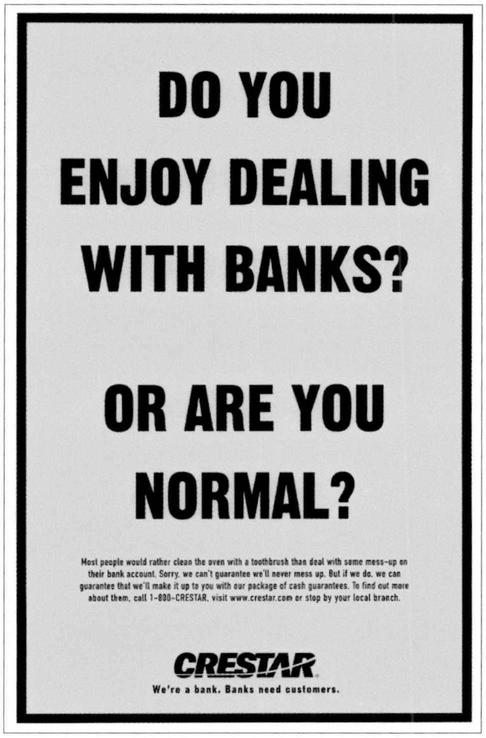

**DO YOU
ENJOY DEALING
WITH BANKS?**

**OR ARE YOU
NORMAL?**

Most people would rather clean the oven with a toothbrush than deal with some mess-up on their bank account. Sorry, we can't guarantee we'll never mess up. But if we do, we can guarantee that we'll make it up to you with our package of cash guarantees. To find out more about them, call 1-800-CRESTAR, visit www.crestar.com or stop by your local branch.

CRESTAR
We're a bank. Banks need customers.

Figure 6-10

*PRINT:
"ARE YOU NORMAL?"*

AGENCY: WORK, INC. / RICHMOND, VIRGINIA

Creative Director: Carolyn Tye McGeorge

Art Director and Designer: Cabell Harris

Copywriter: Kathleen Lane

Client: Crestar Bank

The newspaper campaign used a combination of bold, proactive headlines, spot color, and short copy, and the ads developed were crisp and memorable. Mindful of the mandate to "execute overnight if needed," the agency used all type, thus reducing turnaround time (which would otherwise be extended if illustration or photography had been used).

Figure 6-11

AGENCY: HUNT ADKINS / MINNEAPOLIS

Creative Director and Copywriter: Doug Adkins

Associate Creative Director and Art Director: Steve Mitchell

Client: Mystic Lake Casino

These very amusing ads offer the tagline "You're a lot luckier than you think."

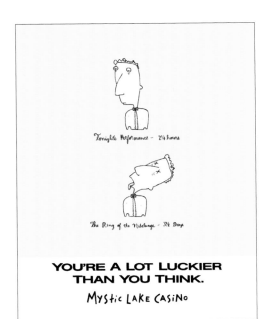

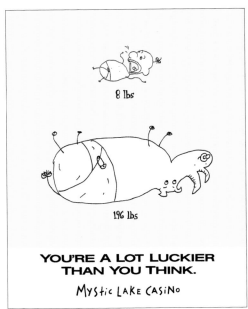

Figure 6-12

PRINT CAMPAIGN: "CIRCUMVOLVE," "AQUEOUS," AND "AMBULATE"

AGENCY: MULLEN / WENHAM, MASSACHUSETTS

Chief Creative Officer: Edward Boches

Creative Director: Jim Hagar

Art Director: Paul Laffy

Copywriter: Brian Hayes

Photographer: Dan Nourie

Digital Artist: Dave Nadeau

Client: Houghton Mifflin
© Mullen

By replacing common words with less-common synonyms, these ads urge us to seek out help from the dictionary.

concept: "Research and account planning revealed that rather than using the traditional 'warm and fuzzy' and overpromising appeals common to the industry, Crestar would be better served by direct, honest, and understated communications. No bank-speak. Instead, Crestar would relate to the consumers from their point of view rather than the bank's. The ads themselves demonstrate that we understand their concerns. The campaign centered around a decidedly unbanklike tagline: 'We're a bank. Banks need customers.'"

THE "DO I SOUND LIKE A SALES PITCH?" TEST

Some lines, such as "Introducing the tingly tang of amazing CheesWhip Dip," sound like a bad advertising sales pitch. Others, less badly written—such as "You'll love our new and improved cheese dip"—still sound like a sales pitch.

Once you've written a line or the body copy, it is highly advisable to test it by saying it aloud. Does it sound stiff? Or like an annoying salesperson trying to sell you something? It should sound like something you'd say in conversation with a friend.

The claim, "You're a lot luckier than you think," for Mystic Lake Casino (figures 6-11) by Hunt Adkins, sounds like a line I can relate to, and it is written in a conversational, natural tone.

STYLE

"The key to coming up with a great ad is finding that one clear, concise, engaging idea. This holds true for all advertising mediums: print, radio, TV, outdoor, etc.," notes Eric Silver, executive creative director, BBDO Worldwide, New York. Once you generate an idea, the way you craft the copy should be appropriately convey the message. The style of the writing contributes to the message, just as the choice of typeface contributes to the voice.

The style of copy in Mullen's campaign for Houghton Mifflin (figure 6-12), is a perfect fit for the call to action: "Upgrade Your Language."

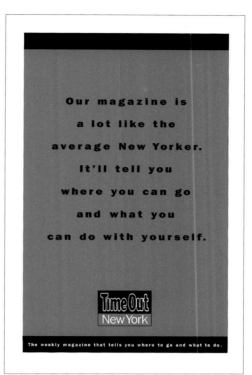

Figure 6-13

PRINT: "OUR MAGAZINE IS A LOT LIKE THE AVERAGE NEW YORKER."

AGENCY: DEVITO/VERDI / NEW YORK

Creative Director: Sal DeVito

Art Directors: Abi Aron and Rob Carducci

Copywriters: Abi Aron and Rob Carducci

Client: *Time Out New York*

With a clever play on words, this ad communicates the benefit of the magazine.

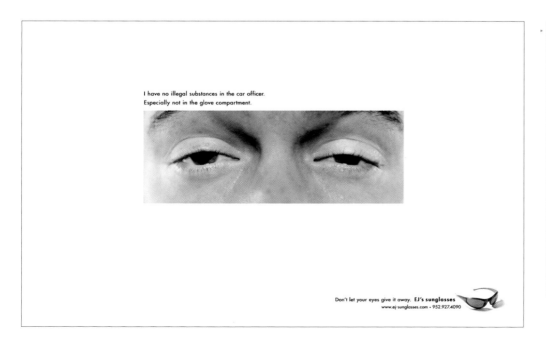

Figure 6-14

PRINT: "DON'T LET YOUR EYES GIVE IT AWAY."

AGENCY: CARMICHAEL LYNCH / MINNEAPOLIS

Creative Director: Jim Nelson

Art Director: James Clunie

Copywriter: Tom Camp

Photographer: Ron Crofoot

Client: EJ Sunglasses

The functional benefit of wearing sunglasses is demonstrated by the cropped photograph of a face, focusing on the expression in the eyes, coupled with irreverent copy.

Would you write an antidrug campaign directed at kids and one directed at parents the same way, with the same rhythm, the same language? As always, understanding the audience is key to writing effective copy. To persuade someone to donate blood or give money to a charity, you have to make a connection. You have to touch the reader's emotional core. The reader should be able to recognize something relevant to his or her ex-perience. The reader should be prompted to think: "Oh yeah, that's so true!" "You're talk-ing about me." "You know me." Copy should be completely pertinent to the advertising proposition and entirely appropriate for the audience. An ad aimed at tourists visiting New York City has the tone that tourists ex-pect and find endearing about forthright New Yorkers (figure 6-13).

Whose Voice Is It?

In whose voice is the copy written? Is it writ-ten from the brand's point of view? Does it seem to be the voice of an expert? Is it a tes-timonial? The voice of a character in the ad?

Is it a disembodied voice? Is the copy in the ad telling you what to do or how to behave? Does the headline take on a maternal tone? Does it sound like a friend who is advising you? In any ad, words take on a voice.

Perhaps the headline is in the voice of the person pictured in the ad, as is the case in a wry ad for EJ Sunglasses (figure 6-14). Or does the voice represent the brand, as in a campaign for American Airlines, where the tone is earnest and the words communicate an important message (figure 6-15)?

It is in the context of the entire ad—the words plus the visual—that we can deci-pher who is speaking to us. Copy also sets a tone or mood. It can sound formal, informal, corporate, scientific, friendly, acerbic, or just about anything else. Colle + McVoy's ad for the Minnesota Department of Tourism actu-ally tells us who is speaking (figure 6-16). With what seems to be a glib memo of sorts, one's "coworkers" suggest a much-needed rest and some relaxing fun by exploring Minnesota.

**TAKE your vacation days.
PLEASE.
—your COWORKERS**

www.exploreminnesota.com

Figure 6-16

*PRINT: "TAKE YOUR
VACATION DAYS, PLEASE—
YOUR COWORKER"*

AGENCY: COLLE + MCVOY /
MINNEAPOLIS

Creative Director: John Jarvis

Art Director: Jon Montgomery

Copywriters: Eric Husband
and Dave Keepper

Photographer: Layne Kennedy

Client:
Minnesota Office of Tourism

© 2002 Minnesota Office of Tourism

*A convincing line coupled with
a photograph suggesting a
refreshing vacation communicates the message that many
of us need time to explore
states such as Minnesota.*

THE WRITING PROCESS

Tim Delaney of Leagas Delaney, who is renowned for his wickedly clever headlines and
acerbic wit, advises, "I'm fairly relaxed about
writing, so I just do it. I'm not afraid of it.
I'm not thinking, 'Oh my God, I'll never crack
this.' I learned this when I was young. . . .
Early in my career someone told me that all
you have to do when you get blocked is keep
writing any old rubbish. And it'll come to you,
eventually. But most people don't do that.
They sit there wringing their hands, or they
get up and walk away."[2]

One thought usually leads to another—as you
write, you'll be thinking.

Write a lot. In the act of writing, you may
generate an idea for a headline. Write a good
number of lines.

*Writing should be viewed as an opportunity
to play,* and play hard. Enjoy the process.

*When you first start writing lines, just keep
writing.* Don't judge what you've written until
much later. Later on, you will have to edit.

Edit. Revising and editing are part and parcel
of the art of writing.

FEED YOUR WRITING

Read, read, read.

Read great literature—read dramas and com-
edies. Try different genres. Read a great daily
newspaper, one that wins journalism awards.

The most important thing you can do to improve your writing is to write, write, write. Also,
try any of the following as writing exercises:

> *Keep a journal.*

> *Write letters to friends.*

> *Write funny descriptions of things.*

> *Write song lyrics about the ingredients
> in tomato soup.*

> *Read. Listen. Write.*

Gregg Wasiak, creative director (and copywriter) of the Concept Farm, advises that the
best copywriting exercise comes through
writing radio spots. Writing for radio teaches
timing and storytelling. There are no visuals
to catch someone's attention—it's all about
the words, rhythm, and pace.

07

APPROACHES

DECONSTRUCTING MODEL FRAMEWORKS

Certainly, everyone wants to create imaginative, effective advertising—fresh work that hasn't been done before, ads that make people watch and then act, solutions that make other creative professionals say, "I wish I had thought of that!" Creating the "same old" won't grab anyone's attention.

To create something fresh, you need to know what has already been done. You've seen millions of ads in your lifetime and probably know what looks, feels, and sounds stale by now. The ability to deconstruct and categorize ads is a useful skill for those who aspire to do creative work.

Can something fresh be created using existing structures for the Internet, TV, video-sharing, mobile applications (apps), or any medium? If you decide that it can, in this chapter you will find tactical creative approaches to framing an idea. Creative solutions are provided as examples.

A creative approach is a master general structure that also can be seen as a mode or method of presentation or an underlying schema or framework. These are conventions used in advertising to communicate messages. Analogs to this would be model formats for television programming (think sitcom, reality show, game show, talk show, westerns, soaps) or conventional formats in music or poetry. Model formats, like television program formats, are formulaic and conceived in specific genres.

In a much broader sense, an analogy could be made to storytelling conventions or established narrative frameworks: some people believe there are basic narrative archetypes (for example, the Greek mythological model, Northrop Frye's modes, or archetypal narratives such as comedy, tragedy, quest, rebirth, and others). As with many things, a model format can be utilized in a pedestrian way or in an imaginative way. Some believe certain model formats are more malleable than others, better lending themselves to creative solutions. A creative thinker can utilize any model format to his or her advantage to create an effective and creative solution. Learn the advertising model formats, and then toss them or change them. Or learn them, recognize them, and use them creatively, without being limited by them.

At times, newer media change how stories are told and how advertising is created. The short video format viewed online (YouTube, for example), certainly depends on the element of surprise, unlike the predictable television commercial formats and programming. As Virginia Heffernan, television critic for the *New York Times*, pointed out when writing about contestant Susan Boyle on *Britain's Got Talent:*

The answers still lie in the video, a small, insidious masterpiece that really should be watched several times for its accidental commentary on popular misery, the concept of "expectation" and how cultures congratulate themselves. First off, the Susan Boyle phenomenon truly belongs to the world of online video, whose prime directive is to be amazing. The great subjects of online video are stunts, pranks, violence, gotchas, virtuosity, upsets and transformations. Where television is supposed to satisfy expectations with its genres and formulas, online video confounds them.[1]

Informational videos shared on YouTube. com can be big hits as well; for example, Lauren Luke's homemade makeup tutorials on YouTube became a sensation in the United Kingdom, and thanks to her fame she has launched her own line of makeup at Sephora, a beauty retailer.

Other existing formats are suitable for the Web. Take, for example, a Web-video advertising campaign for FedEx directed by Bob Odenkirk, which appears on a dedicated

YouTube channel (youtube.com/getinfotained) and on FedEx's own Web site. It consists of five three-minute films featuring the actor Fred Willard in skits that parody infomercials "while reaping that format's benefits: using a long-form pitch to be more descriptive than a 30-second spot allows." Michael Smith, a BBDO creative director on the project, said the pace was more frenetic than typical FedEx spots for a reason.

"It's one thing to capture someone's attention, but another thing to hold them for three minutes," Smith said. "And on the Internet, you're competing against everything else on the Internet, which is one finger-click away, so engagement becomes a critical element."[2]

The Appeal of Transformation

In the nineteenth century, American medicine traveling shows, a traveling troupe of performers and hucksters, with origins as far back as fourteenth-century Europe, "were structured around entertainers who could be expected to draw a crowd who would listen to, and then undoubtedly purchase, the medicines offered by the 'doctor' who made two or three sales pitches a night."[3] (You might be surprised to learn that Harry Houdini, as a spirit medium, and Buster Keaton's parents, as performers, were involved with traveling medicine shows; less surprisingly, P. T. Barnum was a medicine pitchman.) The theatrical *strong man* had a featured recurrent role in the traveling medicine show. If we examine the strong man's role, we can better understand one of the basic premises of selling any product or service—the appeal of transformation. A strong man now can perform amazing, entertaining acts (or tricks) of strength. He used to be weak, but the featured cure-all product transformed him. *Without the product,* he was a weakling. Presented on stage pulling horses with his bare hands, or some other clever stunt, the strong man could do all that *by benefit of the product.*

And there you have it: you and your ailment, without this wonderful branded product or

1. Virginia Heffernan, "The Susan Boyle Experience," *New York Times Magazine,* 28 June, 2009, 16.
2. Andrew Adam Newman, "Madison Avenue Will Be Watching FedEx's Web Videos," *New York Times,* 20 July 2009, B4.
3. "A great deal of ephemera is associated with the medicine shows—tickets of admission, broadsides advertising the place and time of the show, forms for proprietors to book halls or hotels for their troupes, songsters for the audience to join in singing with the entertainers, advertising booklets, etc." In "Here Today, Here Tomorrow: Varieties of Medical Ephemera, Medical Show," The United States National Library of Medicine, National Institutes of Health, http://www.nlm.nih.gov/exhibition/ephemera/medshow.html (accessed March 22, 2010).

service, and you and your newly transformed fabulous life with this (miraculous) branded product or service. In the nineteenth century, when a medicine show rolled in, it would have been the only show in town, with no competing entertainments or products in the vicinity. Once competition is introduced in the form of another brand, then a brand or group has to "own" benefits, differentiate, or make grander claims than the others.

Writing about publicity in *Ways of Seeing*, John Berger states: "It proposes to each of us that we transform ourselves, or our lives, by buying something more. This more, it proposes, will make us in some way richer—even though we will be poorer by having spent our money.

Publicity persuades us of such a transformation by showing us people who have apparently been transformed and are, as a result, enviable. The state of being envied is what constitutes glamour. And publicity is the process of manufacturing glamour."[4]

All of us certainly want to distance ourselves from hucksterism, patented medicine and snake oil salesmen, and charlatans. That said, effective advertising is based on strategies of persuasion, whether a commercial ad uses social acceptance to persuade someone to purchase a brand name mouthwash or a public service advertising (PSA) campaign uses humor to encourage people to get tested for colon cancer. Very simply, there is you and your life without the mouthwash and colon cancer screening, or there is the transformed (better) you and your life with it.

goes back to Plato's *Republic* and Aristotle's *Poetics*. Very basically, in advertising, telling is narration—events conveyed by a narrator or presenter; it is also called *diegesis* or summary. Showing is mimetic, directly visually or dramatically representing events; it is also called *mimesis* or scene.

In 1986, William D. Wells, former executive vice president at DDB Needham Chicago, presented a paper discussing two broad categories of means of delivering an advertising message: lectures and dramas.[5] *Lectures* tell; they present information to an audience by *directly* addressing viewers; the actors or models look at the audience and the sales pitch is not disguised or, at the least, is fairly transparent, making no bones about the ad attempting to persuade. Conversely, *dramas* show; they are indirect advertisements in the form of stories or plays, which seduce the audience into watching through (entertainingly) crafted scenarios. Here, the sales pitch is woven into the drama, with the hope that the audience won't focus on the persuasive intent. Some say that audiences tend to be more skeptical of claims made in lectures, whereas dramas tend to disarm, dropping the level of skepticism. Lectures and dramas can be combined into one format, where the drama is interrupted by a mini lecture or vice versa.

Since *interactive* media changed the landscape, we must add *participation*, where the viewer takes an active role in the marketing message. There is no doubt that we have moved from delivering lecturelike monologues pushed at people to attempting dialogues with people.

HOW TO CONVEY THE ADVERTISING MESSAGE

The relative value of "telling" versus "showing" an audience a story is a matter that

Lecture

In a lecture a product or service is featured by discussing it; a brand is presented for your consideration, typified with a presentation by a talking head, where the presenter talks at or to the viewer, announces, describes, highlights, declares, states offers, or provides information, still or in motion in any media. It also is called *presentation*, show and tell, a declaration, see and say, announcements (think new or improved).

---

4. John Berger, *Ways of Seeing* (New York: Penguin, 1990), p. 131.

5. William D. Wells, "Lectures and Dramas," in *Cognitive and Affective Responses to Advertising*, ed. Patricia Cafferata and Alice M. Tybout (Lexington, Mass.: Lexington Books, 1989).

Figure 7-1

INSTALLATION: NOKIA "SUPERNOVA"

PRODUCTION COMPANY: HUSH / BROOKLYN, NEW YORK

Creative Directors: David Schwarz, Erik Karasyk, and Nikolai Cornell

Executive Producer: Casey Steele

Live-Action Director: Peter Rhoads

Producer: Mei-Ling Wong

Director of Photography: Zak Mulligan

Design: Laura Alejo, Graham Hill

Production Design: Sergeo Levitas

Build Design: Jamie Barlow

Editor: David Schwarz

Technical Directors: Obscura Digital / San Francisco

Technical Lead: Niklas Lundback

Music and Sound Design: Antfood

Composers: Wilson Brown and Polly Hall

Executive Producer: Sean McGovern

Client: Nokia

Come on, take a closer look . . . Nokia commissioned HUSH to develop an installation for their retail flagship stores worldwide. Timed with Nokia's launch of the Supernova phone series, we created a physically interactive kiosk that challenges the viewer's notions of voyeurism and provides a unique media experience for customers in the retail environments. Working closely with technical partner Obscura Digital, we creatively directed the project from concept to completion. The project combines beautiful portraiture footage, the form factor design of the kiosk's structure and branding, as well as the back-end C++ code that generates particle animations on the Supernova-shaped mirror display screen. Yeah, it's a lot to juggle.
—HUSH

More specifically, a demonstration shows products or services at work: proving functional benefits (faster connection, higher sheen, more accurate test results); performing tasks (distributes food, drills a cleaner hole, mops floors); or making life easier or safer (helps you speak another language, practically mows your lawn for you, finds your keys, keeps you belted in your seat). For example, the historic Ad Council's Safety Belt Education PSA—sponsored by the U.S. Department of Transportation and the National Highway Traffic Safety Administration (NHTSA) and created by volunteer agency Leo Burnett—used two crash test dummies to dramatize what could happen if you don't wear a safety belt. (See historic campaigns at www.adcouncil.org.)

A demonstration offers useful information since we get to observe a product or service in action, see the product, and, most likely, see its packaging. Naturally, sound and motion in television or on the Web would be best suited for demonstration; however, a demonstration can be done in print as well as incorporated on package design (figures 7-2 and 7-3.)

Comparison

A comparison format compares and contrasts one brand either in relation to a competing brand (or two brands) or to the entire product or service category in order to display the differences between them and ultimately claim that the brand being advertised is superior. Most often, two brands are compared for their *functional benefits* (our brand of nail polish makes your nails harder or our insurance company gets to the scene of the accident faster) or *attributes* (our burgers are broiled on an open flame while the competing brand is fried or our potato chips are unbroken contrasted to the broken chips of the leading brand or our organization treats animals more humanely). Famous comparisons include the "Pepsi Challenge"—asking consumers to take a taste test between Coke and Pepsi (often referred to as "the cola war").

A brand can also be compared to the entire category (this toilet tissue brand is softer than any other or this charity spends less on administrative costs and more on charitable programs than any other organization).

To introduce Apple's Mac, Chiat/Day created the now legendary TV commercial "1984," which aired only once during the 1984 Super Bowl. Borrowing from George Orwell's novel of the same name, the TV spot's concept depicted Apple as the triumphant rebel in contrast to conformity. More recently, with Apple's Mac vs. PC campaign, created by TBWA/Chiat/Day, Apple contrasts itself to PCs (personal computers). In 2008, Microsoft challenged the comparison by repositioning the PC with a positive view in the "I'm a PC" campaign created by Crispin, Porter Bogusky.

A brand or group can even compare its (new and improved self) to its former self. In figure 7-4, print ads for the Nature Conservancy, show a visual comparison between the same places at different times, making a point about the organization's conservation mission.

Spokesperson

A spokesperson is an individual—an average person, actor, model, or other celebrity—who positively represents the product, service, or group. If the role is a recurring one, that individual becomes the face and voice of the brand or group. Some Hall of Fame football players are used in the American Urological Association's prostate cancer awareness campaign. "Get screened," Len Dawson, a former Kansas City Chiefs quarterback, says in a public service television spot: "Don't let prostate cancer take you out of the game." Thomas Gottschalk, a German television celebrity, has been the Haribo spokesperson for over fifteen years. Actress and social activist Marlo Thomas is, like her famous father, Danny Thomas, before her, the longtime spokesperson for St. Jude Children's Research Hospital.

BRAND ICONS AND FICTIONAL SPOKES-CHARACTERS

To put a friendly or trustworthy face on a faceless brand, group, or corporation, brand icons or fictional characters are used. A brand icon is a recurring character used to represent a brand or group. It can be an actor, a proprietary illustrated character, or a cartoon or animation—for example, Tony the Tiger

Figure 7-4

PRINT: "MOUNTAIN LAKE" AND "RAIN FOREST"

AGENCY:
EISNER COMMUNICATIONS / BALTIMORE

Executive Creative Director:
Steve Etzine

Associate Creative Director:
Mark Rosica

Photographers:
Alan St. John, Andy Drumm

Client:
The Nature Conservancy

© April 2000

represents Kellogg's Frosted Flakes, Chick-fil-A uses cows, and the Pillsbury Doughboy represents Pillsbury. A *fictional* spokes-character is a recurring invented persona or character used to represent a brand, cause, or group, for example, the Geico Gecko and Geico Cavemen, Smokey Bear, McGruff the Crime Dog (www.mcgruff.org). In 1921, the fictional model homemaker Betty Crocker was invented to promote and advertise Gold Medal flour for the Washburn-Crosby Company. Betty Crocker remains a brand, and her appearance has been updated many times over the years.

"The power of corporate mascots is that of all icons," writes Tom Vanderbilt. "It becomes a symbol for something larger than the brand itself. It takes mass, impersonal abstractions (i.e., multinational corporations) and condenses them into approachable, charismatic, even cuddly symbols."[8]

The Ad Council has partnered with the U.S. Department of Health and Human Services (HHS) on obesity prevention PSAs. To target children, the Ad Council launched a round of PSAs featuring Shrek characters, who were *licensed from a film*, urging children to get more exercise. The PSAs can be seen at **www.healthierus.gov**.

Endorsement

An endorsement is a public statement of approval for a product or service. It can include verbal statements or depictions of the name, signature, likeness, or other identifying personal characteristics of an individual, or the name or seal of an organization. The party whose opinions, beliefs, findings, or experience the message appears to reflect is called the endorser and may be an individual, group, or institution.[9]

Any product, service, commodity (for example, eggs or milk), company, individual (for example, a political candidate), group (for example, a nonprofit organization or social group), or industry can be endorsed. An endorser can be a celebrity, media personality, politician, or any supporter of the product or

service. An endorsement is when a celebrity certifies a brand or group's claim or gives testimony to a brand or group's quality. Through projection and association, the brand or group acquires the cachet of the celebrity, borrowing the celebrity's regard, social status, or expertise in the field.[10]

When so many brands are parity products and services, a celebrity endorsement can provide a point of differentiation and build brands through the purchase of a celebrity's cachet. In the last twenty years, celebrity endorsers include Michael Jordan and Tiger Woods for Nike, Madonna and Michael Jackson for Pepsi, Beyoncé for L'Oreal, David Beckham for Gillette, and Justin Timberlake for McDonald's. In the past, when former U.S. President Ronald W. Reagan was an actor, he endorsed a hair tonic; actor Gregory Peck endorsed Chesterfield cigarettes; and 1950s radio personality Arthur Godfrey endorsed Pepto-Bismol.

As in the case of Rachel Ray for Dunkin' Donuts and Michael Jordan for Nike, a celebrity can both endorse and be the brand spokesperson.

In the case of nonprofits, many celebrities endorse charities and causes that they believe in or have been affected by. Celebrities draw attention to causes, and they can be instrumental in social or political marketing. For example, in the Harvard Alcohol Project's National Designated Driver Campaign sports celebrity Magic Johnson stated that "a designated driver is the most valued player." In a public service announcement campaign titled "Standing Up to Cancer," celebrities who endorsed the cause's message included Sidney Poitier, Christy Turlington, Susan Sarandon, New York City Mayor Mike Bloomberg, Morgan Freeman, Lance Armstrong, Keanu Reeves, Tobey Maguire, Casey Affleck, and Jodie Foster.

We encounter all types of endorsements—from endorsements by experts to endorsements by consumers on Internet blogs and product review sites. For example, when we see an excerpt from a book critic's review of a novel cited on the book's back cover, that is considered an endorsement,

---

8. "The 15 Most Influential, Important, Innocuous, Inane, and Interesting Ad Icons of the Last 500 Years (In No Particular Order)," *Print* 54, no. 6 (2000): 116.
9. *Guides Concerning Use of Endorsements and Testimonials in Advertising* (Washington, D.C.: Federal Trade Commission, 2009); http://www.ftc.gov/os/2009/10/091005revisedendorsementguides.pdf.
10. Ibid.

since it is viewed by readers as a statement of the critic's own expert opinion of the book and not the opinion of the book's author, publisher, or distributor. When we go to purchase a book on Amazon.com, we can read reviews by both experts and consumers. An *expert* is any individual, group, or institution possessing a great deal of knowledge about or training in a particular field, superior to that generally acquired by the average person. And when an expert makes an endorsement, we can expect that he or she is a bona fide user. In the United States, the Federal Trade Commission (FTC) has guidelines about what constitutes expert endorsements.[11] When consumers enthusiastically review a book or other product offered for sale on Amazon.com, that is an endorsement, even though those people are not experts related to the particular book or product.

Testimonial

A testimonial is a favorable message delivered by an expert, the gal or guy next door, or a celebrity (purportedly) reflecting his or her opinions, beliefs, findings, or experiences in support of the sponsoring advertiser. An expert's testimony can engender trust in the audience. In the case of a testimonial by an average Joe or Jane, the hope is that people will relate to that individual's opinion or experience—and it is a voice other than the sponsor. When people read or hear a celebrity's testimony, that celebrity's cachet will add value, even if that individual does not have related expertise. There are innumerable early examples in United States of advertising testimonials. They are found in broadsides, brochures, newspaper ads, booklets, and post cards; for example, in 1880, for the "Boss" Cotton Press, there are many featured testimonials as well as a list of parties using their presses. Around the turn of the nineteenth century, Kodak featured a testimonial by Rudyard Kipling for pocket Kodak cameras: "I can only say that I am amazed at the excellence of the little Kodak's work." In 1924, in an ad for Pond's Cold Cream and Vanishing Cream, there are testimonials by

Let a robot do your dirty work.

Figure 7-5

TV: "ANIMAL HOUSE"

AGENCY: THE GATE WORLDWIDE / NEW YORK

Writer: David Bernstein

Art Director: Bill Schwab

Producer: Bob Samuel

Director: Simon Cole, HIS

Director of Photography: Andrzej Sekula

Editor: Chuck Willis

11. Ibid.

Figure 7-6

PRINT:
"BUNNIES" AND "WORM"

AGENCY: MULLEN
/ WENHAM,
MASSACHUSETTS

Chief Creative Officer:
Edward Boches

Art Director: Mary Rich

Copywriter: Stephen Mietelski

Photographer: Craig Orsinni

Client: Boeri Helmets

the Princess Matchabelli, the Dutchesse de Richelieu, the Princesse Marie de Bourbon, Lady Diana Manners, the Vicomtesse de Frise, and Mrs. Conde Nast.

Problem / Solution

The problem/solution approach is sometimes used when the product, service, or group successfully solves an actual problem (think flaking skin, stains, identity theft, cleaning, cyberbullying) in one's life and/or the greater community. For example, concerning figure 7-5, and iRobot: "Small and silent, this robotic vacuum doesn't come across as a serious vacuum cleaner. Yet it's much more expensive than a Dustbuster. So we positioned it between the two — as a home maintenance product that does the cleaning for you. The Brand Idea: Cleaning between major cleanings" (from the Gate Worldwide Web site).

Historical examples of problem / solution are those campaigns directed at minor afflictions such as bad breath, acne, and dandruff or at household nuisances such as resistant stains on clothing. An early twentieth century (1919) social-problem and melodramatic ad campaign for Odo-Ro-No deodorant for women warned that "B.O." is short for body odor and would ruin a woman's life, rendering her socially unacceptable; but, if a woman were to use Odo-Ro-No, she would pass the "Armhole Odor Test." In the late 1940s, in a socio-drama print campaign, Listerine promoted their product as a solution to halitosis, featuring the case of pitiable Edna as she was approaching her "tragic" thirtieth birthday unmarried. You see, Edna had halitosis, therefore, was "often a bridesmaid but never a bride."

Assuming anonymity and no accountability, some tweens and teens send or post harmful or cruel text or images using the Internet or mobile devices. To combat cyberbullying, Saatchi & Saatchi (volunteer agency through the Ad Council for the National Crime Prevention Council [NCPC], U.S. Department of Justice) created a PSA campaign. To drive people to the Web site (www.ncpc.org/cyberbullying), they created a television

PSA using a problem-or-solution format, a "Talent Show," which dramatically illustrates that cyberbullying is equal to a hurtful public presentation to a big audience. The NCPC initiative urges teens to solve this problem as follows: "Delete cyberbullying. Don't write it. Don't forward it." (Visit www.adcouncil.org, look for the Cyberbullying Prevention campaign.)

In figure 7-6, humorous analogies show a clever chocolate bunny and a worm, who protect their respective skulls, reminding us: "Remember to ski and snowboard responsibly."

Slice of Life

In advertising, slice-of-life format is a drama *showing* a realistic portrayal of life, featuring everyday situations to which average people can readily relate. Often, a real-life problem (a headache, mortgage mismanagement, being overweight) is dramatically depicted. In literature, the term "slice of life" is used to describe the works of certain nineteenth-century novelists, such as Émile Zola, George Eliot, and Leo Tolstoy. During the "golden age" of American television, writers such as Paddy Chayefsky and Reginald Rose wrote teleplays that were described as a slice of life.

Storytelling

Storytelling is a narrative format in which a tale is told to an audience utilizing voice, gesture, and/or imagery; we have the story, the teller, and the listeners. Since the active imagination of the audience (and the creation of illusion) is key, media such as radio can allow for conjuring. Some consider storytelling to be interactive—a two-way interaction between storyteller and listeners. Therefore, interactive media can be particularly effective for this format, allowing the listener (visitor to the Web site) to become a cocreator of the story. According to the National Storytelling Network:

Figure 7-7

TV: "MASK"

AGENCY: WIEDEN + KENNEDY / PORTLAND, OREGON

Executive Creative Directors: Mark Fitzloff and Susan Hoffman

Creative Directors: Hal Curtis and Mike Byrne

Art Director: Storm Tharp

Copywriter: Mark Fitzloff

Producer: Jeff Selis

Client: Nike

Wearing Pro Combat apparel brings out your inner beast. Basically, you put on this apparel and you kick ass at your sport. Athletes used were Torii Hunter, [Albert] Pujols, LaDainian Tomlinson, Mariano Rivera, Brian Urlacher and Ben Roethlisberger. Each of those athletes has a certain inner strength. In this spot, we attempted to show that strength through masks portraying their inner image that comes out when they are competing in Pro Combat on their skin.
    —Wieden + Kennedy

Storytelling involves a two-way interaction between a storyteller and one or more listeners. The responses of the listeners influence the telling of the story. In fact, storytelling emerges from the interaction and cooperative, coordinated efforts of teller and audience.

In particular, storytelling does not create an imaginary barrier between the speaker and the listeners. This is part of what distinguishes storytelling from the forms of theatre that use an imaginary "fourth wall.". . . The interactive nature of storytelling partially accounts for its immediacy and impact. At its best,

storytelling can directly and tightly connect the teller and audience.[12]

Think of the many stand-up comedians who are good storytellers, relying on audience reactions or interaction. A great example of contemporary storytelling is American Public Media's *A Prairie Home Companion* with Garrison Keillor.

Figure 7-7, a TV spot for Nike by Wieden + Kennedy proves that an intensely compelling story can be told in seconds, conjuring mythic imagery and grabbing our attention as the story unfolds, through bold imagery, camera angles, and music.

An historic example of storytelling format is a TV spot for Dodge, created around 1958:

This is a story, a story of an industry in action." [A man sings lyrics reminiscent of a Broadway musical such as Carousel *or* Oklahoma.] *"How many dreams can you shape in a minute? In an hour? Ask the people of Dodge. I Built a Dodge!*

A classic example of storytelling is by George Lois and Julian Koenig for Wolfschmidt vodka (figure 7-8).

Cartoon

A *cartoon* is a single panel pictorial sketch or a sequence of drawings (also called a cartoon strip) that tells a very short story or comments on a topical event or theme. In a single panel cartoon there is a cooperative action between drawing and caption, such as those in the *New Yorker* magazine.

According to cartoonist Lee Lorenz, around 1930, the *New Yorker* magazine's editors reconceived the cartoon format as a "fresh new way of commenting on life in a blend of drawing and caption." Lorenz explains that during this time period, *New Yorker* cartoons "were collaborations between artists and writers, and the final push toward captions with the rhythm of natural speech was provided by writers James Thurber and E. B. White."[13]

12. For more information, see National Storytelling Network, www.storynet.org/resources/knowledgebank/whatisstorytelling.html.
13. Lee Lorenz, "Back to the Old Drawing Board: The Evolution of the *New Yorker* Cartoon," www.cartoonbank.com.

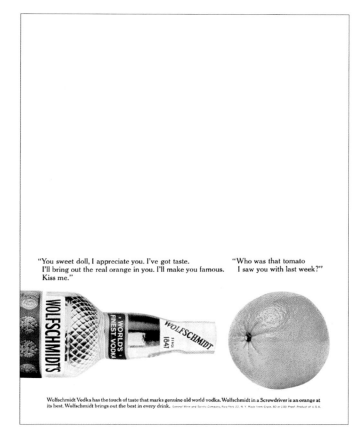

A contemporary comic strip most often contains elements such as panels, dialogue balloons, and visual iconography; noncommercial comic strips often have continuing storylines. In *Comic Strips and Consumer Culture, 1890–1945*, Ian Gordon argues that from their inception comic strips were themselves commercial projects, and they "played a definitive role in the creation of a mass culture of consumption."[14]

Most cartoons used for the purpose of advertising are humorous, aiming to engage and endear through witty entertainment, as well as setting a tone or voice. This format usually has high readership, since people either may not realize it is an ad or, even if they do, they are hoping to be entertained or provoked. Related to this is the format of an *animated cartoon*, or animation, which is a (narrative) film or pictures consisting of a series of drawn, painted, or modeled scenes and characters used to tell a story.

Commercialization and merchandising have been a part of cartooning since comic strips first began appearing in newspapers. The level of merchandising increased in the 1980s, however, as several cartoon programs were built around already existing commercial products: Strawberry Shortcake, the Smurfs, He-Man, etc. Unlike the merchandising of, for instance, Mickey Mouse, these cartoon characters began as products and thus their cartoons were little more than extended commercials for the products themselves.[15]

Musical

In advertising, a musical is a narrative or play that is music-based and where music, singing,

Figure 7-8

PRINT:
WOLFSCHMIDT (1962)

AGENCY:
PAPERT, KOENIG, LOIS

Art Director: George Lois

Copywriter: Julian Koenig

Client: Seagram

14. Ian Gordon, *Comic Strips and Consumer Culture, 1890–1945* (Washington, D.C.: Smithsonian Institution Press, 1998), 12.

15. Jeremy G Butler, "Cartoons"; http://www.museum.tv/archives/etv/C/htmlC/cartoons/cartoons.htm

PRINT CAMPAIGN:
"INTERESTING, SI?"

AGENCY:
FECHTOR ADVERTISING /
COLUMBUS, OHIO

Creative Director and
Copywriter: Stephen Fechtor

Art Director: Rocco Volpe

Illustrator: Zach Volpe

Client: Arte Mexicano

*You would think that an art gal-
lery that specializes in art and
crafts from Mexico would have
limited appeal. And you would
be right, hence the need for a
little strategic positioning. This
campaign is a tongue-in-cheek
look at the "upscale" crowd. It
positions Arte Mexicano as the
place where everyday people
can find unique, attention-
getting work. Work that not
only makes their homes more
interesting, but makes them
more interesting, as well.*
  —Stephen Fechtor

and/or dancing are the main vehicles for telling the story.

"Let's face the chicken gumbo and dance!"

sang Ann Miller in the Great American Soup
commercial by Stan Freberg, humorist and
ad creative, in 1970. Miller, a tap-dancing
star of 1940s and 1950s musicals, lampooned

American commercials by dancing and sing-ing in the character of a housewife in this thoroughly entertaining commercial.

In a more recent campaign created by BBDO Worldwide in New York, "Why settle when you can Select," for the Campbell's Select line of premium soups, actor John Lithgow dances and sings exaggerated tributes to the brand, written by David Yazbek, who also wrote the music and lyrics for the songs Lithgow performed in his hit Broadway show *Dirty Rotten Scoundrels.*[16]

As in popular films, musicals are making a comeback in commercials, for example, in a TV campaign for Procter & Gamble's Swiffer brand dust mop and in ads for the FTC combating Web sites offering "Free Credit Reports."

In 1948, the early days of television, we saw stop-motion animation of square dancing Lucky Strike cigarettes to "You just can't beat a Lucky Strike." From 1948 to 1954, the Texaco Star Theater was a popular Tuesday night program. Four men in matching gas sta-tion uniforms opened the show singing lyrics by Buddy Arnold and Woody Kling (and set in part to Liszt's Hungarian Rhapsody No. 2): "Oh, we're the men of Texaco, We work from Maine to Mexico."

Misdirection

Misdirection ads start out one way and then suddenly change direction. Thinking the TV commercial is about one thing, viewers are surprised by the real message.

These ads can work for a variety of reasons. One reason is the element of surprise; we are being led one way but are surprised to find ourselves taken somewhere else. Certainly, there is a risk with this type of approach: once you've seen the ad, you know the surprise ending. Of course, if the idea and execution are excellent, then you might not mind seeing it again.

This category is often used to spoof other commercials. Pepsi's agency, BBDO / New York, used a misdirection ad during Super

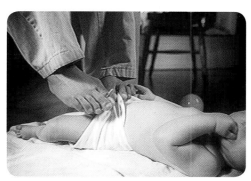

Figure 7-10

TV: "FEET"

AGENCY: CLIFF FREEMAN & PARTNERS / NEW YORK

Creative Director: Eric Silver

Art Director: Kilpatrick Anderson

Copywriter: Kevin Roddy

Director: Rocky Morton

Producer: Nick Felder

Client: FoxSports.com

Taking irreverence to an ex-treme, this commercial leaves the audience completely sur-prised by the time it's over.

Bowl XXXV that played on a Viagra commer-cial featuring spokesperson Bob Dole. In the Pepsi ad, Dole was drinking a Pepsi to get "rejuvenated."

We are completely misled in a satiric TV spot for the Fox Sports Web site (figure 7-10). At first we see a close-up of a man attempting to fasten a baby's diaper with his toes, which leads us to believe that we are watching a heartrending PSA, perhaps about a man triumphing over adversity.

Gradually, it is revealed that the man is a sports-obsessed father who is using his fingers on the computer keyboard to visit the Fox Sports Web site. Likewise in figure 7-11, an ad for a paper company, we expect it to end how the usual story of Old Yeller turns out, but end up chuckling over how the misdirection cleverly explains that "Everything Turns Out Better on Domtar Paper."

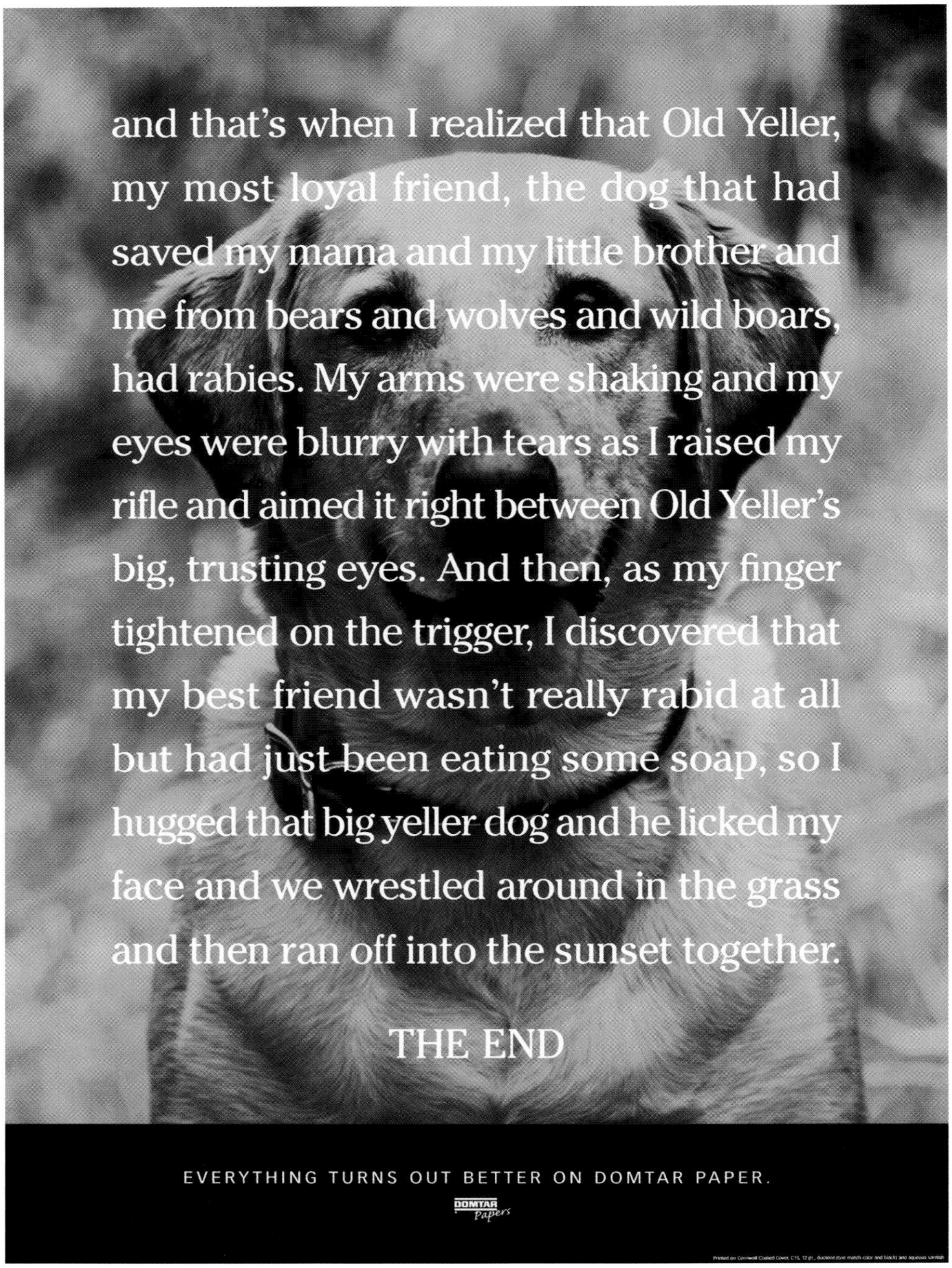

Figure 7-11

PRINT: "OLD YELLER"

AGENCY: HUNT ADKINS / MINNEAPOLIS

Creative Director and Copywriter: Doug Adkins

Associate Creative Director and Art Director: Steve Mitchell

Client: Domtar

Unexpected story line twists, along with the tagline, clarifying the ad concept while making a declaration about the paper.

and that's when I realized that Old Yeller, my most loyal friend, the dog that had saved my mama and my little brother and me from bears and wolves and wild boars, had rabies. My arms were shaking and my eyes were blurry with tears as I raised my rifle and aimed it right between Old Yeller's big, trusting eyes. And then, as my finger tightened on the trigger, I discovered that my best friend wasn't really rabid at all but had just been eating some soap, so I hugged that big yeller dog and he licked my face and we wrestled around in the grass and then ran off into the sunset together.

THE END

EVERYTHING TURNS OUT BETTER ON DOMTAR PAPER.

DOMTAR Papers

One day, Franchise Fred came to town. "I want to build my one zillionth Clone-A-Burger right here," he grinned. So all the people held a meeting. Mr. Snowboarder was there. Mrs. Hiker, Mr. Skier and Ms. Ski Instructor were there too. "No, no," they told Franchise Fred. "Your idea is not so good. We have come here to laugh and play and ride and ski all the livelong day. Your eyesore will ruin our happy mountain town." Franchise Fred made a big fuss. Finally, everyone said, "Well, there is some land above treeline." Then they took him way up there and left him. Maybe Franchise Fred made it home. But with 311 inches of annual snowfall, no one will really know for sure until the spring thaw. Telluride. A land where people come to play. The end.

Figure 7-12

PRINT: "FRANCHISE FRED"

AGENCY: CRISPIN PORTER + BOGUSKY / MIAMI

Creative Director: Alex Bogusky

Art Director: Paul Keister

Copywriter: Bob Cianfrone

Illustrator: Doug Jones

Client: Telluride

Taking a format from another form of printed matter, this ad playfully explains the advantages of Telluride.

Adoption

At times, adopting or appropriating another form of visual art, such as fine art, or another form of artistic work, such as a children's book, makes sense, as in figures 7-12 and 7-13.

In these cases, adopting other forms is whimsical. In nineteenth-century England, controversy erupted over the use of fine art—Sir John Millais's painting *Bubbles*—in a poster advertising Pears Soap, by Thomas Barratt, who built Pears Soap into one of the world's great brands in the nineteenth century. Many people objected to the use of fine art for commercial purposes. Barratt's intention was to borrow the reputation of "high art" for his Pears Soap brand.

▸   Figure 7-13

PRINT:
"RIVER" AND "PEAK"

AGENCY: M&C SAATCHI /
SINGAPORE

Creative Director:
Shane Gibson

Art Director: Eddie Wong

Copywriters:
Nicolas Leong and Paul Tan

Illustrator: Heng-Chia Oi Yong

Retoucher: Sally Liu, Procolor

Client:
Performance Motors BMW

These ads promoted the X5,
which is an off-road car. The
Mandarin headline reflects the
position of the car. The tagline:
"Ultimate driving machine."

Documentary

A documentary is a presentation of facts and information, usually about a social, historical, or political cause. In advertising, a documentary-style format is most often used for public service advertising. For example, the "Ready Campaign" public service advertisements, sponsored by the U.S. Department of Homeland Security in partnership with the Advertising Council, "take a documentary style approach using real people with honest, unscripted answers in regards to their family's emergency preparedness plans." The PSAs direct audiences to www.ready.gov, a Web site "that helps to educate and empower Americans to prepare for and respond to all kinds of emergencies."[17]

Sometimes, political advertising uses a *faux* documentary format, co-opting and creating the look and feel of a documentary to make a political message more authentic or believable.

Mockumentary

A mockumentary (that is, a mock documentary) is a spoof created or shot in the style of a documentary. "The whole purpose of the mockumentary is to say, 'This isn't a commercial, this is real,'" said Chuck Bennett, former creative director at TBWA Chiat/Day. Successful, major mockumentary films include Rob Reiner's *This is Spinal Tap* (1984), which is about a rock band on tour. There have been several other popular films in the mockumentary style. For example, *A Mighty Wind* (2003), directed by Christopher Guest, is about a reunion show of three folk singing groups, and *The Blair Witch Project* (1999), directed by Daniel Myrick and Eduardo Sánchez, is about a trio of film students who disappear when searching the woods for the Blair Witch (this mockumentary film was mocked numerous times). Often, a captivating film genre spawns an advertising format or creative approach.

---

17. www.dhs.gov/xcitizens/gc_1163610715312.shtm

Figure 7-14

TV: "EINSTEINS" AND "PHONELANDIA"

AGENCY: BUTLER, SHINE, STERN & PARTNERS / SAUSALITO, CALIFORNIA

Client: Radio Shack

© Radio Shack & BSSP

These animated TV spots are part of an integrated campaign including: digital media, out of home, direct, in-store signage, and a three-day bicoastal event as well as a live broad- cast video.

To illuminate one of the functional benefits of shopping at Radio Shack, an animated TV spot titled "Einsteins" lets us know that the Shack has more "expertise than a truck full of Einsteins." Set to the beat of European dance music, "Phonelandia" is an animated TV spot featuring phones and PDAs, dressed in wigs and hats, partying against the backdrop of a mountain range.

Wieden + Kennedy created a successful moc- kumentary campaign for "Sports Center" on ESPN, the cable sports network, which began in 1995. In this campaign, we are taken be- hind the scenes of the "This Is SportsCenter" report. One spot featured Evander Holyfield, heavyweight boxing champion, in charge of ESPN's day care center, feeding raw eggs to the children and telling them, "Don't forget your gloves."

"The ESPN commercials use either people from the show or sports stars and throw them into absurd situations. The campaign has become such a cultural hit that star athletes ask to appear in the commercials—and ESPN does not pay them for doing the spots."[18]

Because the commercials promoting its sports news program were so well liked, in 2007, ESPN devoted an entire hour of its broadcast time to showing them.

18. Greg Farrell, "TV Commercials Offer Too Much of a Good Thing All Over Again," *New York Times*, 1 October 1998.

Figure 7-15

INTERACTIVE-VIDEO BASED MARKETING CAMPAIGN: TARGET / CONVERSE ONE STAR FILMS

AGENCY: SCHEMATIC

Creative Lead and Senior Creative Director: Jen Koziol

Senior Vice President and Client Services: Bill Melton

Client: Converse One Star

© Schematic, Inc.

The Situation

Converse and partner Target agreed to sponsor a short film competition that would culminate at the Wanderlust Festival at Squaw Valley [in California] in July 2009. They asked Schematic to design and develop a viral-video marketing campaign around the One Star line that would appeal to the decidedly nonmainstream target audience of music fans, yoga aficionados and health/wellness enthusiasts. The timeline: 6 weeks.

Our Contribution

Schematic recognized that successfully reaching the target demographic would demand a subtle strategy; this audience identifies as countercultural and is not likely to be impressed, or swayed, by overt marketing. To encourage grassroots participation in the film competition, we created a 90-second video featuring indie director, Suzie Vlcek, shown in various stages of low-budget filmmaking in and around her neighborhood. This was designed to democratize submissions, making it clear that anyone with a video camera, a few friends, and a cause could make a film worthy of entry. For this specific audience, we came up with the contest as a "change the world" challenge under the rubric: "Challenge. Fix. Change." We also created a "branded" YouTube channel page on which to show the videos.

The Impact

The Target and Converse One Star film competition launched on May 24, 2009. This project marks the beginning of Schematic's foray into interactive-video and video-based marketing for Target, including campaigns for the Fall 09 (Style) and Holiday 09 collections.
    —Schematic

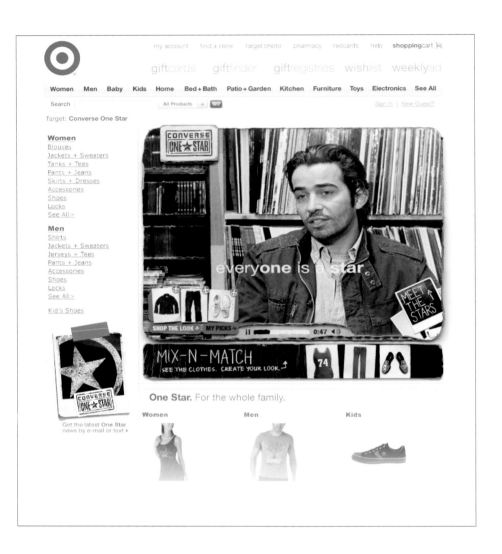

Montage

Montage is the assembling of various short clips or images into a sequence, usually married by look and feel or theme, music, or voice-over narration. The montage is carefully cut and edited together to create a unique whole. In advertising, a montage usually is used to highlight advantageously a single subject or brand or to quickly differentiate aspects or clips; for example, a promotion for a fitness DVD might take advantage of montage to very quickly illustrate the variety of the regimen. Montage also can be used to illustrate the passage of time, though many think it tends to fragment spatial unity.

Assemblage (a work created by combining and composing a collection of different objects) and photomontage (a technique of combining a number of photographs to form a composite whole) are similar to montage.

Animation

Animation is a moving image that consists of a series of drawn, painted, or modeled scenes. In advertising, animation can be thought of as a method or technique for visualizing an idea.

Consumer-Generated Creative Content

Whether a brand or group sponsors a short film competition, as in figure 7-15, or a cover competition, as with the cover of this book, or a competition for a TV spot to be aired during the World Series, it is a way to generate enthusiasm among people while acquiring creative solutions for the brand. (See "Gotta Love It," page 10.)

Pod-busters

Pod busters are very short-form content created to complement the TV program and commercials containing sponsor messages, called *bitcoms*, *minisodes*, or *microseries*; they are customized spots sponsored by marketers that interrupt commercials that interrupt shows. More specifically, bitcoms are skits about sponsors; microseries are two-minute shows that integrate advertisers into plots; and customized spots feature cast members promoting sponsors. They are used to keep viewers' interest during commercial breaks in the TV programming by asking viewers to interact by doing such things as looking for clues, texting, and nudging people to the web.

Entertainment

What does a gorilla playing drums to the sounds of Phil Collins have to do with Cadbury Dairy Milk chocolate? In Cadbury "Gorilla," a format that does not fit conventions or obvious logic related to the product, created by Fallon, London, and Glass and a Half Full Productions, there is no chocolate, no functional benefit, no one experiencing the product. "We felt that the time was right for the brand to not tell people that it made you feel good—but to elicit that feeling," remarked Lee Rolston, director of marketing for block chocolate and beverages at Cadbury. And this piece certainly found a great life on video-sharing sites, too![20]

A film-themed marketing campaign for Bloomingdale's, called "Lights, Camera, Fashion," includes a partnership with Young Indie Films and other groups, in-store screenings, and an interactive Web effort to drive people into stores. "The viral aspect of movies is amazing," commented Anne Keating, senior vice president of public relations, special events, and corporate philanthropy at Bloomingdale's. Young Indie Films assigned "five of its emerging filmmakers to shoot and produce four-minute films dubbed Bflix. The films, which take place in New York City over the course of 15 days, include subtle references to the brand and feature actors in Bloomingdale's apparel. . . . Additionally, Bloomingdale's worked with casting director Jennifer Venditti to launch a http://bloomingdales.com/screentest microsite where consumers can view a promotional casting video."[21]

GAGS, STUNTS, AND PRANKS

As Heffernan pointed out, "the great subjects of online video are stunts, pranks, violence, gotchas, virtuosity, upsets and transformations."[19] Online video sharing, microsites, and mobile platforms will continue to spawn their own formats; some will be much like vaudeville or variety shows, with short blasts of entertainment that pull our collective legs and makes us happy to watch for the punch lines.

19. Heffernan, "The Susan Boyle Experience," 16.

20. www.dandad.org/inspiration/creativityworks/08/gorilla.html

21. Alexandra Bruell, "Bloomingdale's Reveals Film-Themed Fall Campaign," *PR Week*, 14 August 2009.

08 TYPOGRAPHY AND VISUALIZATION

DESIGNING WITH TYPE

Typography makes language visual. In graphic design, typography is designed on two levels—*denotation*, the literal meaning of the words, and *connotation*, the meaning suggested by the design of the typography and the type's relationship with the images. Because type is visual communication, concerns are the clarity of the literal communication—legibility for headlines and readability for body copy—and the aesthetics and expressive quality of the typographic design. Typography is the design of letterforms and the arrangement of them in two-dimensional space (for print- and screen-based media) and in space and time (for motion and interactive media). Type is used as display or as text. *Display type* functions as a dominant typographic component and is usually large or bold. Titles and subtitles, headlines and subheadlines, headings and subheadings are all set in display type. *Text type* or *body copy* is the main body of written content, usually in the form of paragraphs, columns, or captions. Type can be created in a variety of ways—for example, computer generated, hand drawn, handmade, found, or photographed.

Facilitating Reading

Type should be readable. Determining the proper point sizes, spacing, line length, alignment, column depth, variation, and contrast will facilitate reading. Letter and word spacing can make or break communication. Through visual hierarchy, rhythm, and the use of other design principles, you can arrange a *flow* of information, guiding the reader from the most important information to the least.

Letter, word, and line spacing is critical in typography. Spacing should enable comprehension, making the reading experience effortless and agreeable. *Spacing is about transitions—from letter to letter, from word to word, from line to line, from paragraph to paragraph, from page to page, from screen to screen.* Seventy percent of how you design with type depends on how well you craft transitions! *You should always judge the spacing optically.* When designing display type, it is feasible to adjust the spacing of individual characters.

Readability means body copy that is easy to read, thereby ensuring a frustration-free reading experience. How you design with a suitable typeface, with considerations of size, spacing, margins, and color, contributes to readability.

General pointers:

> *It is difficult to read typefaces whose strokes are extreme—too light or too heavy. Those typefaces with too much thick-thin contrast may be difficult to read if they are set very small, as the thin strokes may seem to disappear.*

> *Expanded or condensed faces are more difficult to read due to the distortion.*

> *Body copy set in all caps is difficult to read.*

> *Value contrast between type and ground increases readability.*

> *It is more difficult to read highly saturated colors, especially when positioned on other highly saturated colors.*

> *Type over imagery is harder to read.*

> *Small white type on dark backgrounds is harder to read, especially on screen.*

> *People tend to read darker colors first.*

Selecting a Typeface

The structure and individual characteristics of a typeface matter greatly to communication and how well any typeface will integrate

Figure 8-1

*POSTERS:
"CRIME REPORTS,"
"COLLEGE SCHOLARSHIPS,"
AND "CROSSING STREETS"*

AGENCY: CARMICHAEL
LYNCH / MINNEAPOLIS

Art Director and Illustrator:
James Clunie

Copywriter: Tim Cawley

Client: Cub Scouts

with the characteristics of an image, as in the fine integration in figure 8-1. Evaluate each typeface for its structure, characteristics, aesthetic value based on proportion, balance, visual weight, positive and negative shapes of each individual letter, as well as shape relationships between and among letters. For both display and text, many esteemed designers utilize "classic" typefaces, those that have endured due to their grace (proportion and balance) and are eminently readable.

Classic typefaces also possess visual qualities that have survived changes in fashion, those without eccentricities or trendy qualities. Conversely, decorative or novelty typefaces are not considered classics, because they tend to be highly ornamental, tending to overwhelm a design. If you must use a decorative typeface, use it for display type in very small quantities and mix with a timeless typeface for text. Handmade or hand-drawn type or lettering, most often, is reserved for display; of course, there are situations where handmade works overall. The headline script typeface in figure 8-2 helps communicate the feeling of passion and beauty.

When selecting a typeface, there are at minimum five general criteria to consider:

> Idea. *Each typeface has a specific character; and it should be appropriate for the advertising idea and message.*

> Content. *Readers need to able to make out the message. A typeface must be readable, legible, and appropriate for the nature of the content.*

> Audience. *Just like aiming an ad idea at an audience, considering who comprises the audience—the demographics (the selected population characteristics)—should affect how you select and design with type.*

> Integration with images. *If type and image are components of a composition, then they are in a relationship, a marriage. You determine the nature of that relationship. Will the typeface and image share defining characteristics, such as line, shape, textural quality, or proportion? Will their characteristics contrast one with the other? Will one partner be neutral?*

> Context and media. *Some consideration should be given to how display type will be seen. Will it be on screen (on a small, bigger, or huge screen) or in print (in a magazine or on an outdoor poster)? Will the impact be the same at some distance? What about varying lighting conditions? These factors, among others, should be considered.*

Each typeface has qualities that communicate visually and may or may not be appropriate for an idea, the content (literal message), or the target audience. Choose a face whose character is appropriate to the idea and message. For example, using black letter typeface for a book about contemporary culture aimed at an audience comprised of

---

Figure 8-2

PRINT:
"PASSION" AND "BEAUTY"

AGENCY: CRISPIN PORTER
+ BOGUSKY / MIAMI

Creative Director:
Alex Bogusky

Art Director: Tony Calcao

Copywriter: Rob Strasberg

Photographer: Mark Laita

Client: Giro

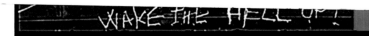

Figure 8-3

PROJECT: *2008 CLEVELAND*
INTERNATIONAL FILM
FESTIVAL CAMPAIGN

FIRM: TWIST CREATIVE INC.
/ CLEVELAND

Creative Director:
Michael Ozan

Art Director: Connie Ozan

Designers:
Brittyn DeWerth, Christopher
Oldham, and Mark Nizinski

Illustrator: Brittyn DeWerth

Copywriter: Michael Ozan

Printer:
Oliver Printing Company

Client: Cleveland International
Film Festival

For five years, we have
worked with the Cleveland
International Film Festival
to improve patronage and
cultural relevance. For 2008 we
wanted patrons to understand
that the festival was a horizon
broadening artistic experience,
thus: How will it change you?
—TWIST

third graders would be highly inappropriate. Related to these criteria is the need to select or create a typeface that works in concert

body copy typefaces from Martin Holloway, Professor Robert Busch School of Design at Kean University, Union, New Jersey.

Diagram 8-3

Graphic interpretation

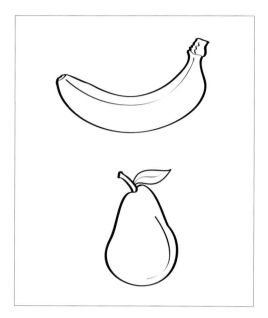

> Motion graphics: *time-based graphics that integrate visuals, typography, and perhaps audio; created using film, video, and computer software, including animation, television commercials, film titles, promotional and informational applications for broadcast, broadband, and mobile media.*

> Diagram: *a graphic representation of information, statistical data, structure, environment, or process (the workings of something).*

> > Chart: *a specific type of diagrammatic representation of facts or data.*

> > Graph: *a specific type of diagram used to indicate relationships between two (or more) variables, often represented on axes.*

> > Map: *a specific type of diagrammatic representation used to depict a route or geographic area, to show location.*

Found images are existing images or objects found in environments, and the category also includes images from the public domain or copyright free images (woodcuts, lino-cuts, etchings, patterns, rules, and more), historical

imagery, ephemera, old postcards, old letters, old maps, family photos, old photos, old playing cards, stamps, old greeting cards, old wrapping paper, old cigar box labels, old labels, old signs, and more. When using found images, you may need to secure necessary intellectual property rights, if any are required.

ALTERING IMAGES

It may be necessary to alter a found image, or even a commissioned or self-generated illustration or photograph. In the workplace, if you need or choose to alter a commissioned or found image created by an illustrator or photographer, you most likely have to obtain approval to make changes to that person's intellectual property. A photographer or illustrator, or the licensee for stock images from an archive or stock house would offer rules about alterations or edits. Altering your own image is of course up to you.

A common decision a designer faces is whether or not to use a visual *as is*. Perhaps extraneous information in the background of a photograph interferes with the foreground. Perhaps colorizing a black and white photo would help communication or perhaps adding a texture would enhance the tactile quality. An *alteration* is a modification or change to the appearance of an image. You can *edit* an image by taking out or adding in visual information. You can *combine* images, merging two or more different or related visuals into a unique whole. You can *present* an image differently, which we will discuss in the next section of this chapter. If you think back to Osborn's Checklist (page 36), there are many ways to alter an image.

PRESENTATION

How you present an image affects the ultimate communication. An image that fills the page communicates differently than an image surrounded by a lot of blank space. An image seen from up close will affect the viewer differently than an image seen from afar. When you visualize and compose, you need to consider the following:

Margins: the blank space surrounding a visual on the left, right, top or bottom edge of a page can present or frame a visual, almost presenting it in a formal manner (see diagram 9-4).

Cropping: cutting a photograph or illustration to use only part of it, not using it in its entirety. Cropping is used to: bring the object seen closer to the viewer; dramatize; delete visual information that might distract

Figure 8-6

PRINT:
"TICKETS" AND "KEYS"

AGENCY:
SAWYER RILEY COMPTON /
ATLANTA, GEORGIA

Web Site:
www.brandstorytellers.com

Creative Director:
Bart Cleveland Associate

Creative Director and
Copywriter: Al Jackson

Art Director: Laura Hauseman

Photographer: Parish Kohanim

Client: Elliott City Infiniti
© 2002

the viewer from the communication; or for a specific effect. Cropping alters the original by changing its outer shape, its internal scale, and how the inner content is framed; it can change the original's focus.

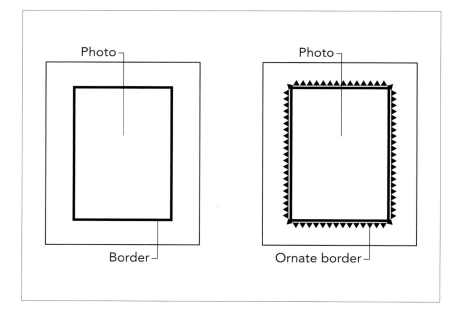

Bleed or full bleed: this a printing term that refers to type or to a visual that extends off the edges of the page, filling the page with an image as in figure 8-6. A partial bleed can run off one, two, or three sides.

Rules: thin stripe(s) or line(s) used for borders or for separating text, columns of text, or visuals. Most often, rules function best when used to separate, as dividers, attracting little notice to them, as in figure 8-7.

Borders: a border is a graphic band that runs along the edge of a visual separating it from the background, emphasizing the boundaries of the visual. Borders can be simple, like a thin rule around a visual, or very decorative, like an ornate picture frame around a Baroque painting. A border should never distract from what it frames (see diagram 8-4).

BASICS OF VISUALIZING FORM

As with designing with type, how you visualize an image depends upon the idea, content, audience, integration with images, context, and medium. In the visual arts, there are basic ways used to describe or characterize form. Examine the print and TV spot in figure 8-8 to see how visualizing form contributes to expression.

Some of the following terms originated in fine art and have been modified for advertising design.

> *Linear:* characterized by a predominate use of lines to describe forms or shapes within a composition.

> *Painterly:* characterized by use of color and value to describe shapes and forms, relying on visible, broad, sketchy, or "brushy" description of form rather than the specificity of lines.

> *Sharpness:* characterized by clarity of form, detail, clean and clear edges and

boundaries, saturated color, readable and legible typography, hard or clear edges, hyperrealism, photorealism, closed compositions, and limited type alignment.

Diffusion: characterized by blurred forms and boundaries, transparencies, muted color palettes, layering, the visual effects of the atmosphere on things seen, and painterliness.

Accuracy: viewers believe an object or subject to be accurately depicted when it conforms with what they know or to common knowledge of that form.

Distortion: when an object or subject is twisted, stretched, bent, warped, buckled, or significantly altered from its normal appearance, then it is distorted.

Economy: images are stripped down visually to fundamental forms, using as little description and few details as possible for denotation.

Figure 8-8

PRINT: "THANKS USA: WHEN JOHNNY . . ."

AGENCY: THE GATE WORLDWIDE / NEW YORK

Writer: David Bernstein

Art Director: Bill Schwab

Photographer: Stock

OUTDOOR: "THANKS USA: MONUMENTS"

AGENCY: THE GATE WORLDWIDE / NEW YORK

Writer: David Bernstein

Art Director: Bill Schwab

Photographer: Bill Schwab

TV: "THANKS USA: PARADE"

AGENCY: THE GATE WORLDWIDE / NEW YORK

Writer: David Bernstein

Art Director: Bill Schwab

Director: Tim Bieber, Mr. Big Film

Editor: Dave Smallheiser

The Background: *This non-profit group was formed to give Americans a lasting way to thank the troops. So instead of offering vets a parade on Veteran's Day, ThanksUSA offered them college scholarships.*

The Brand Idea: *A genuine thank you.*
    — *The Gate Worldwide*

PRINT: "ENJOY"

AGENCY:
RETHINK ADVERTISING
/ VANCOUVER, BRITISH
COLUMBIA

Art Director and Copywriter:
Ian Grais

Photographer: Hans Sipma

Client: Playland

If you cover the image and read the headline and vice versa, you don't get the full communication. Together, the headline and image communicate the thrill of an extreme amusement park ride with great humor.

Intricacy: visualization is based on complexity, on the use of many component parts, and/or on details to describe and visually communicate.

Subtlety: visualization is based on low contrast, muted color palettes or tints, static compositions, transparencies, layering, limiting fonts and alignment, distant vision, and atmospheric perspective.

Boldness: forms are conveyed with big, brassy, aggressive movements and compositions, saturated color palettes, thick

lines, high contrast, cropping, or images that are near.

Understated: visualization is less dramatic, subtle, and restrained.

Exaggeration: visualization uses a visual hyperbole and might be bigger, grander, more prominent, more dramatic, embellished, or amplified.

Predictable: pattern, symmetry, absolute consistency of elements and their treatment, stable compositions, even

Figure 8-10

PRINT: "WE HAVE A SUGGESTION FOR WHOEVER SUGGESTED IT"

AGENCY: DEVITO/VERDI /
NEW YORK

Client: Daffy's

Figure 8-11

PRINT CAMPAIGN: "TRAIL SIGN" AND "DRIVE-IN THEATER"

AGENCY: LOEFFLER KETCHUM MOUNTJOY / CHARLOTTE, NORTH CAROLINA

Creative Director: Jim Mountjoy

Art Director: Doug Pedersen

Copywriter: Curtis Smith

Photographers: Olaf Veltman and Stuart Hall

Client: North Carolina Travel & Tourism

Figure 8-12

PRINT:
"SHOWER CURTAIN RAIL"
AND "POTATO PEELER"

AGENCY: FORSMAN
& BODENFORS /
GOTHENBURG, SWEDEN

Art Directors: Karin Jacobsson
and Anders Eklind

Copywriters:
Filip Nilsson, Fredrik Jansson,
and Hjalmar Delehag

Photographer: Karolina Henke

Client: IKEA Sweden

*Targeting men, these ads
utilize unexpected visuals in a
slice-of-life setting.*

weights, among other things, would be considered predictable.

Spontaneous: sketchiness, abrupt movements, asymmetry, change in pace, staccato lines, open forms, changes in case, or blurring of edges could communicate spontaneity.

Opaque: forms and elements are dense, solid seeming, not see-through.

Transparent: type and visuals can be see-through; we see through from one image to another, from one letterform to another, from one texture to another.

Digital transparency: visualization involves altering the opacity of any graphic element or image, in print or motion. The contrast of an element is lowered so that it appears transparent in relation to its original opaque form. Visualization can also rely on a juxtaposition of transparent and opaque components.

Patterns often employ *graphic transparency* where layers of lines, shapes, textures, forms, letterforms or fields, or bands of color overlap. Related to graphic transparency, *linear transparency* refers to

transparent layering of linear forms, lines, or outline type.

Pastiche: visual appearance is palpably created by imitating a style, recombining ideas, appropriating or referencing; also referred to as *sampling* or (negatively as) *appropriation.*

INTEGRATING TYPE AND IMAGE

When coupled, type and image should equal a sum greater than the separate parts. Type and image work together in a cooperative duet, in a synergistic relationship, as in figure 8-9, a humorous ad for Playland, or in the classic ad by DeVito/Verdi for Daffy's (see figure 8-10).

When visualizing and composing your idea, the following questions are useful to answer:

> *How will type and image interact?*

Figure 8-13

PRINT: "BULLDOZER"

AGENCY: R & R PARTNERS / LAS VEGAS

Creative Director: Ron Lopez

Copywriter: Gage Clegg

Art Directors: Jean Austin and Becca Morton

Photographer: Gary Jensen

Client: Laughlin Shoot Out

© 2001

Figure 8-14

PRINT: "ALL SIX OF THEM"

AGENCY:
PUSH ADVERTISING /
ORLANDO, FLORIDA

Creative Director:
John Ludwig

Copywriter: John Ludwig

Art Director: Ron Boucher

Client: Middleton

*The linear quality of the type
and illustrations correspond
and are unified, working
together to communicate the
benefits of Middleton.*

Integration Categories

Type and image form specific relationships. Let's categorize the broadest possible relationships:

Starring role: Either type or image takes the lion's share of the attention—it is the star—with the other component acting in a more neutral fashion, like a supporting actor. If the image is the star, then type might be selected to contextualize the visual, as in figure 8-12. When type is *purposely understated* in contrast to a strong visual statement, that constitutes a complementary relationship, where the type simultaneously contextualizes the image. When the type is the star, then the visual is subordinate, as in figure 8-13.

Similar characteristics: Type and image are sympathetic, possessing similar characteristics resulting in agreement, in harmony (figure 8-14). Or type and image share a thematic purpose. Congruency relies on agreement in: shape, form, color palette, proportions, weights, widths, thin-and-thick strokes, lines, textures, positive and negative shapes, and time period.

Contrast: Type and image possess different characteristics (figure 8-15). Their contrast produces an effect, either a complementary relationship or a formal ironic relationship.

In a complementary relationship, a typeface or handmade type works in op-position (or in juxtaposition) to an image, depending on contrast in shape, form, proportions, weights, widths, thin-and-thick strokes, lines, textures, and positive and negative shapes. For example, slab serif type versus a sinuous image, smooth-textured image versus distressed type, detailed image versus loosely rendered image. Mixing styles and historical periods can also create opposition.

In a formal ironic relationship, when the typeface and image are coupled for in-congruity, the result is ironic.

> *Will the type drive the composition, or will the image drive the composition?*

> *Will one be emphasized and the other deemphasized?*

> *Will the type and images share characteristics?*

> *Will the type and images work in opposition, be contrasted in style or form?*

> *Will they touch, overlap, fuse, become emblematic, be juxtaposed, be words that incorporate images, or be images that incorporate words?*

In figure 8-11, a campaign for North Carolina Travel and Tourism, the type and visuals are emblematic, and the type is embedded in the visual.

Figure 8-15

POSTERS:
THEATRE PROJECT

DESIGN STUDIO:
SPUR DESIGN / BALTIMORE

Designer and Illustrator:
David Plunkert

Client: Theatre Project

With an emphasis on concept and form, although the thicks and thins of the typeface share some characteristics with the illustrations, Spur Design's David Plunkert has created contrast between the formal nature of the typeface and the whimsical personality of the illustrations.

SHOWCASE

ROBYNNE RAYE
MODERN DOG DESIGN CO. / ARTWALK POSTERS: 1996–2009
moderndog.com

Since cofounding Modern Dog Design Co. in 1987, Robynne Raye has continued to do work for entertainment and retail companies—both locally and nationally—and counts poster, packaging, and identity projects as some of her favorite work. Recent clients include Coca-Cola, Adobe Systems Inc., Blue Q, Olive Green Dog Products, Shout! Factory, and Live Nation. Robynne has received recognition from every major design organization in the United States. Her posters are represented in the permanent archives of the Louvre (Rohan Marsan wing) the Library of Congress, El Centro de Desarrollo des las Artes Visuales (Havana, Cuba), Hong Kong Heritage Museum, Bibliothèque Nationale de France, Museum für Kunst und Gewerbe Hamburg, the Warsaw National Museum, and the Cooper-Hewitt National Design Museum, among others. In March 2008, Chronicle Books published a twenty-year retrospective focusing on Modern Dog's poster work. For more than sixteen years she has lectured and taught workshops, both nationally and internationally. Currently, Robynne is an adjunct instructor at Cornish College of the Arts in Seattle, Washington.

TITLE: ARTWALK 1996

Designer and Illustrator:
Robynne Raye

Client: Phinney Neighborhood Association

This was our first poster for the annual Greenwood/Phinney ArtWalk. The illustration was first created very large with stencils and spray paint. Then we shrunk the whole thing down on the photocopier and tried to fit it back together. We couldn't get things to line up perfectly, but we liked the look of the bad fit and went with it.
—Modern Dog

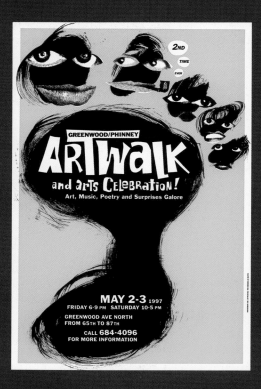

TITLE: ARTWALK 1997

Designer and Illustrator: Robynne Raye

Client: Phinney Neighborhood Association

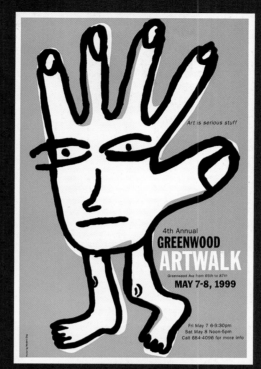

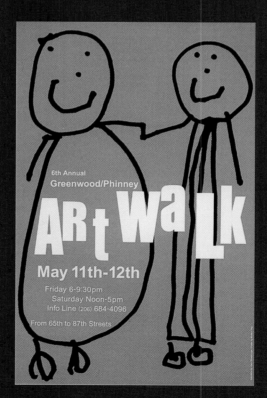

▸ **TITLE: ARTWALK 2000**

Designer and Illustrator: **Robynne Raye**

Client: **Phinney Neighborhood Association**

▸ **TITLE: ARTWALK 2001**

Designer: Robynne Raye

Illustrator: Alice Strassburger

Client: Phinney Neighborhood Association

09

COMPOSITION

WHAT IS COMPOSITION?

In the design process, composition gives form to content. The coherence of the composition depends upon how the content is ordered and shaped. An interesting form results from a good idea and a finely honed visualization and composition.

A composition is the form, the whole spatial property and structure resulting from the intentional visualization and arrangement of graphic elements (type and visuals) in relation to one another and to the format. For each and every composition, you use the formal elements (line, shape, color, value, and texture) to visualize type and images, employing basic principles (balance, emphasis, unity, rhythm, and proportion) in the process of composing.

For some, such as product design legend Eva Zeisel, design "starts with a thought, then proceeds from sketches and notes to working drawings that lead to the finished design."[1] For others, the process of producing ideas and designing—like any creative process—is largely nonlinear. Design, ultimately, is an iterative process.

When designing a single surface, static application, most designers compose spontaneously rather than use a compositional device, such as a grid or template, which are commonly employed for multiple page applications. Whether you compose spontaneously, proceed from thought to final sketch, use a grid or other device, or revise and rethink, clear and interesting visual communication is the goal.

1. http://exhibitions.cooperhewitt.org/Design-USA/designer/10

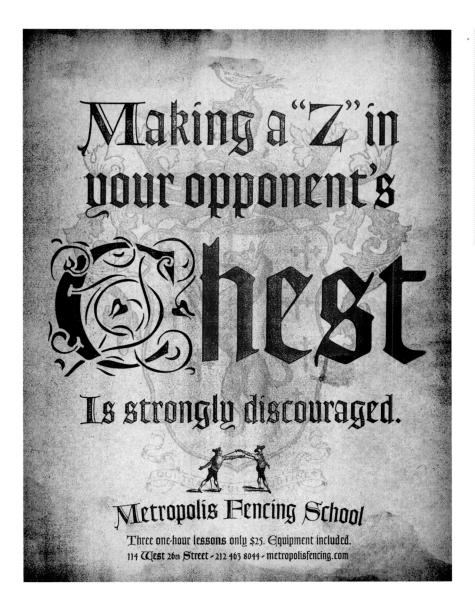

Figure 9-1

PRINT: "Z"

AGENCY:
DEVITO/VERDI / NEW YORK

Creative Director: Sal DeVito

Art Director: Jim Wood

Copywriter: Peter Lipton

Client:
Metropolis Fencing School

Historically appropriate type incisively carries the message of this fencing school.

THE BASIC COMPOSITIONAL STRUCTURES

Once you have generated an advertising idea (and perhaps thought out its visualization), how do you begin to compose it? The ad *idea* should serve as the catalyst for visualization and composition, including determining *content* and *context*. For novices, guidelines are helpful. To begin the process of developing your ad idea, you will need to determine:

> *what you want to say and to whom you want to say it;*

> *the main point of the communication and which graphic elements best carry the message;*

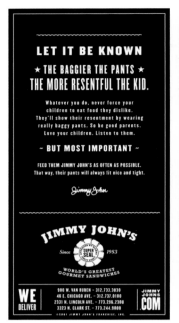
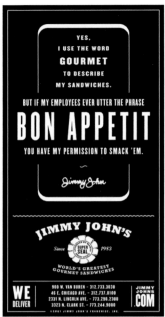
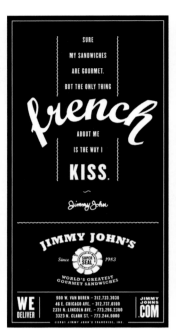
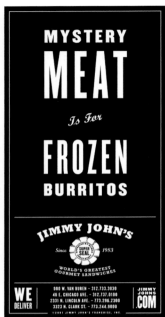

Figure 9-2

*PRINT AD CAMPAIGN,
PACKAGE DESIGN, STORE
SIGNAGE: JIMMY JOHN'S*

COMMUNICATION
COMPANY:
PLANET PROPAGANDA /
MADISON, WISCONSIN

Creative Director: Kevin Wade

Designers:
Dan Ibarra and Mike Krol

Copywriter: Seth Gordon

Client: Jimmy John's

© Planet Propaganda

Figure 9-3

*CAMPAIGN:
MELTED PEOPLE*

Creative Director and
Copywriter: Stephen Fechtor

Art Director: Rocco Volpe

Photographer:
Carmon Rinehart

Retoucher:
Pat Dignan, Image Arts

Client: Graeter's Ice Cream

© 2008 by Fechtor Advertising

*All we wanted to say was, "This
is the best damn ice cream
you've ever tasted."
    —Stephen Fechtor*

> *how to organize the graphic elements
to best communicate to (and grab the
attention of) your audience;*

> *what to emphasize and de-emphasize.*

There are several basic compositional structures, but the focus in this chapter will be on
three: type-driven compositions, image-driv-
en compositions, and verbal-visual synergistic
compositions.

Type-driven compositions emphasize type
and de-emphasize visuals (figure 9-1). Indeed,
type might be the sole element of a composition (figure 9-2).

Image-driven compositions emphasize image
and de-emphasize type. The image becomes
the "hero" (figure 9-3).The composition may
employ no copy at all (a no-copy solution),
where the visual says it all.

An image-driven composition can be built
around a dominant image, to which all other
images and graphic elements are subordinated. The dominant image can be singular
and large or, instead, a major compositional
movement or thrust.

You can build an image-driven composition
without one overtly dominant image; here,
relationships are built through sequence,

pattern, grid, modular structure, repetition,
stair structures, axis alignment, edge alignment, positioning and flow, or some unifying
principle. Though no one image dominates,
the imagery still carries the message, and the
type is subordinated.

Another consideration for image-driven compositions is whether you employ a singular
image or juxtapose images to communicate
meaning—two or more visuals juxtaposed
communicate in a synergistic fashion.

An ad can also have no headline (figure 9-4).

Visual-verbal synergy happens when the
headline and the main image work together
to communicate the meaning. In such a
composition, all other graphic elements are
subordinate to the synergistic relationship
between the headline and the main image.
This is a fundamental structure in advertising
(figure 9-5). The image plus headline equals
greater communication.

Figure 9-4

PRINT: "CORKSCREW"

AGENCY:
RETHINK ADVERTISING
/ VANCOUVER, BRITISH
COLUMBIA

Art Director: Ian Grais

Copywriter: Ian Grais

Photographer: Hans Sipma

Client: Playland

Figure 9-5

PRINT: "WEDDING"

AGENCY:
BMP DDB / LONDON

Photographer: Paul Reas

Agent: John Wyatt Clarke

Client: Volkswagen

BASIC DESIGN PRINCIPLES

Here is a primer of basic design principles that apply to single surfaces, multiple surfaces, and motion graphics.

Format

Every application starts with a format, which is the defined perimeter, as well as the field it encloses, essentially the outer edges or boundaries of a design. The format is the field or substrate (piece of paper, mobile phone screen, outdoor billboard, etc.) for the design. A screen or page's boundaries are full participants in the composition, as much as any element that is added to the format, such

Figure 9-6

PRINT: "CONDIMENT / SPAGHETTI SAUCE"

AGENCY: DEVITO/VERDI / NEW YORK

Creative Director: Sal DeVito

Art Director: Susanne Macarelli

Copywriter: Erhan Erdem

Client: eCampus.com

as type or an image. The term format also is used to describe specific applications, such as a magazine ad or Web site.

SIZE OF FORMAT AND DISTANCE FROM FORMAT

Advertising images and messages are ubiquitous. There are many screens and many surfaces loaded with images. When we are on the go, we use our mobile screens, see outdoor boards, taxi toppers, or public screens. When we are at work, we see our mobile and computer screens and perhaps newspapers, magazines, and kiosks. When we are at home, we see our mobile, computer and TV screens, plus any printed matter. Therefore, we must consider:

Context: where and how we see a format

Size: the dimensions of the page or screen

Distance: viewing position relative to the page or screen

When discussing distance from the screen, Dale Herigstad, chief creative officer at Schematic, terms the mobile and computer screen "personal media" and plans for a one- to two-foot navigation distance; for a traditional family and friends TV-viewing experience, a 10-foot navigation distance is optimal; and public media screens can vary from close (touch screen) to a 200-foot navigation distances.

Balance

Balance is stability created by an even distribution of visual weight on each side of a central axis, as well as by an even distribution of weight among all the elements in a composition. A balanced composition tends to be harmonious. Consider several interrelated visual factors to create balance:

Visual weight refers to the relative amount of visual attraction or emphasis a graphic element carries in a composition due to its size, shape, value, color, and texture.

Where you *position* a mark or graphic element on a page also affects its visual weight. In visual perception, different areas of the page seem to carry more or less visual weight.

A balanced composition can be *symmetrical* or *asymmetrical*. Symmetry is a mirroring of equivalent elements, an equal distribution of visual weights, on either side of a central axis.

▸ ▸   Figure 9-7

PRINT:
"COUCH" AND "RESUME"

AGENCY: BUTLER SHINE STERN PARTNERS / SAUSALITO, CALIFORNIA

Client: Greyhound

© Greyhound and BSSP

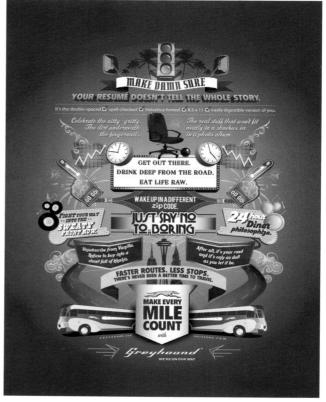

Approximate symmetry is very close to symmetry. Imagine a vertical axis dividing this poster (figure 9-7) in half; you can see an equal distribution of weight on either side of it.

Asymmetry is an equal distribution of visual weights achieved through weight and counterweight by balancing one element with a contrasting element *without mirroring* elements on either side of a central axis (figure 9-7). To achieve asymmetrical balance, the position, visual weight, size, value, color, shape, and texture of a mark on the page must be considered and weighed against every other mark. Every element and its position contribute to the overall balancing effect in a design solution.

When designing asymmetrical compositions, we balance opposing visual weights and forces. One visual weight is strategically counterpoised by another. Think of every visual weight you position in a composition requiring a contrasting counterbalancing force strategically placed in the composition, as in figure 9-9.

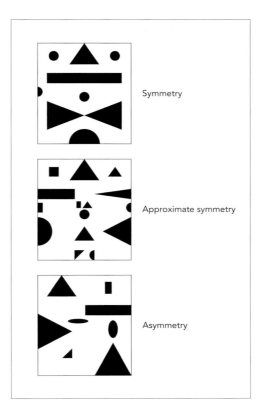

Symmetry

Approximate symmetry

Asymmetry

▸ **Diagram 9-1**

Types of balance

Visual Hierarchy

Since people do not spend much more than a few seconds glancing at an ad, the principle of visual hierarchy creates order and coherence, facilitating rapid message communication. Visual hierarchy is the arrangement of *all* graphic elements according to emphasis, and it is employed to guide the viewer, as in figure 9-10. Emphasis is the arrangement of visual elements according to importance, stressing some elements over others, making some graphic elements dominant and others subordinate. What do you want the viewer to see first? Second? Third? And so on.

When you determine what to emphasize and what to de-emphasize, you are establishing a focal point. Position, size, shape, direction, hue, value, saturation, texture of a graphic element, or an anomaly (a graphic element or image that deviates from the rest), all contribute to creating the focal point of your ad.

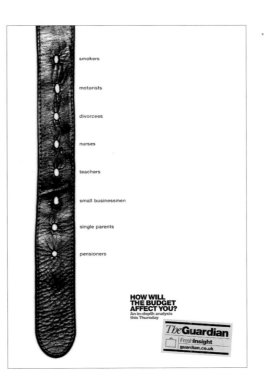

smokers

motorists

divorcees

nurses

teachers

small businessmen

single parents

pensioners

HOW WILL THE BUDGET AFFECT YOU? An in-depth analysis this Thursday

The **Guardian** FreshInsight guardian.co.uk

▸ Figure 9-8

PRINT: "BUDGET BELT"

AGENCY: DMP DDB / LONDON

Photographer: Alan Mahon

Agent: Horton Stevens

Client: Guardian Unlimited

The belt on the left side is counterbalanced by the thoughtful positioning of the headline and the angle of the Guardian logo.

DYNAMIC VISUAL HIERARCHY

When touch screens with multitouch capabilities or gestural interface technology are used, then visual hierarchy becomes dynamic; it changes. When designing for these devices, you will need to consider distance (near and far) and the position and size of what is seen in relation to the viewer, screen, and other graphic elements. A touch screen responds to touch—when someone zooms in on a graphic element, pulls it forward by pinching, then it moves closer; it appears bigger and nearer to the viewer.

Unity

To achieve unity, all the graphic elements must look as though they belong together.

Figure 9-9

PRINT:
"NEVADA: BRING IT ON"

AGENCY: R & R PARTNERS / LAS VEGAS

Creative Director and Copywriter: Tim O'Brien

Designer: Mike Corbitt

Photographer: Jim Erickson

Client: Nevada Commission on Tourism

© 2001

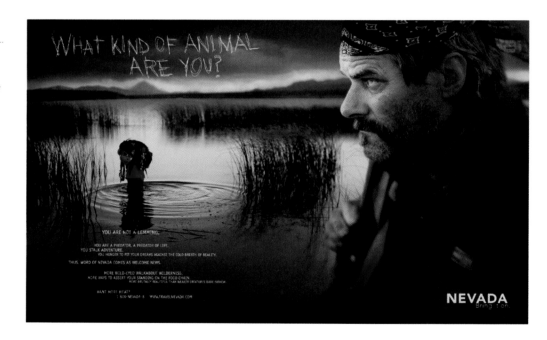

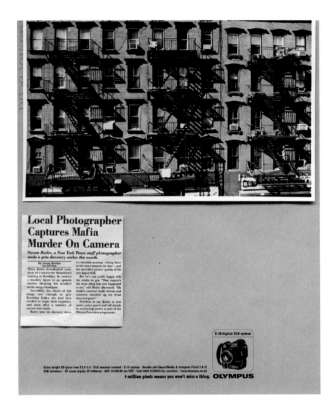

Figure 9-10

PRINT CAMPAIGN:
"MURDER," "CONGRESSWOMAN," AND "TOURIST"

AGENCY: LOWE / LONDON

Creative Director: Charles Inge

Art Director: Steve Williams

Copywriter: Adrian Lim

Photographer: David Preutz

Client: Olympus

The camera produces such high-quality pictures that you won't miss a thing. The line ("4 million pixels means you won't miss a thing") plus the photos convince us of the claim. Also, this campaign engages viewers' attention by making them search the photo for the evidence.

CASE STUDY

Schematic

*Creative Lead and Chief
Creative Officer: Dale Herigstad*

*User Experience Lead and
Executive Vice President, User
Experience: Jason Brush*

*Account Lead and CEO:
Trevor Kaufman*
© Schematic, Inc.

Cannes Lions Touchwall

The Situation

Schematic has a history of taking on internal research and design (R&D) projects and training our teams on emerging technologies like Microsoft Surface, Google Android, and Facebook Connect, to name a few. We believe that the best way to deliver innovation for our clients is to prepare for what's on the horizon by becoming experts ourselves. We also believe that the best way to reach customers, regardless of the channel, is to actually offer them something they will value.

One area of the digital landscape we identified as having great opportunity for growth is interactive out of home. More and more digital screens are becoming incorporated into public spaces, and they have the potential to be so much more than the video-content delivery systems they are today.

That is why Schematic decided to take on an innovation project at a scale and level of sophistication that no one had tried before. We selected the Cannes Lions Festival as the venue to launch our new interactive platform, called the Touchwall, because we wanted to demonstrate the power of offering something with real utility. We also hoped to inspire this group of the greatest creative minds in our industry about what interactive out of home and touch technology have to offer.

Our Contribution

Partnering with the Cannes Lions organizers to ensure that the Touchwall would offer attendees the most value, Schematic designed and built a 12' x 5' multiuser touch screen to serve as the information and connection hub of the 2009 festival. The 3840 x 1600 pixel glass screen delivered high-resolution interactive graphics and allowed multiple users to have personalized interactions with festival information at the touch of a finger.

The Touchwall allowed festival delegates to explore and interact with three-dimensional maps of both the city of Cannes and a detailed expandable map of the festival hall, called the "Palais." It also enabled users to send themselves e-mails with information about restaurants, bars, and hotels in the surrounding area and directions from the venue. Along the top of the screen, there is a Gantt-chart style visualization of the entire week's schedule, which is packed with overlapping seminars, workshops, master classes, and award shows. Each event was expandable into a unique "event widget" and sharable via e-mail. The schedule was also strategically positioned above the heads of up close users, so that it would be visible by people who were using it from afar.

Along with providing a lot of detailed information, the Touchwall also gave users another valuable tool—the ability to connect with one another. People could search for other users by name, and then send a request to exchange information. Or, if they were standing side by side, they could exchange contact details through the Touchwall via e-mail by pulling the "drag-tag" attached to their personalized avatars to one another.

Perhaps the most striking element of the Touchwall was the use of radio frequency identification (RFID) technology. By embedding RFID tags in the delegates' festival badges, the wall was able to identify users as they approached the sensors behind the glass and offer them a personal and unique experience alongside other users.

Technical Innovations

Over the course of designing, developing, and building the Touchwall, the team was presented with a number of unique challenges. In order to deliver the final solution, Schematic developed several proprietary pieces of software for the Touchwall. These included a user interface built in the (then

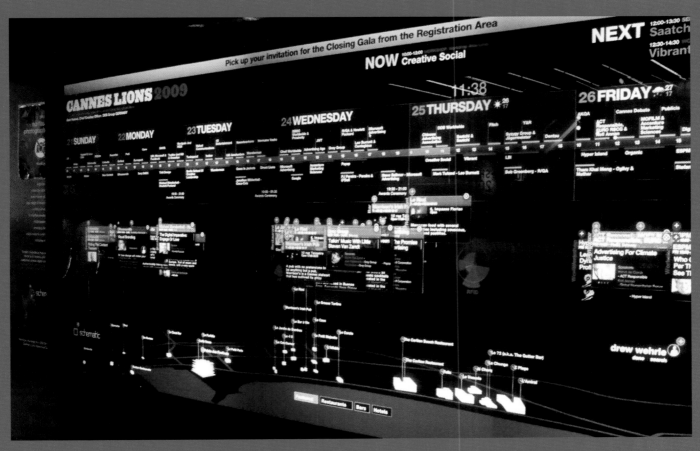

pre-beta) Adobe Flex 4, a unique multitouch framework to interpret individual touches on the wall, and custom .NET RFID Middleware. The wall also required tight integration with the Cannes Lions festival database—to allow real-time updates to schedule information—and connection with registration information.

On the hardware side, we partnered with Motorola to choose the optimal RFID tags (which are typically used on inanimate objects, not people), as well as the RFID antennae used to detect delegate badges from behind the glass. And, in order to achieve the 6.14 million-pixel screen, six short-throw projectors needed to be seamlessly stitched into a single, flawless image. Finally a series of infrared lasers had to be mounted and calibrated to make sure every touchable inch of the sixty-square-foot glass surface was accurately detecting touch inputs.

In addition to building new technology solutions for the Touchwall, Schematic also developed new multiuser single-touch interaction models. This new platform requires an entirely new set of actions, unlike using a keyboard, a mouse, or even a smart phone that uses touch technology. Careful consideration had to be paid not only to designing individual interactions between users and the interface but also among and between users working side-by-side. In addition to the visual design, each interaction type had its own unique sound, designed by Man Made Music, to reinforce the new touch behaviors.

The Impact

During the weeklong Cannes Lions Festival in June 2009, there were more than 6,000 users identified by the Touchwall, and people spent an average of four minutes per interaction. At peak traffic times, literally dozens of people crowded around the wall at the same time, and 90 percent of the e-mails sent from the wall requesting to exchange contact information were accepted.

The launch also attracted over 25 million media impressions worldwide, and it was featured in *Fast Company, USA Today, Creativity,* and *Boards,* among dozens of other media outlets. The new technological innovations and unique interaction models we developed for this multiuser public interface have potential applications for retail spaces, museums, airports, and a variety of other venues. Anywhere large groups of people convene and need better ways to interact with the information around them.

Perhaps the most important result of the launch of our Touchwall at the Cannes Lions festival is the set of lessons we learned about developing beautiful, powerful out of home solutions that we can now bring to bear for our clients. Schematic set out to make ourselves experts in large, interactive touch-screen technology, and we are now well on our way.

—Schematic

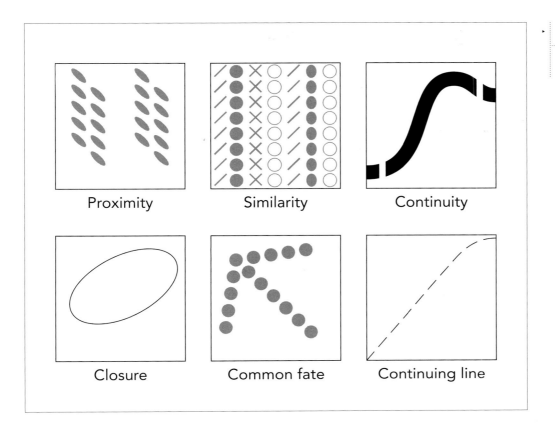

▸ **Diagram 9-2**

Laws of perceptual organization

The notion of *gestalt* (from the German for "form") emphasizes the viewer's perception of *an integrated whole,* not unrelated component parts. By grouping—perceiving visual units by location, orientation, likeness, shape, and color—we tend *to seek a whole* form (see diagram 9-2). According to the principle called the law of *prägnanz* ("precision"), we seek a coherent, elegant experience. These are the gestalt laws of perceptual organization[1]:

Proximity. Elements near each other, those in spatial proximity, are perceived as belonging together.

Similarity. Like elements, those that share characteristics, are perceived as belonging together. Elements can share likeness in shape, texture, color, and direction. Dissimilar elements tend to separate from like elements.

Continuity. Perceived visual paths or connections (actual or implied) among parts establishes continuity; elements that appear as a continuation of previous elements are perceived as linked, creating an impression of movement.

Closure. The mind tends to connect individual elements to produce a completed form, unit, or pattern in order to produce closure.

Common fate. Elements are likely to be perceived as a unit if they move in the same direction.

Continuing line. Lines are always perceived as following the simplest path. If two lines break, the viewer sees the overall movement rather than the break; this is also called *implied line.*

When elements such as color, value, shape, texture, or parallel directions are repeated or

1. From Max Wertheimer, "Laws of Organization in Perceptual Forms," *Psycologische Forschung* 4 (1923): 301–350.

Figure 9-11

PRINT: "ALL SIX OF THEM"

AGENCY:
PUSH ADVERTISING /
ORLANDO, FLORIDA

Creative Director:
John Ludwig

Copywriter: John Ludwig

Art Director: Ron Boucher

Client: Middleton

© 1997-2003

*The linear quality of the type
and illustrations correspond
and are unified, and they work
together to communicate the
benefits of Middleton Lawn
and Pest Control.*

when you establish a style (a linear style, for example), you establish a visual correspondence among the graphic elements. Related to correspondence is continuity, which is the handling of design elements—like line, shape, texture, and color—to create similarities of form, as in a family resemblance (figure 9-11).

For example, if you were designing print magazine ads, outdoor boards, taxi toppers, and Web banners, you would want to handle the type, shapes, colors, and any graphic elements on all the applications in a similar way to establish a family resemblance among the pieces in the campaign. Not only are correspondence and continuity critical to each composition, they are critical across an ad campaign, where each unit must bear some visual resemblance to each other (figure 9-12).

You will also need to apply correspondence in these cases:

> *Correspondence throughout a Web site.* A clear sense of place or geography created by consistent position of menus will help guide the viewer.

Figure 9-12

*PRINT CAMPAIGN:
"MORE TURN. LESS BURN"
AND "DRIVE LIKE THERE IS
NO TOMORROW"*

AGENCY: BUTLER, SHINE,
STERN & PARTNERS /
SAUSALITO, CALIFORNIA

Client: MINI

© MINI and BSSP

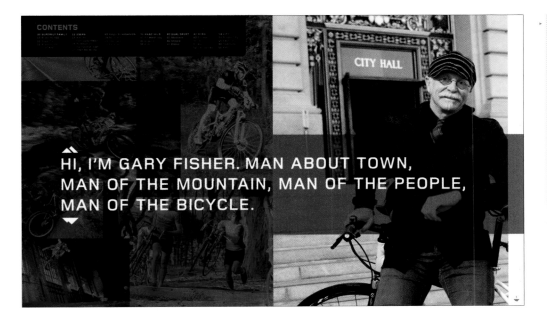

Figure 9-13

INTEGRATED CAMPAIGN:
GARY FISHER

COMMUNICATION
COMPANY: PLANET
PROPAGANDA / MADISON,
WISCONSIN

Creative Director: Dana Lytle

Art Director and Designer:
David Taylor

Copywriters: Andy Brawner
and Ann Sweeney

Photographers:
Justin Nolan, Michael Kirk,
Winni Wintermeyer, Russell
Lee, Alan Davis, Jason Van
Horn, Steve Milanowski, Colin
Meagher, Michael Martin, and
David Nevala

Interactive Director: Ben Hirby

Developer:
Marcus Trapp, Trent Simon

Web Designer: Zack Schulze

Client: Gary Fisher

© Planet Propaganda

Correspondence across screens. A clear sense of how to change content within a Web site establishes correspondence across screens. Should the pages move up and down with the main navigation remaining constant? Should the page "turn"? Should the viewer's gaze remain centered and the next page or screen come to the viewer?

Correspondence in a series. When designing for a series of individual but related units (for example, a campaign that crosses platforms such as print, mobile, and Web), establish parameters to define a typographic system (palette and usage) along with a common visualization language, compositional structure, and color palette to ensure continuity across the individual units as well as to ensure that viewers see the individual units as belonging to a campaign (figure 9-13).

CONTRAST CREATES DYNAMICS

A composition needs a dynamic quality to engage the viewer. Contrast adds dynamics. Contrast is a visual effect created by the use of differences, by comparing (dissimilar) elements. Big is bigger in relation to small. Slow is slower in relation to fast. If a newscaster delivered the news in a monotone voice, it would be very difficult to glean information, or if a dancer moved at one pace or level, that too would be uninteresting. Think of a snow globe. When shaken, there is great movement and energy. As the snowflakes settle, there is less movement and finally no movement. The swirl of snowflakes looks more exciting because it is contrasted to the calm before and after.

The two overarching purposes for differentiating visual elements are to create visual variety (or dynamics) and to compare dissimilar elements, thereby enhancing the uniqueness of each, to show its differences and to make distinctions. For example, if you contrast saturated colors with muted colors, then the viewer is treated to variety. If you contrast small graphic elements with big graphic elements, then there is dynamic

scale. If you contrast a sans serif headline against a serif body copy, then readers will be able to more easily distinguish the copy.

In figure 9-14, contrasting near and far—close-ups of objects with a distant view of the Casbah club—creates very interesting space and communicates the benefit of this music venue.

Through contrast, the viewer is better able to understand each graphic element. Short juxtaposed to tall looks shorter. Bright looks more saturated compared to dull. In dance, we understand quick in relation to slow.

"Polar contrasts" was a theory of oppositions put forth by Johannes Itten, artist, professor, author, and color and design theoretician. Itten's list of contrasts includes:

> *big/small*

> *long/short*

> *straight/curved*

> *pointed/blunt*

> *much/little*

> *light/heavy*

> *hard/soft*

Rhythm

A strong and consistent repetition of graphic elements (color, line type and quality, texture, shape, position, etc.) can set up a rhythm, reminiscent of a beat in music, that guides the viewer's eyes around the page. Rhythm—a sequence of graphic elements at prescribed intervals—across multiple-page applications and motion graphics (including Web site, magazine design, and motion graphics) is critical to developing a coherent visual flow from one page to another (moving the eye like a strong dance beat moves bodies).

Variation is introduced to punctuate, accent, and create visual interest. In design composition, the key to establishing rhythm is to understand the difference between

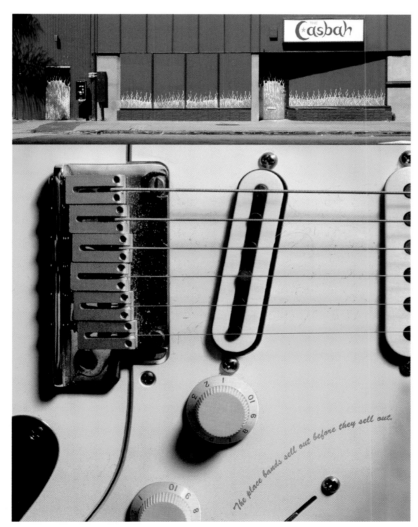

Figure 9-14

PRINT: "CORPORATE RADIO," "ARROGANT," AND "SELL OUT"

AGENCY: MATTHEWS | EVANS | ALBERTAZZI / SAN DIEGO

Art Director and Photographer: Dana Neibert

Copywriter: John Risser

Client: The Casbah

© 2002 Matthews | Evans | Albertazzi

Juxtaposing cropped images that appear to be near the viewer with the faraway image of the Casbah creates a dynamic contrast. Placing the sharp-witted copy on the cropped images, as if it were a natural part of them, gives fluidity to the ad idea.

The "Corporate Radio" tagline reads: "Bands so new and fresh, corporate radio hasn't had a chance to ignore them yet."

The "Arrogant" tagline reads: "Where crass, arrogant, multi-millionaire musicians played when they were only crass and arrogant."

Figure 9-15

PRINT: "SOUL PATCH" AND "FRIENDS MOVE"

AGENCY: MCCLAIN FINLON / DENVER, COLORADO

Creative Directors: Gregg Bergan and Jeff Martin

Art Director: Dan Buchmeier

Copywriter: Eric Liebhauser

Photographer: Jeff Martin

Client: Vespa

The lines humorously explain the emotional benefits of buying a Vespa, while the cropped close-ups illuminate the beauty of the product design.

Figure 9-16

POSTER:
"DANCING ON HER KNEES"

DESIGN FIRM:
PENTAGRAM / NEW YORK

Partner: Paula Scher

Client: Public Theater

Not only does the background become an active participant due to the color and division of space, but one element directs our eyes to the next.

repetition and variation. *Repetition* occurs when you repeat one or a few graphic elements a number times or with great or total consistency. *Variation* is established by a break or modification in the pattern or by changing elements, such as the color, size, shape, spacing, position, and visual weight. Some variation is absolutely necessary to create visual interest; too much variation might destroy rhythm.

Rhythm, in part, is about a sense of movement from one element to another. Major vertical, horizontal, and diagonal movements help structure the composition and thus guide the viewer. Elements should be arranged so that the audience is led from one element to another through the design. *Flow* is also called *movement* and is connected to the principle of rhythm. Position graphic elements to promote flow from one to the other.

Harmony, Proportions, and Scale

Harmony is a congruent arrangement of parts. Combining parts to form a harmonious composition begins with consideration of how each graphic element relates to the others. Parts must be in accord.

Proportion is the comparative size relationships of parts to one another and to the whole. Elements or parts are compared to the whole in terms of magnitude, measure, and/or quantity. *Scale* is the size of an element or form *seen in relation* to other elements or forms within the format. Scale is based on proportional relationships between and among forms. In general, we best understand the size of visual elements in relation to other visual elements.

Figure/Ground Shape Relationships

Figure/ground, also called positive and negative space, is a basic principle of visual perception and refers to the relationship of shapes, of figure to ground, on a two-dimensional surface. To best understand what is being depicted, the mind seeks to separate graphic elements that it perceives as the figures from the ground (or background) elements. In figure/ground relationships, the observer seeks visual cues to distinguish the shapes representing the figures from those that are the ground. The figure or positive shape is a definite shape; it is immediately discernible as a shape. The shapes or areas created between and among figures are known as the ground or negative shapes. Viewers tend to be drawn to the figure as opposed to the ground, they hunt for the figure to make sense of the visual. Negative spaces also create passageways, promoting movement, unity, harmonious shapes, and rhythm—and they direct our eyes (figure 9-15).

DIRECTING THE VIEWER THROUGH A COMPOSITION

The viewer seeks a point of entry into a composition. The entry can be the focal point, the key component established through visual hierarchy, or a dominant image (people tend to prefer visuals over copy). An obvious focal point will provide a point of entry; for example, a dominant image or dominant headline provides a point of entry (figure 9-16). Eye tracking studies have proven that people do indeed respond to compositional structures; their eyes move, scan, and rest on a page, screen, or a Web site, due in part to the composition. Your composition facilitates the viewer's reading of it—think of your composition as if it is an architectural space the viewer has to walk through.

Arrangement: The arrangement is the structure of the composition in terms of position of elements: *where* you place the graphic elements and negative spaces and *how* you facilitate the viewer's reading of the composition through entry point, flow, and eye direction. Visual flow should not be interrupted; there should be no "road barriers." Any movement or graphic element that pulls the viewer's eyes from the preferred path or from important information is counterproductive.

Movement: A static page or screen can give the illusion of movement through skillful manipulation. Any design can appear still, imply motion, or even incorporate intervals of stillness and movement. Action-oriented relationships—diagonal counterpoints, acute shifts in scale, extreme value contrasts, and more—can create the illusion of movement.

In time-based media, such as motion graphics, commercials, and animation, motion occurs from frame to frame, over time. (See chapter 12.)

Alignment: In a composition, every graphic element—type or image or graphic ornament—is positioned in graphic space. You determine those positions and their resulting alignment with other visual components either through purely optical means (by eye) or with the aid of a grid or some other structuring device (which still requires optical judgments).

Congruity of alignment enhances unity and creates clarity. Designers who compose optically or spontaneously seek inherent ways to align type and visuals by finding movement within the graphic elements that can be paralleled or echoed. They also look for sympathetic relationships among the forms, places where alignments could occur and be capitalized on. Other than the several basic alignments—flush left, flush right, centered, justified—there are wraparound or edge alignments. In figure 9-7, a print campaign for Greyhound, the type and image are architectural and emblematic, working together, aligned on a center axis, hugging the midline of the page, yet relating to the edges of the format.

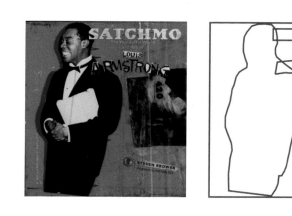
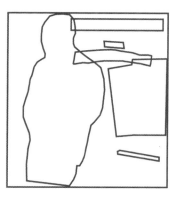

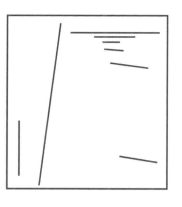

Transitions: A transition is the passage or progression connecting one graphic element or movement to another in a design, a spatial interval; often, the transition is negative space or a subordinate element (figure 9-17).

Consider each and every interval and every transition from shape to shape, letter to letter, form to form, visual component to type component. If you focus on the interstices—those spaces between shapes, forms, and type—then the entire composition will appear organically interconnected and taut. Imagine choreography composed of individual dance moves with awkward or unconsidered

› Figure 9-17

BOOK COVER: SATCHMO: THE WONDERFUL WORLD AND ART OF LOUIS ARMSTRONG

Art Director: Michelle Ishay

Design: Steven Brower

Diagrams: Steven Brower

Art: Louis Armstrong

Client: Harry N. Abrams

Each transition in this composition helps you navigate through the design. The spaces between the forms help connect the forms to one another.

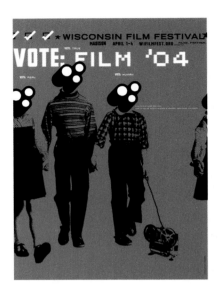

Figure 9-18

CAMPAIGN: WISCONSIN FILM FESTIVAL

COMMUNICATION COMPANY: PLANET PROPAGANDA / MADISON, WISCONSIN

Creative Director: Dana Lytle

Designer: David Taylor

Copywriter: James Breen

Interactive Director: Ben Hirby

Developers: David Huyck and Brian Wilson

Client: Wisconsin Film Festival

© Planet Propaganda

transitions, and you will understand the importance of efficient transitions to smooth visual moves (figure 9-18).

Point of View

A designer must consider *point of view*—the viewer's position in relation to what he or she is looking at and from which angle. When elements or visuals are very large in relation to the size of the format, they appear to be physically closer to the viewer. Cropping also brings the viewer closer to the visual, so close that sometimes the viewer cannot see the entire image. When elements are small in scale in relation to the size of the format, they seem to be further away from the viewer. These two compositional approaches relate to human perception and how we perceive objects in an environment. Also, within a composition, you can contrast cropped images or big visuals with small ones to create a sense of depth. In "Legends Don't Die in Bed" (figure 9-19), we are looking at the man from slightly above him, which increases the illusion of depth from his hand holding the hammer down to the floor where we read "bed." In the other ad in this campaign, "Sex," the place where the wall meets the floor at a corner creates the illusion of spatial depth in this composition.

A subject can be seen and visualized from the following orientations:

> *near (near and far are important for touch screen and gestural interfaces)*

> *far*

> *above*

> *below*

> *at eye level*

> *from the side (three-quarter view)*

> *profile*

Figure 9-19

PRINT:
"LEGENDS" AND "SEX"

AGENCY: HEIMAT / BERLIN, GERMANY

Client: Hornbach

Illusion of Spatial Depth

When you design on a two-dimensional surface, you begin with a blank, flat surface called the picture plane, the front plane of a page or screen. As soon as you make one mark, you begin to play with the picture plane and possibly create the illusion of spatial depth. The illusion of spatial depth means the appearance of three-dimensional space, where some things appear closer to the viewer and some things appear farther

Figure 9-20

PRINT:
"SALMON" AND "APPLE"

AGENCY: D'ADDA,
LORENZINI, VIGORELLI,
BBDO / MILAN AND ROME

Creative Director:
Stefano Campora

Art Director: Sara Portello

Copywriter: Andrea Rosagni

Photographer: Carlo Facchini

Client: PLASMON

© May 2000

distance or behind the most important part. Most observers look at foreground elements first. Understanding this is critical to both static and motion graphics.

In print, in a regular composition, those major planes are fixed. In a disjunctive composition, those planes may seem to shift. However, on-screen, in mobile and Web applications, the position of graphic elements is dynamic, where the user can change the position of elements in the graphic space by zooming, by pulling elements forward or pushing them back. The middle ground seems to remain constant, while elements can move forward or back.

The illusion of spatial depth can be achieved through a variety of means:

> Progressive change: *A gradual or progressive change from one color to another or a progressive arrangement of an element according to size or characteristic can contribute to the illusion of depth or motion.*

> Overlapping: *When an opaque flat plane or form is placed in front of another, that overlap creates the illusion of depth (figure 9-22). Successive overlaps create the illusion of a recessive space, which can be manipulated to appear shallow or deep. When a transparent flat plane is placed in front of another, an ambiguous space is created, which could appear shallow.*

> *Overlapping can be used for various stylistic and visualization goals; for example, overlapping functions well in collage, where elements are cut and pasted over others. Collage is a technique invented and first utilized by the Cubists, particularly Pablo Picasso and Georges Braque. (You can use the cut-and-paste function in software to simulate collage.)*

> *To denote associations, overlaps function to display a familial relationship among related information or visuals. Overlapping can aid emphasis when used with nest and*

away—just as in actual space (figures 9-20 and 9-21). The illusion of spatial depth can be shallow or deep, recessive or projected.

In two-dimensional design, we describe the illusion of spatial depth in terms of three major planes: the foreground, which is the part of a composition that appears nearest the viewer; the middle ground, an intermediate position between the foreground and the background; and the background, which is the part of a composition that appears in the

stair structures, among others. It can also create fractured space, as in the Cubist style, where multiple viewpoints are seen simultaneously.

> Layering: By overlapping parts of an image simultaneously or in a sequence, the illusion of shallow space is created.

Layers can be opaque or transparent, aligned or purposely misaligned, typographic layers in any design application, layers of information on maps or layers of data on charts, layers of images in motion graphics, subtitles on film and in motion graphics. Layers can imitate actual textures found in

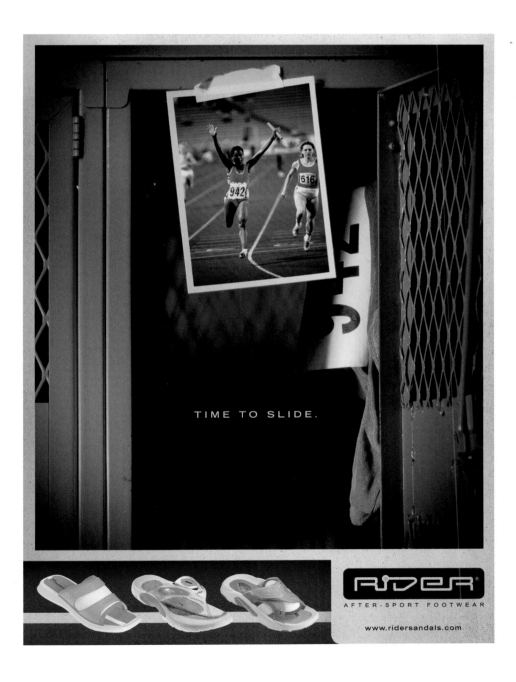

TIME TO SLIDE.

Figure 9-21

PRINT: "RUNNER"

AGENCY:
PUSH ADVERTISING /
ORLANDO, FLORIDA

Creative Director:
John Ludwig

Copywriter: Gordon Weller

Art Director: Ron Boucher

Photographer: Doug Scaletta

Client: Rider Sandals

The three-dimensional illusion of the photograph hanging from the locker heightens the visual impact.

Figure 9-22

*MICROSITE AND ONLINE MEDIA
CAMPAIGN: CONVERSE ONE STAR*

AGENCY: SCHEMATIC

Creative Lead and Senior Creative
Director: Jen Koziol

Senior Vice President Client Services:
Bill Melton

Client: Converse One Star

© Schematic, Inc.

The Situation: *When fashion-con-
scious retail giant Target decided to
partner with one of the most iconic
American pop culture brands,
Converse, they turned to their lead
digital agency Schematic to help build
awareness, create excitement and
drive sales in store and online among
multiple customer segments—most
importantly, the hip and "wired" teens
and twenty-plus demographic.*

  Our Contribution: *Working closely
with Converse, Target's marketing
department and Target's off-line
agencies, Schematic helped craft one
of the most visually consistent and
integrated campaigns Target has ever
launched. The Target.com experience
was supported by a variety of online
media campaigns offering different
collections throughout the year. Many
of the rich media units had integrated
video and allowed users to interact
with the various product lines in the
unit. The goal of the online experience was to drive interaction and
encourage users to adopt a desirable
"identity" that can be achieved only
through Converse shoes and clothing.*

  The Impact: *The Converse One
Star collection, featuring sportswear
and accessories for men and women
and footwear for the whole family,
launched exclusively at Target stores
nationwide and on Target.com in
February 2008. Not only was the microsite well received, but it garnered
a lot of attention for our sponsors.
Pandora, for example, a free online
streaming music service, was "thrilled'
with performance to date for the
entire campaign—in fact, one video
had a phenomenal 55 percent click-
through rate.*
  —Schematic

Figure 9-23

POSTER:
"THE PRINTED WOMAN"

DESIGN STUDIO:
LUBA LUKOVA STUDIO/
NEW YORK

Designer and Illustrator:
Luba Lukova

Client: La MaMa e.t.c.

© Luba Lukova

Often, Luba Lukova uses her own hand-drawn lettering to ensure that the type and visual act in concert to communicate expressively.

environments (think peeling layers of outdoor boards or layers of scrapbook elements on pages). Layering conveys movement, thought, and the passage of time.

> Diagonals and tilted planes: *A shallow or deep illusion of depth is created by planes comprised of diagonals or by elements that oppose the edges of the format. A recessional space created by a titled plane moving back in perspective can create a heightened illusion of three-dimensional space.*

> Atmospheric perspective: *This illusion simulates the effect the atmosphere has on color, shape, form, texture, and* detail when seen from a distance; it is also called aerial perspective.

The Illusion of Movement

A static composition represents a fixed position; it neither moves nor implies motion. The illusion of movement can be created through a variety of means—for example, by focusing on action-oriented arrangements, that is, receding diagonals; using a figurative image that relates to our sense of kinesis; capturing an archetypal movement (think Myron's *Discus Thrower*); and using angle or point of view, visual multiplication, "before and after" images implying duration, large shifts in

Figure 9-24

PRINT:
"KOSKIE" AND "GUZMAN"

AGENCY: HUNT ADKINS /
MINNEAPOLIS

Creative Director and
Copywriter: Doug Adkins

Associate Creative Director
and Art Director:
Steve Mitchell

Client: Minnesota Twins

scale, extreme value contrasts, and more. In figure 9-23, Luba Lukova creates the illusion of movement as the "Printed Woman" rolls, and in figure 9-24 the illusion of movement is created by the angle of the ball player's gestures in relation to the horizontal headlines.

A visual sequence is a number of things, elements, or events in an order that might imply time, interval, or motion over a period of time (duration). A sequence can be established on a single surface, sequential pages, or in motion graphics. For example, a storyboard or comic graphic format can visualize a sequence. Or when a reader turns a page, that kinetic experience can be utilized to represent a sequence of events over a short period of time. Certainly, motion graphics and film are natural media for depicting sequence.

Arrangements can seem ordered or random. Sequential arrangements have a discernible

and specific order, or they can form a particular sequence. Also, one element or frame can seem to be the consequence or the result of the previous element. The quality of randomness in composition stems from an intentional organization where elements belong, yet no discernable pattern, uniformity, or regularity is readily apparent.

Sequential elements can also denote the illusion of motion through visual multiplication. Multiple positions (think a comic book rendering of a dog with many legs to denote running), blurred boundaries or edges, repetition, shift, and layers contribute to the illusion of motion.

MULTIPLE PAGES AND MODULARITY

In graphic design, modularity is a structural principle employed to manage content using modules. A *module* is a self-contained, fixed unit that is combined with others to form a larger foundational structure comprised of regular units. Modularity helps manage content as well as complexity (think of all the content on a governmental Web site). Modularity has three main advantages: (1) the underlying structure produces unity and continuity across a multipage application, (2) the content within each module can easily be replaced or interchanged, and (3) modules can be rearranged to create different forms yet still remain unified.

A module is also defined as any single fixed element within a bigger system or structure. For example, a unit on graph paper is a module, a pixel in a digital image is a module, a rectangular unit in a grid system is a module, and a fixed encapsulated chunk of a composition is a module.

Modularity is used to create modular alphabets, hand-lettering, typographic treatments, signage systems, symbol systems, pixel effects, or any modular-based imagery (for example, a transformation or sequence developed in modular units or figures composed of units).

Chunking

A technique related to modularity in graphic design, where content is split or information is grouped into chunks, is called *chunking*

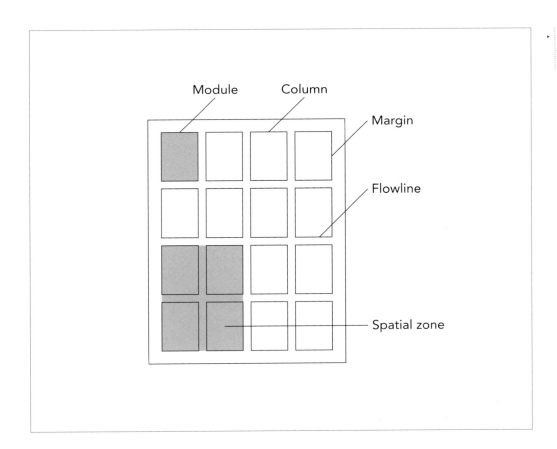

Module   Column

Margin

Flowline

Spatial zone

Diagram 9-3

Grid anatomy

▸ **Diagram 9-4**

Margins

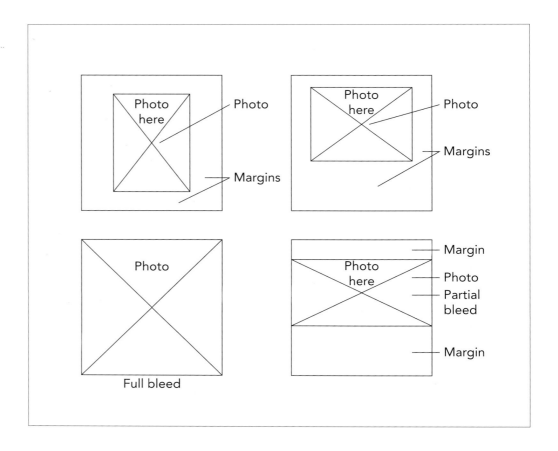

or *encapsulating*. You do this by combining units or capsules of content or information into a limited number of units or chunks. The aim of chunking is to make information easily understood: it affords the viewer digestible amounts of content at a time. Chunking is utilized to facilitate memory and in other disciplines, such as musical composition.

THE GRID

All the elements, display and text type, and visuals (illustrations, graphics, and photographs) in applications with multiple pages, such as a Web site or magazine, are almost always organized on a grid. A grid is a guide—a modular, compositional structure made up of verticals and horizontals that divide a format into columns and margins (see diagram 9-3).

Grids organize type and visuals. If you have to organize the enormous amount of content in any given corporate, museum, social cause, or editorial Web site, you would want some type of structure to ensure that readers would be able to easily access and read an abundance of information. A grid affords a skeletal structure that can provide continuity, congruence, unity, and visual flow across many print or digital pages.

A grid is about maintaining order. If you think of the pool lanes in a swim meet and how they efficiently keep the swimmers where they are supposed to be, then one reason for using a grid structure becomes clear. A grid defines boundaries and keeps content in order.

Figure 9-25

TV: "INSPIRATION"

AGENCY: BUTLER, SHINE,
STERN & PARTNERS /
SAUSALITO, CALIFORNIA

Client: The San Francisco
Jazz Festival

© The San Francisco Jazz Festival & BSSP

In this witty TV spot, a close-up of a hand finger snapping provides a visual and sound transition from each person attempting to play jazz to the next. The color not only provides a look and feel but also acts to unify the spot.

Designer's Checklist

> Be mindful of how all graphic components relate to the midline of the format.

> Relate all graphic components to the format's edges.

> Consider all negative space.

> Consider all transitions among graphic components.

Basic Compositional Checklist

> Have you established a clear visual hierarchy?

> Have you used alignment to foster unity?

> Have you arranged the composition to guide the viewer through the space?

> Have you chosen a compositional approach that best enables communication?

> Have you employed action to create visual interest or dynamics through contrast?

> Have you created visual interest?

> Is your arrangement firm or seem tentative?

> Have you paid attention to the interstices?

> Does your visualization of the concept enhance communication and meaning?

A designer can strictly adhere to a grid or break a grid. For the sake of visual drama or surprise, you can occasionally break the grid. If you break the grid too often, however, the armature it provides will be lost. Often, large Web sites have several grid options that work together.

Margins

Defining boundaries starts with margins—the blank space on the left, right, top, or bottom edge of any printed or digital page (diagram 9-4). Basically, in grids as well as on any single surface, margins function as frames around visual and typographic content, concurrently defining active or live areas of the page as well as its boundaries. When planning margins for a bound book, magazine, or annual report, allow for the space needed for binding in the gutter margin, the blank space formed by the inner margins of two facing pages of a book.

VISUAL BASICS FOR SCREEN-BASED MEDIA MOTION

An individual frame is an individual picture, a single static image. The illusion of motion is created when we see a series of frames in rapid succession. All that applies to print also applies to creating visual communications that move over a period of time. Each frame must be considered, as well as how each frame flows into the next frame and the overall impact of the frames as a group. Equally, each Web page must be considered, as well as how each page flows into the next page and the overall impact of the entire Web site. When considering the overall screen-based piece, the following are critical to create impact.

> Visual hierarchy *builds clear levels of information in motion from frame to frame to help guide the viewer, enhancing communication and comprehension.*

> Contrast, *an effect created by arranging very different graphic elements, generates visual variety and makes distinctions among visual elements and helps set up the hierarchy of information in the screen-based application. It also creates impact by the use of differences.*

> Repetition *establishes an underlying structure that holds a piece together over time. Just as in music, we count on repetition to form continuity. With motion graphics, percussive sounds or musical beats can be combined with visual repetition or rhythmic animation to enhance the effect.*

> Alignment *set up throughout motion graphics creates a pattern the viewer can recall, to anchor the piece in his or her mind, creating a sense of order.*

> Conceptual interplay *between type and visuals communicates meaning, both literally and symbolically.*

> Positive and negative shape relationships *will have enormous effect on establishing flow from one frame to another.*

> Varying *scale or size relationships will add depth, a sense of front to back, or even the effect of coming to the front of the screen.*

Creative Prompts

Here are some creative prompts that will help you to start composing by experimenting:

> Formally driven creative directives: *contrast; illusion of three-dimensional space, movement, or sound; exaggerated scale; exaggeration; near and far; image manipulation; synthesis; visual merge; unexpected juxtapositions; abstraction; among others.*

> Media-driven creative directives: *collage; photograms; photomontage; experimental materials; mixed media; painting; sculpture; three-dimensional illustrations; photography; sewing or stitching; weavings; rubbings or blottings; monotypes; printmaking; among many others.*

> Style-driven creative directives: *primitivism; techno; homemade; flat color; period or retro, and historical references or homage; among many others.*

PART 03

DESIGNING ACROSS MEDIA

10

CAMPAIGNS AND STORYTELLING

WHAT IS A CAMPAIGN, AND WHAT MAKES IT EFFECTIVE?

An *advertising campaign* is a series of coordinated ads, based on an overarching strategy and closely related ideas and connected by look and feel, voice, tone, style, imagery, and tagline, where each individual ad in the campaign also can stand on its own. An *integrated media ad campaign* works across channels, which might include print, broadcast, interactive, mobile, video-sharing, other screen-based media, out-of-home media, and unconventional media. Walter Gropius, as leader of the Bauhaus, provided

its slogan: "Art and Technology: A New Unity." As a spur to a program, this couldn't be more relevant today, when each idea in a campaign must be strategically formulated to work for each and every specific medium.

As Daniel Stein, CEO and founder of Evolution Bureau, says: "Integration is never an afterthought. Forcing together disparate parts and shoehorning creative doesn't make a campaign 'integrated.' Instead, strive for ideas that are integrated at the core and work gracefully together between platforms."

For MINI USA, Butler, Shine, Stern & Partners created the MINI Covert campaign, an integrated campaign that is based on insights into the audience, brand, and media that carries the messages (see p. 190).

At times, an integrated campaign (see figure 10-1) entails designing the brand identity through applications for various media, such as print, a primary Web site, and corporate

A HIGHER FORM OF FUNCTION   BRETFORD

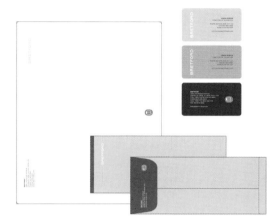

Figure 10-1

INTEGRATED CAMPAIGN: BRETFORD

AGENCY:
PLANET PROPAGANDA /
MADISON, WISCONSIN

Creative Director: Dana Lytle

Designer: Geoff Halber

Copywriter: Rodney Oman

Interactive Director: Ben Hirby

Developer:
David Huyck, Brian Wilson

Client: Bretford

© Planet Propaganda

Focusing on the aesthetic and functional benefits of the Bretford products, this campaign is unified with a consistent look and feel that is completely appropriate for the brand.

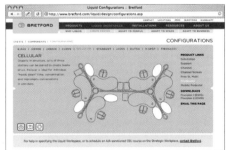

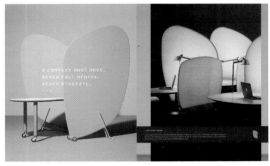

CASE STUDY

CAMPAIGN: MINI COVERT

AGENCY: BUTLER, SHINE, STERN & PARTNERS / SAUSALITO, CALIFORNIA

Client: MINI USA

© MINI USA & BSSP

MINI Covert

Our Story

From the start, we felt that the greatest untapped strengths of MINI were the passion and devotion of its owners. So we decided to do something a little different. We decided to advertise to the people who had already purchased a MINI. Sound strange? Here's why it worked. Since its U.S. launch in 2002, MINI has exceeded sales goals, but by 2006 it had gone from having no direct competitors to having over a dozen. This development made the early adopting owners of the vehicle more important than ever. MINI owners are passionate. They're

borderline evangelical. In that way, they're more effective than any print ad could be at converting others who haven't quite bought in. With that in mind, we created a super-secret, integrated campaign with messages only MINI owners could see. We called it the MINI Covert campaign.

Book

First, we sent a book to 150,000 MINI owners called "A Dizzying Look at the Awesomeness of Small." This book included an introduction with a secret compartment that housed the Covert Kit. This kit included instructions and three decoder tools that would help owners decipher the rest of the campaign. The blogosphere responded with that much-desired thing people refer to as "buzz," not only on dozens of independent blogs but also on many automotive sites and general mass sites such as Flickr and YouTube.

Decoder

After the book was sent, three print ads in targeted publications let MINI owners know how to use their tools to decipher the secret messages. And, for the uninitiated, we even had an "overt" message in the ads. For example, "Non MINI Owners: Get your complimentary decoder with the purchase of any MINI." In the first print execution, owners were asked to use their decoder. The message led them to a super-secret Web site, and the adventure was on.

Decryptor

This ad used the sophisticated spy language known as Pig Latin to throw the curious off the scent. Again, owners were directed to a site and nonowners grew more intrigued. (One message read: "BINGO: You're a natural at this spy stuff. Now check out AsWeC-FiT. org to continue your. Journey. This message will self destruct in five seconds.")

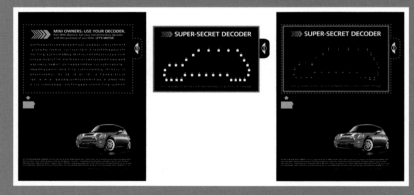

Glasses

What is a good espionage operation without some cool spy glasses? OK, maybe ours weren't really that cool, but the results were.

Citizens for Fair Insect Treatment (c-Fit)

The mysterious print ads led curious readers to corresponding Web sites. The sites required a little more investigation in case "outsiders" happened to find them. The first was dedicated to the protection of insects. It included short videos promoting that cause. (One featured an attack by an enormous killer bee that bore a strange resemblance to one of our office canines.) But more importantly, it led MINI owners to an invitation to participate in a cross-country road rally called MINI Takes the States.

MINI Takes the States

Not only did tens of thousands of people find the reward from the c-Fit site (www.aswecfit.org), but thousands followed through and participated in the cross-country driving extravaganza that stretched from Monterey, California, to beautiful Jersey City, New Jersey. Three-thousand MINIs cruising down the highway is not a bad way to spread the love.

Spy Gear

Every good sleuth needs good spy equipment. So on this site, we presented cover for the next reward with some gag spy stuff. Of course, there were more videos, including the musical stylings of a paleontologist turned singer. But again, the true payoff was another reward for MINI owners.

Adventure Toggle Switches

This reward let MINI owners further customize their vehicles by adding a little intrigue to their control panels. What car couldn't use an ejector switch or cloaking device?

Awesomeness of Small

The final site was a look at the benefits of being small. It featured another informative video showing the adventures of a butterfly with a bad attitude and a black belt. It also featured the final reward.

Medallion

For completing the final leg of the Covert print campaign, MINI owners could order proof of their participation and incredible investigative abilities. This reward came in the form of a medallion to be hung from the rearview mirror or to be worn around the neck while wearing a tuxedo at Monte Carlo casinos.

Motorby

In addition to creating a new way to talk to MINI owners, we created an entirely new way to directly communicate with drivers on the road. Using RFID (radio frequency identification) technology embedded into a key fob, outdoor boards literally talked to MINI owners on the road.

Results

We preached to the choir. And the choir sang. Loudly.

—Butler, Shine, Stern & Partners

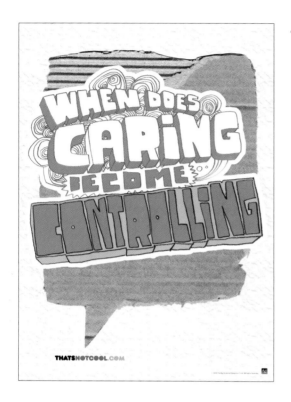

Figure 10-3

PSA CAMPAIGN: "THAT'S NOT COOL"

SPONSOR ORGANIZATION: THE FAMILY VIOLENCE PREVENTION FUND
AND THE OFFICE ON VIOLENCE AGAINST WOMEN

Campaign Web Site: www.thatsnotcool.com

Volunteer Agency: R/GA / New York

Courtesy of The Ad Council

The Ad Council asked us to help them spread awareness of teen-dating violence. But when we talked to teens, we realized there was a related problem that no one knew was happening: digital abuse. Almost every teen has experienced it, from incessant, harassing texts, to pressure for nude pics to the loss of privacy resulting from hacked personal accounts. We created the 'That's Not Cool' digital platform to help teens get informed, cope with digital harassment, and draw their own digital line separating acceptable from inappropriate.
—R/GA (http://www.rga.com/work/thats-not-cool)

Figure 10-4

PRINT: "FAN" AND "PIZZA"

AGENCY: COLLE + MCVOY /
MINNEAPOLIS

Creative Director: John Jarvis

Art Director: Liz Otremba

Copywriters: Eric Husband
and Dave Keepper

Photographer: Curtis Johnson

Client:
League of Women Voters

This campaign seeks to compel young and first-time voters with the argument that an election is yet another opportunity to express their opinion—something every young person is prone to do, a point made here through images evoking the love of a team and the enjoyment of a pizza. This campaign got young voters out in record numbers in Minnesota.

interpersonal dynamics, and other of life's everyday dramas can yield ideas. Basing ideas on personal life experience or observing others can help make your ad ideas relevant to others' lives (figures 10-3 and 10-4). People should react: "Yep, that's how it is!" When we can relate to the story, we feel a kinship with the brand or group being advertised.

A story has to address the brand and make it the "hero" or even the "action hero" of the story. Good brand stories have a conflict, as exemplified by these classic campaigns:

> *Person against himself/herself ("Just Do It")*

> *Person against environment ("Don't leave home without it.")*

> *Person against person ("I Want My MTV!")*

To generate an appropriate conflict for your brand story think about change and choices:

Change

> *What kind of change do people want*

> *How things change*

> *Why things change*

> *How you can affect change yourself*

Choices

> *How people make choices*

> *What are the consequences of those choices*

> *How the brand or group can change those choices or consequences*

Finally, my favorite creative thinking or story-generating prompt is:

"What if...?"

If you examine the premises of some extremely creative films and books, you will notice "What if...?" thinking: for example, in Woody Allen's *Purple Rose of Cairo* (1985), a movie character walks off the screen and into the real world; in Cornelia Funke's *Inkheart* (New York: Scholastic, 2003), a girl discovers her father has the talent to bring characters out of

Ad Campaign Checklist

An advertising campaign is a series of coordinated ad units, based on an overarching strategy and highly related ideas, connected by look and feel, voice, tone, style, imagery, and tagline, where each individual ad in the campaign also can stand on its own. That means:

> **Ideas:** *Each ad unit is based on an idea. Each ad unit has a main visual plus verbal components that work cooperatively.*

> **Brand Identity:** *Any campaign must work with the visual and verbal brand identity.*

> **Media:** *What can this story do in each specific medium? What can it do for its audience?*

> **Unity and Variety of Messages:** *A campaign needs to have an overarching story or theme. Each ad unit has the same tagline.*

> **Unity and Variety of Design:** *Imagery and typeface choices should contribute to the audience's understanding, recognition, and memory of the campaign. Too much variety in images, color palette, and type may result in a loss of coherence across the campaign. Each ad unit looks like it belongs to the other; they all have a family resemblance.*

> **Style:** *A visual look and feel based on consistency in imagery and type, the particular characteristics that contribute to the overall appearance. Typeface choices, color palette, textures, patterns, compositional modes, kinds of images (illustration, photographs, etc.), graphic elements, and nature of the imagery all contribute to a look and feel.*

> **Brand Experience:** *Each ad unit creates a brand experience, such as marketing as service or utility, entertainment, enlightenment, or any other engaging experience.*

their books; or in J. K. Rowling's *Harry Potter and the Sorcerer's Stone* (New York: A.A. Levine Books, 1998), where an orphaned boy discovers he is a wizard.

HOW TO USE: WHAT IF...?

To get ideas flowing use "What if...?" scenarios. Feel free to pose the most absurd possibilities or inspired question related to your product, service, or group:

> *What if you could invent a new way to communicate with another person?*

SHOWCASE

THE POWER OF STORY
ALAN ROBBINS
www.alanrobbins.com

Alan Robbins is the Janet Estabrook Rogers Professor of Visual and Performing Arts (2006–2010) at Kean University in New Jersey. He is also the founding director of the Design Center, which produces exhibitions, publications, and products in various fields of design and which has won numerous design awards.

Robbins is also an award-winning writer and the author of twenty books in the areas of mystery, science fiction, puzzles, and humor. His cartoons, illustrations, graphics, and games have appeared in dozens of publications and exhibitions. His unique series of mystery jigsaw puzzles has millions of fans around the world and his featured YouTube channel has over 3.5 million hits.

His work can be seen at www.alanrobbins.com.

"The World Is Made of Stories, not Atoms."

We live in stories.

I am not referring to a method of communication here or even to a marketing technique. I mean something much deeper and more fundamental than all that. I mean that stories are a form of consciousness, a way we think, a means by which live in a complex world.

There is a theory of mind that suggests that we experience the world in disparate moments—quantum bursts of awareness—and only weave them into coherence in the storytelling part of the brain, in the same way you might have a series of unrelated dream images and only tie them together by telling someone about your dream. Narrating it, in other words, turning it into a story.

The simple words "and then . . ." become a kind of glue that pulls it all together.

I like this idea of the centrality of stories to consciousness. I once wrote a sci-fi story called "The Edge of Time" in which people stop the end of the universe by reading fiction to each other, so bound up are stories with the very fabric of our existence.

But even if this idea is too radical for your own way of thinking, it is easy to see that we also live in stories in another sense . . . we love them. We have carved, scratched, painted, printed, and inked our stories onto wood, hide, skin, paper, bamboo, ivory, clay, stone, silk, canvas, film, and now onto evanescent digital bits. We watch and read and remember and are influenced by stories for our whole lives—and we tell them all the time. The growing science of *narrative medicine* suggests that the stories we keep about ourselves can affect our own healing. And,

in any case, what is most of our common communication if not an elaborate trading of stories? We are *Homo fabula,* the storytelling creature, and anyone involved in creating visual communications should have this in mind as a powerful tool.

In even the most basic way, every picture tells a story.

The simplest mark—like the handprints found on the walls of the Ice Age caves—says, "I was here." A person, a place, an action. Story 101. Jump thousands of years and you get to the TV show *Lost,* which presents dozens of characters whose entire lives are revealed through interweaving parallel narratives looping backward and forward in time. Story to the nth degree. Yet our ability to recognize, absorb, and react to both those simple marks and that complexity of storylines shows just how comfortable we are with story as a basic cognitive ability.

In fact, we recall stories better than facts. Think of any teacher you had who made the material vivid through great anecdotes rather than a clear recitation of details. Think about telling your friends something interesting you heard that, no doubt, was not a list of specifics (not if you want to keep your friends) but a story. A funny joke, a good single-panel cartoon, and a memorable anecdote all share this power. The best of the one-minute TV spots is a classic of the form.

A true study of the power of storytelling involves a lot of things from genre and style to mode and method, controlling idea and theme to plot and antiplot, character, climax, setting, and much more. Yet all stories also have one fundamental thing in common that is a bit easier to keep in mind as we work on our visual communications. Every good story has a simple narrative structure . . . a beginning, middle, and end.

To create a wildly popular three-minute video for YouTube—nothing more than a simple visual gag—I immediately divided it into those three basic narrative segments: beginning, middle, end. Act I was the introduction: the character and basic props were presented. Act II was the action: a series of events took place but were left unresolved, and it was not clear what would happen next. Act III was the resolution: character and action came together to create the final upshot. In other words, the video was not so much a gag as a short story or tale that lured the viewer along by creating a series of mysteries from start to finish. Who? What? Why?

As any fiction writer knows, this structure—with its unresolved segments—creates a suspense that compels the reader to keep reading or the watcher to keep watching. For visual communicators, it is crucial that we keep this ability—this need, this fascination—in mind. We use words and images and graphic elements to communicate concepts, of course, but what ties these components together most powerfully is a unifying story.

So we should work with that story in mind. Any consistent attempt to package products for marketing should have a storyline behind it. And every iteration of advertising for it should expand on that storyline. What is the tale we are telling? What is the storyline that we want our audience to know and remember? How does it start, what happens next, how does it conclude? How do we reveal some information but hold back other things to create suspense?

This is especially critical as the forms and forums of new media continue to expand. In an era of transmedia entertainment, every brand plays itself out across the maximum number of media platforms: television, comics, the Web, games, and products, as well as participatory medialike blogs, fanzines, Wikis, videos, and more.

Yet behind all those approaches, all that marketing information and user feedback, all the moving images and the tidal wave of words, someone has to keep in mind the narrative engine, that consistent tale to tell and retell. The facts, the details, the benefits of any product get lost, but the story stays, even more powerfully if the viewer or listener becomes part of that story. Thus a branding strategy may become a form of complex interactive storytelling experience. Designers need to understand the story and how it works because it will, inevitably, influence all other decisions. In fact, mastering storytelling is as important to designers in the new world of wraparound media as typeface, composition, and color.

How do you do it?

Same way you get to Carnegie Hall: practice, practice, practice.

Here's a good exercise for visual communicators: the Web abounds with spoken jokes, comedy routines, comic books, interactive graphic novels, videos, and award-winning TV commercials. Find the best ones and study the stories they tell. Write down the structures. Narrate the tale. See how they work. Steal from the best.

Think of yourself not just as a graphic designer or ad major or picture maker, but as a storyteller—narrator, director, scribe—of everything you make.

PRINT CAMPAIGN: "CORK," "HARDWARE STORE," AND "REALLY GOOD CHEESE"

AGENCY:
MULLEN / WENHAM, MASSACHUSETTS

Chief Creative Officer: Edward Boches

Creative Directors: Jim Garaventi and Greg Bokor

Art Director: Dylan Lee

Copywriter: Monica Taylor

Photographers: Ray Meeks, Stock

Client: Swiss Army Brands

© Mullen / Wenham, Massachusetts

This campaign plays off the brand's reliability, precision quality, and famous red color.

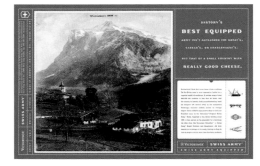

> *What if there were no telephone?*

> *What if all foods tasted the same?*

The follow-up questions usually provide the story's premise:

> *What could your brand do?*

> *What would your brand do?*

General Campaign Considerations

BRAND IDENTITY

Any campaign must work with the visual and verbal brand identity.

Any campaign should relate to the brand's visual identity, its look and feel. That does not mean you have to use the brand colors as the main palette. It also does not mean that you just use the brand logo as the main image. It does mean that the kinds of imagery, the qualities and characteristics of the imagery, typefaces, and color palette should be appropriate for the brand or group. If it works, it is deemed *on brand*. If it does not fit the brand construct, then it is *off brand*. It should fit into the entire branding strategy and not be generic (able to fit any other brand). For example, the history and heritage of the Swiss Army knife are communicated through the brand's color (red) and the concept of always being prepared and properly equipped (figure 10-5). The ads are designed with compartments, to link to the design of the knife's different utility areas. This template also allowed for ease of displaying not one but two logos. The ad idea of being equipped is highly flexible; it highlights brand attributes, relying on what most people know about the Swiss Army knife's heritage. This campaign demonstrates just how specific one can be to a brand's spirit; this is the complete opposite of a generic campaign idea.

The verbal identity is the brand name and the tagline. A simple exercise to help clarify the verbal identity is to complete the following phrases:

> The brand personality is . . .

> The visual appearance is characterized by . . . and communicates this kind of personality . . .

> The campaign personality is . . .

MEDIA

What can this story do in each specific medium? What can it do for its audience? What can you offer: a utility, an entertainment, information, or a worthwhile experience? Each brand-person point of contact is an opportunity to endear the brand to the consumer. Very basically, different media can do different things for people. I use my mobile phone for different purposes than my computer or my iPad or my morning newspaper.

We've moved from the age of interruption to the age of engagement, from a passive consumer to an active consumer who basically doesn't just sit back and wait for things to be delivered but who goes and seeks things out. A whole new mind-set is needed in the way you create and develop work and how you plan your media.
—John Hegarty, Bartle Bogle Hegarty (BBH)

UNITY AND VARIETY OF MESSAGES

A campaign needs to have an overarching story or theme. It must have a unified and varied message.

The larger, overarching story has a duality: each ad should be unified with the other, and yet each offers some variety so that people are curious enough to receive the next message. Different parts of the brand story can be told in different media and in each individual ad; yet all add up to a larger, broader brand story and experience (figure 10-6). Often, there are stories within the larger brand story. For example, each ad unit can tell its own story and still belong and contribute to the larger brand theme.

Designing Campaigns

Throughout the life of a campaign, which can run for a short (months) or long period of time (years), you create and maintain a visual look or framework. We do this so that people will recognize each ad unit within a campaign, feel familiar, and make connections among the various messages. For this reason, some designers and many clients prefer ads, across media, that have an identical or near identical layout, look, and feel.

The *form* of the design should be appropriate for the content, the message, and the story or theme. In other words, how you visualize and compose should be in sync with what you want to say. Form and content together should express the overall campaign theme. For example, if your core idea has a soft, sentimental tone, then the visualization should not be hard-edged or rough in appearance.

Figure 10-6

PRINT, BANNERS, TV, TIMES SQUARE EXTRAVAGANZA: TOSHIBA HD DVD, "SO REAL YOU CAN FEEL IT"

AGENCY: DELLA FEMINA/ ROTHSCHILD/JEARY & PARTNERS / NEW YORK

Creative Director: Michael "Mac" McLaurin

Client: Toshiba

Challenge: *Toshiba HD DVD and Sony Blu-Ray were in the early stages of a "format war," competing for the right to be the high-definition DVD player of choice among consumers.*

Solution: *Capture the feeling of being totally immersed in a movie. Focus on the shared experience of watching movies at home—especially on a Toshiba HD DVD player, when the movie is "so real you can feel it."*

Result: *While being outspent nearly ten-to-one by Sony, Toshiba HD DVD sold out of its entire inventory of early product, secured sellthrough agreements with all targeted retailers, and got the endorsement of virtually every major movie studio not owned or affiliated with Sony.*

Movie Trailer-Like, HighDefinition TV Commercial: *We launched the campaign with a Times Square Extravaganza that included running the TV commercial continuously on the giant TV screens of both the NASDAQ and Reuters buildings.*

—Michael "Mac" McLaurin

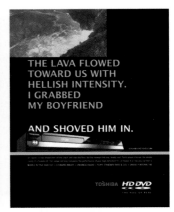

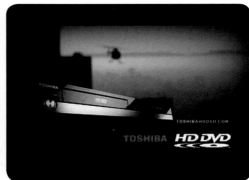

TRIPLETS VERSUS COUSINS

If you study campaigns, you will notice that there often seems to be an underlying compositional structure or template that is utilized for individual ad units in a campaign. ("Template" is used here to mean a master layout designed by you, the art director, or the designer, not a premade template found in a software program.) When a designer chooses to design a master layout, he or she retains a number of graphic elements and positions them similarly from ad unit to ad unit. I call this campaign structure "triplets," because each composition is identical or almost identical to the others; this is the way many campaigns are designed. For each ad unit in a triplet structure, the visual may change, the line may change, but the compositional template stays the same or very close to the same. Other elements that are maintained might include: the color palette, typefaces, method of visualization, style, or work from the same photographer or illustrator.

In Mullen's campaign for L. L. Bean, the template is constant: the photograph, line, and catalog are all positioned in the same place in each individual ad (figure 10-7). The specific visual feel of each ad is different due to the mood and subject of the photographs. Each photograph depicts different types of people—families, individuals, groups—enjoying the outdoors. These images of the outdoors are relaxing; they do not depict extreme conditions or arduous activities.

Forcing us to do a double take, BMP DDB's campaign creatively urges us not to forget to put Lurpak butter on our food (figure 10-8). Each ad in the campaign has a plate of food centered on the page against a blue background with the sign-off at bottom right; a strict (identical) template is used for each ad.

Some designers and art directors reject the notion of "triplets" and create what I call "cousins"—a campaign where, among the ad units, there is a greater degree of variation in the composition, color palette, and visualization, yet the campaign still holds together and manages to maintain a look and feel. Here, variation increases the visual interest of the entire campaign, but it does not hinder unity. Unity with variety is the goal.

What Makes a Good Campaign?

Viewers will notice it.

Each individual ad unit will grab the viewer's attention.

It is distinctive to the brand.

It differentiates the brand or group.

It is consistent with the brand voice.

The idea makes sense for the brand or group.

It endears the brand or group to the public.

It starts a dialogue between the brand and consumers.

Your core idea is elastic—you can create many ads based on the original theme.

It could run forever (almost).

It will surprise people.

It will start a conversation in pop culture.

It strikes a chord in its target audience.

The core idea is flexible enough to work specifically and effectively across media.

Other art directors wish they had thought of it!

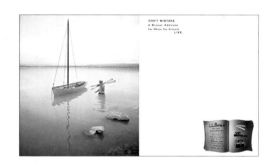

Figure 10-7

PRINT CAMPAIGN: "STREET ADDRESS" AND "RECESS"

AGENCY:
MULLEN / WENHAM,
MASSACHUSETTS

Chief Creative Officer:
Edward Boches

Creative Directors: Jim Garaventi and Greg Bokor

Art Director: Greg Bokor

Copywriter: Jim Garaventi

Photographer: William Huber

Client: L. L. Bean

© Mullen / Wenham, Massachusetts

Mullen wanted to capture the outdoors that most people want to spend time in—a less extreme, more friendly outdoors—to make consumers feel that L. L. Bean is for them.

Figure 10-8

PRINT CAMPAIGN: "PEAS," "CRUMPET," AND "SWEET CORN"

AGENCY: BMP DDB / LONDON

Photographer: David Gill

Agent: Siobhan Squire

Client: Arla Foods—Lurpak

Using yellow sticky notes to look like butter, this campaign "reminds" us to use Lurpak on all types of food.

Figure 10-9

POSTER: "FLAMING LIPS"

Designer and Illustrator: Michael Strassburger

POSTER: "THE HIVES"

Designer and Illustrator: Robert Zwiebel

POSTER: "BLUE SCHOLARS"

Designer and Illustrator: Shogo Ota

Client: Seattle Theatre Group

AGENCY: MODERN DOG DESIGN CO. / SEATTLE

Client: Seattle Theatre Group

© Modern Dog Design Co. 2008

Many clients and creatives believe that repetition is crucial and so tend to prefer "triplets" across media; triplets ensure viewer recognition of the brand message. The logic is that the more times we see each ad unit, the more likely that we will receive and remember the message. Antithetically, other experts think once a viewer has seen one ad unit in a series, they will be bored if the next ad in the campaign looks almost exactly the same, and they will ignore it. One could make a case either way. A moderate viewpoint would be to maintain a unified campaign look and feel to ensure that the ad and brand don't have to reintroduce themselves, while creating enough *variety to engage* the viewer each and every time he or she sees an ad in the series. Edward Boches, chief creative officer at Mullen, offers this advice: "A campaign can be unified in any number of ways. Layout, color, tone of voice, personality. Usually, the smaller the budget or the less familiar the brand, the more disciplined you need to be in making everything come from the same place. For larger clients, say a Nextel, you can take more liberties."

STYLE OF A CAMPAIGN

Style is a visual look and feel based on the particular characteristics that contribute to the overall appearance (figure 10-9). In any media, typefaces, color palette, textures, patterns, compositional modes, kinds of images (illustration, photographs, etc.), the nature of the imagery, and graphic elements all contribute to the look and feel of an advertisement or ad campaign (figure 10-10).

Most art directors prefer consistency in imagery and typeface(s)—for example, if photography is used in one aspect of the campaign, then it is used throughout. Furthermore, if the photography has dramatic light-dark relationships, that is maintained. If flat color illustrations are used in one ad unit, then it is used throughout. The ratio of unity and variety will affect how well the campaign holds together in the audience's mind over each ad unit and how each contributes to recognition.

The style you determine should be appropriate for the brand and for the core ad idea; for the audience, differentiate the campaign from the competition and add freshness. That said, just because a brand has a look and feel

Figure 10-10

PRINT CAMPAIGN: "RAISE THEM ON ROBINSONS"

AGENCY: BARTLE BOGLE HEGARTY / LONDON

Art Director:
Rosie Arnold / Gary McCreadie / Wesley Hawes

Illustrator: Adrian Johnson

Client: Robinsons' Fruit Shoot

should not prevent you from experimenting with various styles, so long as it is on brand. For example, speaking to the serious guitarist, the look and feel of the print ads for Gibson guitars by Carmichael Lynch capture a mood without a commercial tone (figure 10-11).

GRABBING ATTENTION

Figure 10-11

PRINT: "EMOTIONAL BAGGAGE" AND "NO DISTORTION"

AGENCY: CARMICHAEL LYNCH / MINNEAPOLIS

Creative Director: Brian Kroening

Art Director: Randy Hughes

Copywriter: Glen Wachowiak

Photographer: Shawn Michienzi

Client: Gibson Guitar Corp.

© 2000 and 2001 Gibson Guitar Corp.

Mood is created by the photography and the copy, which speaks to the artist within and conveys the benefit of playing a Gibson.

A campaign must have visual impact, whether a visual surprise, graphic interest, visual drama, or a breakthrough appearance. A creative approach in advertising must be appropriate for the product or service, and it must communicate and enhance the client's message—form follows function. For example, the creative visual surprises that constitute Bartle Bogle Hegarty Asia Pacific's campaign for Levi's explain the nature of the product—"The classic men's 501 now re-cut for women" (figure 10-12).

The jeans are a female version of the timeless 501 men's jeans, and the idea is based on the even more timeless connection between a man and a woman.

The poses were constructed in such a way as to form one intertwined being out of two people. The models swapped around until a natural connection was apparent and different poses were experimented with on the shoot day to achieve the best possible combinations.

The campaign was shot in a London studio by the prolific Nadav Kander. A veteran commercial and art photographer, Nadav was selected because the creative team felt that he could best capture the intimate and seamless connection the idea required. He was well up to the task.
—*Bartle Bogle Hegarty Asia Pacific*

Not only do you need to think critically about formulating a core campaign idea, you must think critically and creatively about communicating something specific about the brand or group, not a generic message or pedestrian design. Often, a client will say, "Can you give me something like that campaign that's getting all the buzz?" If that happens, it is your job to help the client understand that the brand needs a distinctive look, not one that has already been done. Here is a little test: Could another brand, product, service,

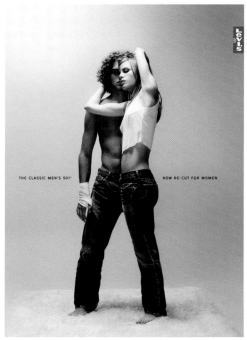

© Levi Strauss/Photo by Nadav Kander

© Levi Strauss/Photo by Nadav Kander

© Levi Strauss/Photo by Nadav Kander

Figure 10-12

CAMPAIGN: "STANDING," "HUGGING," AND "LYING"

AGENCY: BBH (BARTLE BOGLE HEGARTY) ASIA PACIFIC / TOKYO

Creative Director: Steve Elrick

Art Directors: Marthinus Strydom and Alex Lim Thye Aun

Copywriters: Marthinus Strydom and Alex Lim Thye Aun

Photographer: Nadav Kander

Digital Imaging.: Metro Imaging, Anthony Crossfield

Client: Levi Strauss Japan K.K.

This campaign found its way onto almost every printable surface, ranging from magazine ads and billboards to painted buses and free postcards.

A compilation CD features a collaboration of male and female artists.

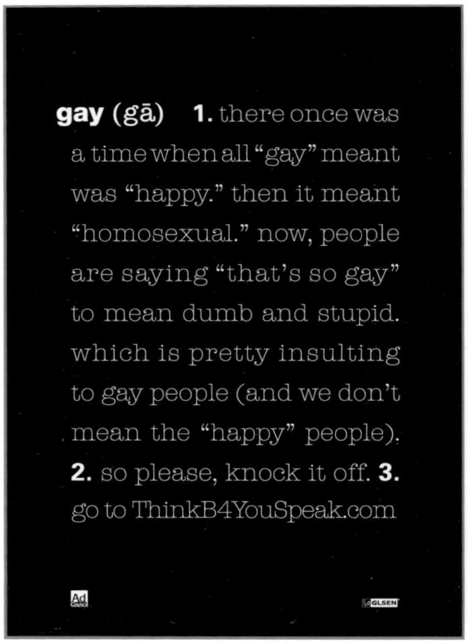

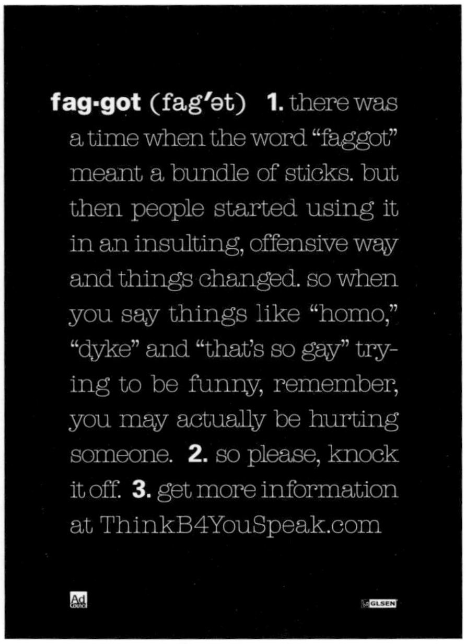

gay (gā) **1.** there once was a time when all "gay" meant was "happy." then it meant "homosexual." now, people are saying "that's so gay" to mean dumb and stupid. which is pretty insulting to gay people (and we don't mean the "happy" people). **2.** so please, knock it off. **3.** go to ThinkB4YouSpeak.com

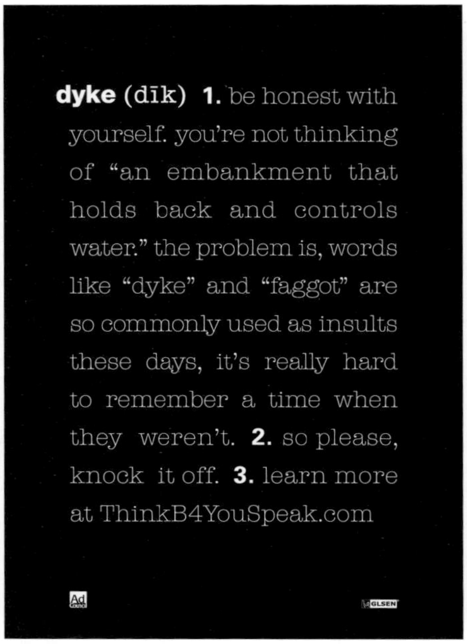

dyke (dīk) **1.** be honest with yourself. you're not thinking of "an embankment that holds back and controls water." the problem is, words like "dyke" and "faggot" are so commonly used as insults these days, it's really hard to remember a time when they weren't. **2.** so please, knock it off. **3.** learn more at ThinkB4YouSpeak.com

fag·got (fag'ət) **1.** there was a time when the word "faggot" meant a bundle of sticks. but then people started using it in an insulting, offensive way and things changed. so when you say things like "homo," "dyke" and "that's so gay" trying to be funny, remember, you may actually be hurting someone. **2.** so please, knock it off. **3.** get more information at ThinkB4YouSpeak.com

Figure 10-13

PRINT: "THINK BEFORE YOU SPEAK"

CAMPAIGN SPONSOR ORGANIZATION: GAY, LESBIAN, AND STRAIGHT EDUCATION NETWORK (GLSEN)

Campaign Web Site: www.ThinkB4YouSpeak. com

Volunteer Agency: ArnoldNYC / New York

Courtesy of the Ad Council

Senior Vice President, Director of Business Leadership: Jamie Talley

Senior Vice President, Director of Connections Planning: Nate Swenberg

Senior Vice President, Group Creative Directors: Thom Baginski and Gary Rozanski

Associate Creative Director: Susan Pracht

Vice President, Group Digital Director: John Fischetti

Executive Producer: Anthony Migliaccio

Assistant Producer: Katie Kelly

Campaign Objective: *Reduce and prevent the use of homophobic language among teens.*

Background: *Lesbian, gay, bisexual, and transgender (LGBT) teens in the United States experience homophobic remarks and harassment throughout the school day, creating an atmosphere where they feel disrespected, unwanted, and unsafe. GLSEN's research finds that three-quarters of LGBT teens hear slurs such as "faggot" or "dyke" frequently or often at school, and nine in ten reports hearing anti-LGBT language frequently or often. Homophobic remarks such as "that's so gay" are the most commonly heard type of biased remarks at school. Research also shows that these slurs are often unintentional and are a part of teens' vernacular. Most do not recognize the consequences, but the casual use of this language often carries over into more overt harassment.*

Campaign Description: *The new campaign aims to raise awareness among straight teens about the prevalence and consequences of anti-LGBT bias and behavior in American schools. Ultimately, the goal is to reduce and prevent the use of homophobic language in an effort to create a more positive environment for LGBT teens. The campaign also aims to reach adults, including school personnel and parents, because their support of this message is crucial to the success of efforts to change behavior among the target age group.*

Target Audience: *Teens in grades 8–12.*

Did You Know: *Nearly a third of LGBT students missed school in the past month, because they felt unsafe or uncomfortable (more than two-thirds report that they feel unsafe).**

Almost 90 percent of LGBT students reported being verbally harassed at school because of their sexual orientation; almost half were physically harassed at school because of their sexual orientation; also more than half experienced some form of electronic harassment (cyberbullying) in the past year.*

Sexual orientation and gender expression were the most common reasons students were harassed at school.*

—The Advertising Council, Inc.

---

*Based on data from GLSEN's 2007 National School Climate Survey.
The Advertising Council, Inc.

or group easily fit your campaign idea? If you could easily swap the brand, then your theme or idea is probably too generic.

Here are some creative prompts to help you think creatively. If it makes sense for your idea, then a design solution might be based on:

> *Juxtaposition*

> *Texture*

> *An odd point of view*

> *Combining photographs with drawings*

> *Abstraction*

> *Color combined with black and white*

> *Odd scale*

> *Montage*

> *Handmade elements and/or handwriting*

> *Bizarre visuals*

> *An illusion of three-dimensional space*

> *Scent*

> *Motion*

> *Texture*

> *Odd comparisons*

Using visuals that surprise is one way to grab a viewer's attention. Using copy-driven ads that surprise is another. For example, the ads in figure 10-13 begin with a slur, to attract attention, and end in an effort to create a more positive environment for lesbian, gay, bisexual, and transgender (LGBT) teens by helping reduce and prevent the use of homophobic language.

Ping When They Pong

If everyone in a room is wearing a blue denim shirt except for one person who is wearing a green satin shirt, who would stand out from the crowd? If 99 percent of TV ads are in color, then why not think of utilizing black-and-white

or duotone palette? They're ponging, so you ping. Take the least traveled path.

There are fads in most design arenas—trendy color palettes, trendy typefaces, two people everyone is casting for voice-overs, typographic arrangements that are prevalent. At times the introduction of new technology creates a trend. Thus, if everyone seems to be using photo-editing software to create visuals, create yours by hand. If every art director is relying on photography, use illustration or an interesting hybrid. Without a doubt, your ping has to be appropriate for your audience and brand as well as work for your idea.

Make It Your Own

Find a way to utilize something that you can create that others might not think of or utilize. Find inspiration from other arenas, such as art history, interior design, architecture, ephemera, primitive signage, wrapping-paper patterns, eighteenth-century prints, previous eras, industrial design, fashion design, landscape design, product design, floral arrangements, sushi arrangements, crafts, and countless others. Make it your own. Add range to your design repertoire. This means putting your own twist on it, not stealing. For example, how can an Aztec temple inspire a look for an interactive ad? Can celadon-glazed stoneware of the Koryo dynasty inspire a visual for a print ad?

There is an enormous difference between copying another art director and finding inspiration in another discipline or source. Examining typography on old orange crates or cigar boxes, Navajo patterns, or old maps might inspire you. Be open to inspiration from a variety of sources. Try different art-making processes. Experiment.

11

DESIGNING FOR PRINT

PRINT BASICS

Two to three seconds is all someone will give to a print advertisement. Can you grab someone's attention? Can you keep it?

Advertising communication depends on a synergy of visual and verbal components. In other words, the visual-verbal ad equation is: 1 + 1 = 3. Nowhere is this more evident than in print. Whether it is a magazine or newspaper ad, an outdoor poster or billboard, there is no motion or sound to dazzle. In print, words and images alone must convey the idea. Working off one another like a great duet, their synergistic relationship is evident in each ad of this campaign for Prulink Realty (figure 11-1).

The main verbal message is called the line or headline. Most people refer to this line of

copy as the headline, because in the early days of advertising it usually occupied the top of the page. Today's art directors experiment freely with composition—a line can be positioned anywhere on the page or screen, depending upon your design idea and solution, as in the ad for Living Quarters (figure 11-2), where the line is within the photo below the image and the body copy runs up the side of the ad.

The main visual message is called the *visual* or *image*. Together, the line and visual should communicate and express the advertising message. In fact, in a really good ad, the line and visual, in combination, should have an additive effect, as in a classic ad for El Al airlines (figure 11-3).

When the line and visual work off one another, together they create greater meaning. Just like a good comedy team or a musical duet, the total effect is greater than the sum of the separate parts; it is seamless. In Buzz

Figure 11-1

PRINT:
"CASINO" AND "TREE"

AGENCY: SAATCHI &
SAATCHI / SINGAPORE

Executive Creative Director:
Sion Scott-Wilson

Art Director: Simon Yeo

Copywriter: Srinath Mogeri

Client: Prulink Realty

The adage "location is every-thing" is demonstrated by showing how proximity (a pawn shop located next to a casino and a car wash located next to a bird sanctuary) can make your business: "We'll take care of the right place bit."

Figure 11-2

PRINT: "LAKE"

AGENCY:
PUSH ADVERTISING /
ORLANDO, FLORIDA

Creative Director:
John Ludwig

Copywriters: John Ludwig and
Gordon Weller

Art Director: Ron Boucher

Photographer: Doug Scaletta

Client: Living Quarters
© 1997–2003

Disposing of old furniture in a uniquely anthropomorphized way, so that it can be replaced by new furniture, is an attention-grabbing device.

Figure 11-3

PRINT:
"NOAH'S ARK," 1968

AGENCY: JOHN COLLINGS
& PARTNERS / LONDON

Art Director: John Hegarty

Designer: John Hegarty

Artist: Roy Carruthers

Copywriter: Lindsay Dale

Client: El Al Israel Airlines

If you cover the visual and just read the line, you do not get the full meaning of the ad's message, and if you cover the line and look at the visual, you do not get the ad message at all. However, in combination the line and visual yield a greater meaning than either of the parts alone.

Put it out of your misery.

Living Quarters at Millenia Plaza grand opening. October 11-13. Stop by. No questions asked.

directly under the headline, the logo under that, with the Web address in the bottom right-hand corner. The body copy in Hunt Adkins' ad for Dublin Productions makes for entertaining reading (figure 11-6): the line is at the top of the page, with a main visual in the center of the page that is surrounded by body copy and smaller inset photographs. The logo is in the bottom right-hand corner.

CONSIDERATIONS FOR PRINT

> *Grab attention*

> *Keep attention*

> *Be relevant*

> *Serve as a call to action*

Grey's campaign for the Buick Classic, the line and visuals work together to communicate the magic of a golf tournament in New York (figure 11-4).

Four of the usual elements in a print ad are in this visually inviting ad for MINI USA (figure 11-5). The visual is the photograph of the yellow MINI. The line sits at the head of the ad: "Good. Clean. Fun." The body copy is

Yes, it has been known to rain in Israel.

Figure 11-4

PRINT: "DIVOT"

AGENCY: BUZZ GREY,
A DIVISION OF GREY
WORLDWIDE / NEW YORK

Art Director: Mark Catalina

Creative Director:
Robert Skollar

Copywriter: Brian Fallon

Client: The Buick Classic
© 2002

*Merging the worlds of golf and
New York City creates visual
twists.*

Parts of a Print Ad

In print a design usually includes a line, visual, body copy, product shot, tagline, and sign-off. At times, one or more of these elements may not be included. There are times when an ad does not need body copy—for example, an ad for chewing gum does not really need to explain much more than what is communicated through the line and visual. Or, if the main visual of an ad is the product, then there is no need for a product shot.

The usual elements of a print ad are:

Line (headline): *main verbal message*

Visual: *main visual message*

Body copy: *the text of the ad (supports main message)*

Product shot: *a photograph or illustration of the product or packaging*

Tagline: *claim in the form of a catchphrase that embodies the brand campaign strategy*

Sign-off: *this includes the logo and/or product shot, tagline, Web address*

Figure 11-5

PRINT:
"GOOD. CLEAN. FUN."

AGENCY: BUTLER, SHINE, STERN & PARTNERS / SAUSALITO, CALIFORNIA

Client: MINI USA

© MINI USA & BSSP

The visualization and composition are the visible representation of an ad idea (see figures 11-7, 11-8, and 11-9). Regardless of the format—print for magazines or newspapers, direct mail, posters, billboards—the design of a print ad can make or break the communication. Regardless of medium, you can have a good idea with poor execution, and vice versa. Both idea and design count (see figure 11-10).

Print ad design considerations:

> *Make sure the idea is on strategy. Make sure you have generated a valid idea based on insights for the brand and audience.*

> *Set up cooperative action between words and image.*

> *Determine the specific relationship between type and visual.*

>> *Will type and visual share characteristics?*

>> *Will they contrast one another?*

>> *Will one be the star and the other take a supporting role?*

> *Check the quality of the typography (appropriateness of typeface, kerning, interline spacing, readability, legibility), color choices (color can add to legibility and communication).*

> *Apply all the principles of design: balance, unity, visual hierarchy, rhythm, flow, contrast.*

> *Have you guided the viewer through the composition using arrangement, movement, alignments, and transitions (A.M.A.T.)?*

> *Ensure clarity of communication:*

>> *Communicate a functional or emotional benefit.*

>> *Create visual interest.*

> *Ensure the ad unit works within the larger campaign.*

SADISTIC WILLIE,
PINSTRIPE-SUIT CHUCKLES, NAKED BOB
and other
CLOWN HERETICS.

1944. The National Clown Convention. A sea of happy clown faces stretches as far as the eye can see. Surveying this scene, Silly-Shoe Shermie sets his huge clown shoes aside, slips his feet into a pair of dainty size sixes and steps boldly out into the spotlight. The crowd gapes as Shermie proudly strikes several breathtaking poses in his pair of shiny new wing tips. Silly-Shoe's hopes soar; he is doing it! And then they fall on him like jackals and beat him to death with rubber chickens.

The fish clowns' somewhat unique art consists of hitting each other over the head with a small boy.

POWER TO THE CLOWNISTS!

Word of Shermie's shoe martyrdom spread quickly. Within days, other fringe clowns had appeared. One such clown, Friendly Willie, could live the lie no longer. Casting aside his old image, he rose like a phoenix and became reborn as Sadistic Willie. For his new act he filled his squirting flower with battery acid, ran people down in a clown tank, threw jagged-glass-shard pies into people's faces and crammed 21 clowns into one tiny car by first grinding them up in a cuisinart. Others quickly joined Willie in this clown liberation: Armani-Suit Alvin, Vivisectionist Vinny, Cross-Country-Killing-Spree Charlie, Petite-Nose Percy, Ozwald the Pimp. At long last clowns everywhere were casting aside the iron shackles of the controlling clown proletariat, marching into the streets to proudly display their protest signs, banners and tight-fitting leather thongs.

White-Collar Joe is well known for his hilarious list readings that often go on for several days. Here we see him bringing down the house as he recites from a list containing the serial numbers of every urethane squeegee in Liechtenstein.

The famed Clowns of Calcutta. Their bloody regime controls the world's supply of tiny cars with large red-seven-gut horns.

THE CLOWN INQUISITION

The clown fundamentalists, afraid of losing all that was happy and beloved about clowns, worried that little children would not have anyone to laugh with, set about systematically torturing and murdering all suspected clown infidels. Many a clown was stretched on the rack for honking a horn less than the minimum 17 times per minute. Clown S.W.A.T. teams burned art galleries to the ground to drive out Dadaistic clowns. And yet, the revolution prevailed when the clown inquisition forgot to pay their VISA bill and had all their torture devices repossessed. To hear the famous Clown March on Washington, punctuated by the sound of thousands of red noses honking in unison, call 612-332-8864 (Minneapolis) or 213-960-3322 (Los Angeles).

Jerry Pope adds Sadistic Willie for another spanking with the Fustnaky-Buster-2000.

DUBLIN
PRODUCTIONS

Figure 11-6

PRINT: "SADISTIC WILLIE"

AGENCY: HUNT ADKINS / MINNEAPOLIS

Creative Director and Copywriter: Doug Adkins

Associate Creative Director and Art Director: Steve Mitchell

Client: Dublin Productions

Figure 11-7

PRINT: "SOS"

AGENCY: TAXI / TORONTO, ONTARIO

Client: Visine

Using the red veins in the eye to issue a distress call (SOS), this ad explains the benefits of Visine.

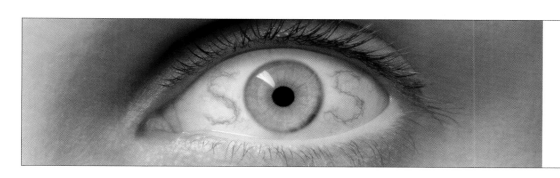

▸ Figure 11-10

PRINT: "ROLLER,"
"STAPLER," AND "ICE CUBE"

AGENCY: MAD DOGS &
ENGLISHMEN / NEW YORK

Creative Director: Dave Cook

Art Directors: James Dawson
Hollis and Vivienne Wan

Copywriters: Jaime Palmiotti
and James Robinson

Photographer:
Kudo Photography

Client: Haribo

© 1992 Haribo

▸ Figure 11-11

OUTDOOR BOARD:
KEYSTONE RESORT

AGENCY: CULTIVATOR
ADVERTISING & DESIGN /
BOULDER

Creative Directors:
Tim Abare and Chris Beatty

Art Director: Chris Beatty

Copywriter: Tim Abare

Sculptor: David Bellamy

Client: Keystone Resort

Figure 11-12

*OUTDOOR BOARD:
COLORADO WILDLANDS
DROUGHT AWARENESS*

AGENCY:
CULTIVATOR ADVERTISING
& DESIGN / BOULDER

Creative Directors:
Tim Abare and Chris Beatty

Art Directors: Chris Beatty
and August Sandberg

Copywriter: Tim Abare

Client: Colorado Wildlands

Critique Method by Sal De Vito / DeVito/Verdi, New York

The following critique method is used by Sal DeVito, cofounder and creative director of DeVito/Verdi in New York. When I studied advertising under DeVito at the School of Visual Arts, New York, he employed a critique methodology of teaching that greatly clarified things for me. DeVito has said, "In the advertising class I teach, I've created a list of critiques that go with the types of predictable ads students create, which I paste up on the wall. . . . Most ads can be placed under one of these critiques. And every now and then you get a good one that doesn't go with any of these critiques."*

When you use these categories, be brutally honest. If your final ad falls into one of these categories, rethink and redo:

Sounds like advertising (a typical sales pitch)

Too damn cute

Sounds like bullshit

I've heard it before

Dull

Good idea but needs a stronger execution

With permission from Sal DeVito.

*. Sal DeVito, "La Vida DeVito," One: A Magazine 6, no. 2 (2002): 8.

12

DESIGNING FOR MOTION, BROADCAST, AND BROADBAND

Entertainment sells.
—Cliff Freeman

AND NOW A WORD FROM OUR SPONSORS...

There you are sitting on your living room sofa, watching the program you've been waiting for all week—and it is periodically interrupted by commercial messages. Although a few critics say that the commercials are better than the programs, television commercials still *interrupt* television programming, whether broadcast or broadband.

Many people are annoyed by those interruptions. Others just zap around for two minutes until their program comes back on or skip ahead. Many people head for the refrigerator. Some stare blankly. A television commercial has to do several things to get people to watch and to keep them from zapping or texting or retrieving a snack or checking their e-mail or doing something else.

Television and Web commercials have to do the following and do it all in fifteen or thirty seconds.

> *Get someone's attention before he or she zaps, skips ahead, or leaves the room*

> *Look or feel fresh (not have the look, tone, and feel of a pedestrian television commercial)*

> *Entertain*

> *Work in the context of television programming*

> *Endear the brand or group to the consumer*

> *Call to action, create awareness, or drive people to the Web*

In print, you have two or three seconds to capture someone's attention. If you lose the consumer in the first second, you've lost 'em. Period. With television, you may lose someone's attention in the first two or three seconds and then recapture his or her attention in the next five seconds, if he or she is still on the sofa. People drift in and out when watching television. Some of what television, online videos, Web commercials, and films have to offer include:

> *Motion*

> *Time: fifteen-, thirty-, or sixty-second ad formats*

> *Sound: music, voice, sound effects*

> *Special visual effects*

> *Narrative: time to tell a longer story than print*

BASICS FOR SCREEN-BASED MEDIA

A temporal relationship exists in screen-based media (the relationship or interplay between two separate events or images), and this involves *chronology* (the order of events). A screen-based design solution is composed of a number of media items (events, frames, images, and sound), each of which has its own duration. These can be combined into a whole by specifying the temporal relationships among the different items.

Consider *spatial relationships* (the distance between the viewer and the thing seen on screen), especially how far or close as well as the shifts between near and far:

Close-up: a zoomed-in shot

Medium shot: seen from a medium distance

Long shot: seen from far away

Consider *temporal relationships,* or how the relationships between frames (preceding or following) contribute to the viewer's understanding of the visual communication and to the impact of the design on the viewer.

For *rhythmic relationships,* the duration of each shot and the interaction of visuals, with contrast, variation, and how the composition flows from one frame to the next are considered and often achieved in the same manner as in print.

Composition basics to consider are:

Proximity: Grouping elements should enhance content and visual communication. Negative space surrounding shapes and forms greatly contributes to how elements relate to one another.

Contrast: Establishing contrast produces visual punch. Contrast creates visual interest through variety.

Repetition and Alignment: When viewers see a repeated element and alignment, or hear a repeated sound, that recurrence helps the viewers perceive the work as a unified whole.

Use of Typography and Graphics in Screen-Based Media

Determine headings and subheadings in terms of color, size, and weight to distinguish the hierarchy of type from one another as well as from visuals. Letterforms or words may stand out by using weight for contrast. The interplay of positive and negative shape relationships will have an enormous effect on establishing flow from one frame to another.

Screen-Based Matters

> **Narrative or Storyline:** *The process of telling a story or giving an account of something, including the chronology, the order in which things happen, with the inclusion of a beginning, middle, and end, though not necessarily in that order.*

> **Sequence:** *The sequence is the particular order in which frames are arranged or connected; also, it is the order of actions or events in the narrative (linear or nonlinear).*

> **Duration:** *Duration is the period of time that the motion exists.*

> **Pacing or Tempo:** *Tempo is the speed and/or rhythm at which the screen-based application unfolds and moves.*

> **Montage:** *The use of visuals composed by assembling and overlaying different visuals or materials collected from different sources.*

The conceptual interplay between type and visuals in print is much the same as in screen-based applications, except the bonus of motion and sound adds potential for heightened dramatic or comedic effect. How type interfaces with visuals in screen-based media, as in print, can effectively communicate meaning, both literally and symbolically.

Music and Sound in Screen-Based Media

We have all heard advertising jingles that we can hum or that stay with us, provoking endearment to brands or nostalgic feelings. Audio provides a strong component in screen-based media, lending to the audience enthusiasm, engagement, and a way to make the piece memorable, to make it stick.

BASIC CONSIDERATIONS FOR MOTION

As with creating concepts and visuals for television commercials, screen-based media can involve narrative or storytelling forms (linear, nonlinear, realistic, abstract, or experimental), sequencing of images and events, composition, and visual and motion variables (characteristics, attributes, or qualities). As always, the underlying concept drives the execution. Basic considerations for motion are:

> *Concept generation based on strategy and brief*

> *Theories fundamental to motion*

> *Narrative forms or storytelling (linear and nonlinear)*

> *Planning of action*

> *Sequencing of images for maximum impact and communication*

> *Integration of different media (if relevant)*

Structuring a Commercial

There are no formulas for structuring a commercial. Or, rather, there are formulas, but they are usually trite or predictable. And that is why it is important to know existing formats and how to use them creatively or ditch them entirely. As Eric Silver, executive vice president and group executive creative director at BBDO Worldwide, says, "We owe it to ourselves to throw out the formulas. And have as much fun as we can in a very stressful business. In the end, our clients will thank us for it."

There also are conventions (see Chapter 7). The *structure* or *form* of a commercial or video refers to the selection and arrangement of the components. There are as many structures for television commercials and commercial videos as there are for film, prose, poetry, or music. The structure should flow out of the brand strategy, the creative brief, the idea (see figure 12-1), the tone you want to set, the feeling, and an insight into the audience. About figure 12-1, creative director Greg Nations explains, "This is a long-running, improvisational comedy television campaign for Sonic Drive-Ins, a chain of drive-through restaurants. Consumers embraced the series of TV spots including "And Tots," "In His Shoes," and "Misleading" because it wasn't the usual over-the-top, fast-food commercial. The client enjoyed it because it was so darn cheap and fun to produce."

Of course, you can think of a commercial as storytelling, as containing characters, goals, conflicts, scenes, and a plot line. When telling a story, one must consider the element of time. How do we experience time in the story or commercial? In what sequence do events occur? Basically, a story moves in either a linear pattern (in chronological sequence, from A to B to C to D) or a nonlinear pattern (not in a chronological sequence).

On creating linear structures, Alan Robbins of Kean University advises:

To me, all stories—whether they are novels, commercials, comics, films—follow the same structure: beginning, middle, and end.

The beginning is the snare, the catch, the lure, the setup. Some image or description that grabs the reader or viewer's attention and sets up a question, a dilemma, a mystery that calls out for an answer.

The middle is the explication or unfolding of events, actions, intentions that are consequences of the beginning.

The end is the resolution of or answer to the beginning setup.

What changes regarding the different formats is the medium of communication (images, words, sounds, etc.) and the length of exposition. The setup in a commercial can take only a few seconds; in a novel, many pages. That's why most story projects begin with a story

Figure 12-1

TV: "AND TOTS," "IN HIS SHOES," AND "MISLEADING"

AGENCY: THE ESCAPE POD

Creative Directors: Greg Nations and Pat Piper

Art Director: Brad Jungles

Copywriters: Greg Nations, Pat Piper, Matt McCaffree, and Brad Jungles

Producers: Charlie DeCoursey and Terry Nichols

Client: Sonic Drive-Ins

When the Sonic "Two Guys" campaign first broke, the two guys were in a car going to competitors' drive-thru windows and ordering breakfast items that the competitors did not have—pancake on a stick, toaster breakfast sandwiches, breakfast anytime of the day, etc.

Sonic was twenty years late getting into the quick-service-restaurant breakfast category, so the agency decided we had to go straight for the throat of McDonald's and Burger King by pointing out their glaring lack of interesting breakfast options.

The breakfast campaign gained such notoriety so quickly that Sonic decided they wanted the two guys to become their main campaign. That's when we took them off competitors' lots and put them on Sonic lots.

Cut to six years later, and they are still going strong with no end in sight.

Early in my career I was fortunate enough to work for Ed McCabe at his second agency in New York City, McCabe and Co. Ed always said one way to judge a good campaign is how long it could keep going and still stay fresh.

—Greg Nations

Figure 12-3

POSTER AND INTERACTIVE FILMS: "THE HIRE" POSTER AND BMW INTERACTIVE FILMS

AGENCY:
FALLON WORLDWIDE / MINNEAPOLIS

Client: BMW

© 2004 BMW of North America, LLC, used with permission. The BMW name and logo are registered trademarks.

The BMW film series pulled people to the Web and brought together leading film directors and BMW cars for a groundbreaking project.

VIDEOS

The short video format viewed online, on video-sharing sites, certainly depends on the element of surprise, unlike the predictable television commercial formats and programming. People enjoy sharing videos that surprise them and their friends, based on pranks or gotchas, as Virginia Heffernan points out.[1] The great subjects of online video are stunts, pranks, violence, gotchas, virtuosity, upsets, and transformations. Commercials that are very entertaining can find a long life on video-sharing sites. People also look for "how-tos" and informational videos.

Videos made for the Web are meant to pull people in, as opposed to pushing TV spots at people. Whether these are films, stories, brand-sponsored series, or any other form, the idea is to engage people enough that they will view it once, twice, maybe more, and share the item (see pp. 196–197).

1. Heffernan, "The Susan Boyle Experience," *New York Times Magazine*, 28 June 2009, 16.

MOTION AND
MOTION GRAPHICS

From Saul Bass's animated film titles of the
mid-twentieth century to contemporary
object-based animation to broadcast and
broadband video, motion graphics play a crucial role in visual communication. The illusion
of motion combined with sound and music
is playing a bigger role than ever due to the
Internet, mobile devices, and other screens.

Working in motion graphics requires the
usual conceptual skills required of a graphic
designer or art director plus the ability to
imagine sequences over time, consider how
form creates impact and motion over time,
and relate the motion graphics to sound.

Screen-based media can support graphics
that move. In order to create motion graphics, one must be well acquainted with the
necessary technical issues, production techniques, and software.

As always, a designer working with motion must consider concept generation,
function, form, aesthetics, meaning,
and—ultimately—communication.

13

DESIGNING FOR WEB SITES

WEB SITES

Imagine your life without your computer, iPod or other MP3 player, video camera, GPS, and mobile phone. Technology has changed people's lives, forcing a key question for advertisers: What do people want to see from brands and groups on the Internet?

People want a variety of *useful* things—tools, utilities, information—and they want rich interactive experiences, including entertainment.

The Internet is a 24/7 global medium that will become even more important in starting conversations, building communities, influencing pop culture, and informing and connecting people worldwide. Any brand or group can offer people opportunities to engage with them and can create something that will make

people want to come back to their Web site again and again.

A brand or group can build an online storefront, information center, or hub. It can build something that informs or entertains for a short period. Or it can build something that lasts and grows. Technological advances have given us all many choices; we can do any number of things with our free time. Why should people spend their time with a brand or group?

The Internet offers many avenues to build relationships with people, from corporate Web sites to entertaining microsites (such as the much celebrated www.subservientchicken.com) to branded programming content, videos, advertising campaigns, and brand platforms.

An online ad campaign is usually short-lived; it either delivers a message, entertains, or informs. Online ad campaigns could be used to drive visitors to a platform, which is an online media destination that people integrate into their lives and come back to again and again.

That said, the most important thing a creative ad professional can learn is to generate ideas, because any effective online site or platform is based on a great idea. Idea generation and designing for interactive media is collaborative, involving a team of experts who develop and execute Web design applications.

Designing for digital media is an iterative process, requiring prototyping and testing, maintenance, campaigns to drive people to the sites, updates, and redesigns.

A *Web site* is a collection of "pages" (or files) linked together and made available on the World Wide Web, and they are authored and owned by companies, organizations, and individuals. Because of constant and rapid innovation in this technology, the page model we are all used to will most likely change—soon. The Web is in its infancy, for the most part. As newer products that utilize touch screen or gestural interfaces become more popular, newer models might replace the page model. No matter—principles such as visual hierarchy, balance, proportion, rhythm, and unity will live on.

Web design involves strategy, collaboration, creativity, planning, design, development, testing, production, and implementation.

WEB SITE BASICS

Any Web site—whether informational, promotional, or a platform—has content, which is the literal communication. Any Web site is designed, which is the form. As Paul Rand said, form and content should be indistinguishable, synthesized to become art. As he advised, although he was talking about print, it absolutely applies to the Web:

When form predominates, meaning is blunted. When content predominates, interest lags. The genius comes in when both of these things fuse.

Couple that thought with Robert Rasmussen's caveat:

Clients are not saying, "Make us ads" or "Make us websites," they're saying, "Create interaction between our brand and our customers." That's our job now.[1]

Visual design is not just about visual impact or aesthetics—it should be a marriage of form and function that ensures an effortless and worthwhile user experience. Visual hierarchy ranks visuals and text in order of importance, which should be a natural outgrowth of content, emphasizing and ordering content from the most important to the least important.

For conventional sites, a grid is most often used as the central ordering structure for a Web site; it is a framework used to create a uniform layout from page to page, while allowing for some variation. The grid splits the page into columns with defined widths, spacing, and margins to establish positions for the standard elements on the page and alignment of text and pictures. Often, there is more than one grid per online design to allow for different types of content and applications.

Web site grids use a master layout to guide the composition and placement of every element—text, headers, and graphics—from screen to screen. By maintaining a visual design grid, the visitor will be able to easily locate titles, information, and navigation graphics, thus enabling a smooth passage around the site. (Software layout programs refer to a stock layout as a template. And nondesigners utilize stock templates in lieu of designing their own grids.)

Unity refers to the level of consistency and correspondence throughout a site. Creating visual correspondence among the pages—unity throughout the entire work, rhythm from page to page, and a flow from page to page—is crucial. Providing a sense of location for the visitor is equally important. For instance, the home page link

---

1. "The Screens Issue: Multiscreen Mad Men," *New York Times Magazine*, 23 November 2008.

Figure 13-1

WEB SITE: LANDS' END | PACKLAND

AGENCY: BIG SPACESHIP, BROOKLYN

Client: Lands' End

Backpacks are a cornerstone of the back-to-school merchandise that Lands' End offers. The company approached Big Spaceship looking to increase engagement with their audience—both online and in store—for this product line.

Lands' End backpacks come in a number of sizes, shapes, and colors. They're customizable. To deliver on that, Big Spaceship created a fantasy backpack creator: Packland. This interactive wonderland gives kids an adventuresome way to design the ultimate backpack, appealing to their sense of imagination.

At Packland, kids choose from various themes and colors as they build their customized backpacks, adding on all sorts of "pack art"— everything from rocket boosters and pirate hooks to tiger tails and butterfly wings. Big Spaceship created all original artwork for the project.

As they build the perfect pack, they can change the theme (say, from "ocean" to "spy lab") select a new color, tack on more art, and give their creation a name. The interactive demo, simple copy, and oversized buttons guide younger kids through the experience. Once they've personalized a backpack to perfection, they can print it, e-mail it to friends, upload it to their social networking sites, or share it on the Lands' End Facebook page.

In emphasizing in-store giveaways, Big Spaceship created a connection between the fantasy backpacks and the actual merchandise, which was a click away. They drew consumers into the Lands' End brand, creating a colorful journey along the way.

—Big Spaceship

Web Site: http://archive.bigspaceship.com/packland

Figure 13-2

*WEB SITE, E-BLASTS,
PACKAGE DESIGN,
STATIONERY: OLIVE*

STUDIO: MODERN DOG
DESIGN CO., SEATTLE

Creative Director and Art
Director: Robynne Raye

Copywriters: Robynne Raye
and Gina Quiroga

Designers: Robynne Raye,
Robert Zwiebel, Shogo Ota,
and Meg Paradise

Illustrator: Vittorio Costarella

© Modern Dog Design Co. 2009

Figure 13-3

DIGITAL PLATFORM: NOKIA URBANISTA DIARIES

AGENCY: R/GA

Executive Creative Director: James Temple

Associate Creative Director: Nathalie Huni

Art Director: Athila Armstrong

Visual Designer: Ennio Franco

Interaction Designer: Kathrin Hoffmann

Copywriter: Neil Starr

Technical Director: Darren Richardson

Senior Flash Developer: Nicolas Le Pallec

Flash Developers: Tomas Vorobjov and Stuart Lees

Quality Assurance: Neil Duggan

Group Account Director: Anthony Wickham

Senior Producer: Dylan Connerton

Client: Nokia

Nokia Client Supervisors
  E-Marketing Director: Arto Joensuu
  Senior E-Marketing Manager: Juuso Myllyrinne
  E-Marketing Manager: Nina Venäläinen

Urbanista Diaries is a digital platform that utilizes a Web site, a mobile application, and personal widgets to allow people to capture and share their lives in real-time through the Nokia N82. The powerful Nokia N82 is enabled with GPS-technology and a five-megapixel camera that allows users to tag each photo to a specific location and instantaneously share their experiences with anyone via widgets posted on blogs or social networking sites, like Facebook.

Urbanista Diaries was rolled out in an extensive three-phase campaign that engaged bloggers, journalists, and everyday people to take photos of their life adventures. For the first phase, four influential bloggers were sent across the globe with a Nokia N82 to record their journeys and share it with guests on the Urbanista Diaries site. For phase two, Nokia partnered with several top media sites such as Wallpaper, Lonely Planet, National Geographic, and CNN to document major world events in real time via journalists, artists and scientists. People could follow the unfolding events both on the site and via widgets. Phase three opens up the experience to everyone with a GPS-enabled Nokia device. Now anyone can upload their personal photos from their journeys to the site or their personal widget for all their friends and family to track. Urbanista Diaries is another example of how Nokia is changing the way people share the stories of their lives.

The driving insight behind Urbanista Diaries was that merely informing people that the new Nokia N82 came equipped with a GPS and a five-megapixel camera was not enough to cut through a crowded market dominated by highly competitive communications. Instead, demonstrating the Nokia N82's capabilities and its benefits would provide a more compelling case.

—Nokia

should be visually consistent (the same shape and in the same spot on every screen page) throughout the site. In addition, each screen should have a title in the same spot so the visitor knows exactly where to look to determine "location" within the site. The visitor should never wonder "Where am I?" without knowing where to look for the answer.

The problem of unity in a Web site design is similar to establishing unity in a song; they are both experienced in "chunks" or recognizable sections. Such a strategy assumes that some aspect of the chunk changes while something else stays the same.

Some Web sites offer a variety of experiences. For example, the Web sites of television broadcast channels offer full episode players. If a viewer does not choose a full screen experience, then the Web site design must accommodate the episode experience while maintaining the Web site context so that the viewer is still immersed in the world of that brand.

Considerations for Web site design:

> *Integrate design of Web site with brand identity: color palette, graphic elements, tone, visualization method, imagery (see figure 13-2).*

> *Engage the visitor throughout the site.*

> *Test at various stages.*

> *Ensure logical information hierarchy.*

> *Offer a rich experience and a branded utility or platform.*

> *Follow the Americans with Disabilities Act (ADA) Standards for Accessible Design guidelines for Web design (www.ada.gov).*

Features of effective Web site design:

> *Content is easy to find, read, print, or download.*

> *Most content should be brought to the immediate attention of the visitor; however, it is acceptable to allow some content to be "found."*

> *Easy to navigate. Make it intuitive!*

> *Content and form are inseparable, with form enhancing the content and content informing the form.*

> *Offers something that print, broadcast, or mobile media cannot.*

> *Offers a media-rich experience.*

> *Respects the user's time. Offer fast content download times (less than 15 seconds) and streaming.*

> *Makes the experience frustration-free.*

> *Provides an interactive experience that draws people back, pulls people in, one that starts a dialogue and a long-term relationship (see pp. 234–235).*

WEB SITE DEVELOPMENT

Besides the usual design process, the Web design application process requires thorough prototyping, where the site is created and tested for usability. There are ten key steps in this part of the Web site development process:

1. Project plan: orientation and analysis to set and guide the goals and form the team of experts

2. Creative brief: to outline creative strategy as it relates to the broader brand or visual identity, positioning, target audience, and all the other objectives of a brief

3. Site structure: plan, map, and prepare content and information architecture (functional specifications) and address technological challenges

4. Content outline

5. Conceptual design: generate design concept based on brand identity strategy and brief

6. Visual design development: design grid/template and element placement, determine visualization method, set color palette, Web type styles, style of navigational cues/graphic interface (link buttons), style of photos, illustrations, and other graphic elements, determine how to integrate media; lay out main screens to determine geography, almost like a storyboard

7. Technical specs

8. Prototype

9. Technology: technical solutions; alpha; beta I and II

10. Implementation: launch, promotion, updating, ongoing testing for usability

comparison tools, which take the Nike+ product experience far beyond just a shoe or an iPod" (www.rga.com/award/nikeplus.html). Ideally, the audience for a platform grows over time, with every ad campaign bringing more people to the platform, unlike traditional ad models where participation drops off.

"Nike and R/GA collaborated on The Human Race, a 10-kilometer running event held in 25 cities worldwide on Aug. 31. Thanks to Nike+, Nike had a ready-built media platform to recruit and connect participants, and set up city and country challenges. Consumers could compete virtually using their Nike+ systems. And the digital platform also informed how Nike marketed the event."[2] For client Nokia, R/GA created an impressive platform that showed off the photographic and geotagging capabilities of Nokia devices, in figure 13-3.

PLATFORMS / OWNED MEDIA

Unlike outbound advertising or a campaign that runs for a period of time in various media, a platform is owned media rooted in utility and built to last, offering a constant connection. Theoretically, people are drawn to a platform again and again. Users revisit and incorporate the platform into their lives. There are excellent examples of owned-media platforms, for example, Nike Football's Head2Head, which is a tool that allows users to compare themselves to any player, at any level, at any stage of their career. The platform was created by R/GA for Nike.

Another example of a well-done platform is Nike+, which is a multichannel, multisensory marriage of Apple and Nike technologies. The ad agency R/GA "built a robust platform of virtual racing, progress tracking, motivational goals and stories, and global community

2. www.rga.com/news/article/2009/2008-digital-agency

CASE STUDY

Web Site: **Swaggerizeme.com**

Client: **Old Spice**

AGENCY: WIEDEN + KENNEDY
/ PORTLAND

Wieden + Kennedy / Portland
Executive Creative Directors:
   Mark Fitzloff and
   Susan Hoffman
Creative Directors: Jason
   Bagley and Mark Fitzloff
Interactive Creative Director:
   Sean O'Brien
Copywriters: Craig Allen, Mark
   Fitzloff, and Jason Bagley
Art Director: Eric Baldwin
Content Writers: Tyler Benson,
   Matthew McFerrin, John
   Zhao, and Angie Ogburn
Interactive Designer: Chris
   Larson, Mark Shepherd, The
   Happy Corp (Vendor)
Producer (Interactive):
   Jeremy Lind
Programmers (Ads): Joshua
   Perez and Laurie Brown
Ad Trafficking: Jonnie James
Photographer: Chris Larson
Account Executive:
   Scott Phillips

Design and Development
Partner: **The Happy Corp.**
Executive Creative Director:
   Doug Jaeger
Art Director: Jeff Baxter
Technology Director:
   Zach Blank
Lead Programmer:
   Adrian Lafond
Producer: Alex Sturtevant

Production Company
Director: Craig Allen,
   Wieden+Kennedy
Executive Producer:
   Ben Grylewicz and
   Wieden+Kennedy
Producer: Lara Gallagher,
   Wieden+Kennedy
Editor:
   David Jahns, Joint Editorial
Post-Production: Joint Editorial

Digital, "Swaggerize Me"

Brief: To translate the Old Spice "Swagger" TV and print campaign into an online experience. Our communications are aimed at men from ages 12 to 34, with a creative bull's-eye of men from ages 18 to 24.

Solution: We created an online application that allows users to enhance their online image, or "Swagger," by creating fake, flattering articles, blogs, and Web sites about themselves that come up when people search their names online. Banners and Web videos were used to draw traffic to the site.

—Wieden + Kennedy

Fights odor all day.

EXPERIENCE IS EVERYTHING.
Old Spice

14

DESIGNING FOR MOBILE ADVERTISING

MOBILE ADVERTISING BASICS

The most important thing to realize about mobile phones is that most people have one, and they have one with them most hours of the day and night. It is the most personal of all media; it resides in our pockets and hand-bags. It has a small screen and is handheld. If we leave home without it, we break into a sweat. People love their mobile phones and have become increasingly dependent upon them. Whether someone is waiting in a line at a theater or store, or sitting on a bus or in a doctor's office, that mobile device can provide entertainment (see figure 14-1 and case study on pages 238–239) or information.

There are applications (or apps) that are essentially branded utilities for just about everything. There are mobile games and programming content. Mobile commerce will increase rapidly, and we will continue to depend upon our mobiles as never before.

A mobile strategy can play a role in most any ad campaign, and it is critical to remember that mobile advertising should not be created in a silo, but be part of an integrated media campaign. It is important to take advantage of any and all mobile-specific capabilities that can extend the reach and breadth of a campaign, such as click-to-call; location and mapping abilities; free mobile content; mobile apps; and camera capabilities, for visual searches and interactive ads.

Mobile phones can be used in a variety of ways. A creative example is the mobile marketing campaign by Saatchi & Saatchi in Sydney for pro bono client the United Nations called "The UN Voices Project" in which you

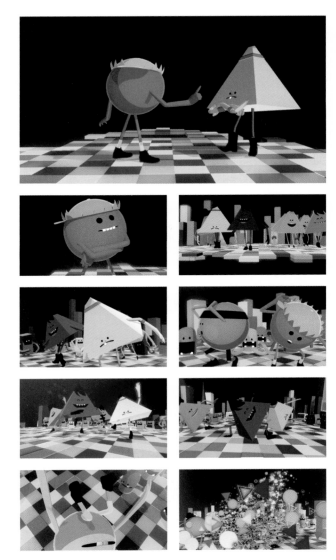

Figure 14-1

MOBILE MEDIA: SONY ERICSSON, "DANCE-OFF"

AGENCY: HUSH / BROOKLYN

Creative Directors: David Schwarz and Erik Karasyk

Lead Designer: Laura Alejo

Design: Jerry Liu

2D and 3D Animation: Joey Parks, Scott Denton, Steve Talkowski, Salih Abdul-Karim, and Jay Cohen

Editor: Amilcar Gomes

Sound Design: Antfood, Wilson Brown, Polly Hall, and Sean McGovern

Producer: Mei-Ling Wong

Production Asst: Melissa Chow

Client: Sony Ericsson

© HUSH Studios, Inc.

For the launch of Sony Ericsson's latest walkman phone, HUSH was asked to concept[ualize] and produce a slew of irreverent, music- and dance-driven animation and design content. In this piece, HUSH pursued a different take on the b-boy dance battle, using simplified, iconic characters, and crews composed of circles and triangles. The piece is a mix of retro music video clichés, 1980s dance subculture, and the in-your-face attitudes associated with the genre. In the end, however, the battle becomes less antagonistic and more Busby Berkeley—the crews fall in sync, performing choreographed moves that transform them into pure dance "energy."
—HUSH

CASE STUDY

Design and Production Company:
HUSH / Brooklyn, New York

Creative Directors: David
Schwarz and Erik Karasyk

Art Director: Darius Maghen

Design: Laura Alejo, Graham Hill,
and Wes Ebelhar

Executive Producer: Casey Steele

**Producer (live action and post
production):** Niabi Caldwell

Production Coordinators:
Michelle Ang and Melissa Chow

Storyboard Artist: Al Johnson

Director of Photography:
Zak Mulligan

Set Design and Art Direction:
Isaac Gabaeff

Stylist: Rich Munsen

2D Animation: Bryan Cobonpue,
Emmett Dzieza, Wes Ebelhar

3D Animation: Scott Denton

3D lighting and texture:
Matthew Wilson

Editor: Nathan Scholtens

Talent: Nina Wray, Esosa
Edosomwan, Eric Linn, Jasmine
Kooun, Mei-Ling Wong

Costume Design: Yvette Helin

Color Correct:
Stuart Levy at Post Works

Producer: JD Marlow

Sound Design and Score:
Antfood

Composers:
Wilson Brown and Polly Hall

Executive Producer:
Sean McGovern

Client: Sony Ericsson

Content Planners: Anderson King
and Emil Kantelius

© HUSH Studios, Inc.

Storyboard, Sony Ericsson "Big Screen"

Written, designed, and directed by HUSH, we responded to Sony Ericsson's desire to promote their new "big screen" phone with our own twisted vision. Thinking back now, it was a rather simple series of mental leaps: a big screen, a drive-in, a giant pissed-off robot, a teenage couple mid-make out, laser beam battles, and some final victorious tongue action. And that was just the opening short. We also delivered a slew of other goodies: video ringtones, demo movies, wallpapers, audio signatures—all part and parcel of SE's latest release.

—HUSH

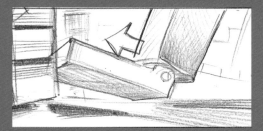

can actually listen to an outdoor poster and press advertisements via mobile phone technology. Saatchi.com explains:

People around Sydney are encouraged to take a mobile phone photo of the featured person's mouth and send it to a number on the poster as a text message. Then using digital image recognition technology and an Australian first call back service, the sender receives a return phone call with a pre-recorded message from the person they have photographed, giving a brief insight into how they live and highlighting some of the issues they face. The message then directs people to a UN website where visitors can leave their own comments and thoughts, turning the original seven voices into thousands.[1]

CONSIDERATIONS FOR MOBILE ADVERTISING

The mobile (or cell) phone provides the most private of all screens. People feel free to use their mobile device in ways that they would not consider on a social networking site. The mobile screen is an opportunity to create a more intimate brand relationship with someone.

Here is the R.U.L.E. for conceptualizing products and ideas for cell phones:

> *Make it Relevant to its audience.*

> *Make it Useful.*

> *Give it Legs (could work across the campaign).*

> *Make it Entertaining (games, programming).*

---

1. http://saatchi.com/news/archive/saatchi__saatchi_sydney_mobilises_voices_for_un

CASE STUDY

UrbanDaddy | The Next Move
iPhone Application

Web site: http://www.thenextmove.urbandaddy.com

Digital Agency: Big Spaceship / Brooklyn

The market is full of mobile apps designed to help you find the right bar, restaurant, or club. Most of these try to be everything to everyone. They're pragmatic. With The Next Move, Big Spaceship took a targeted, narrative-based approach. The application, created for UrbanDaddy (a lifestyle site for hip, upscale guys), is designed for guys who want to stay "in the know." In helping them forge the perfect plan, it tells the story of their day or evening to come.

The UrbanDaddy audience is hungry for this type of app. They want to keep up on all the latest hot spots, but they're also concerned with fashion and appearances. The agency addressed their desires with a tool that marries functionality with style, helping them decide on a destination and placing a premium on design. (Apple has even been featuring The Next Move in its television and print campaign.)

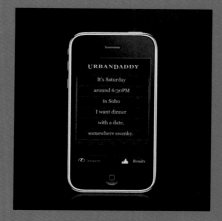

While developing their strategy, Big Spaceship adopted a holistic perspective, factoring in the *who, what,* and *where* of one's plans. The app considers whom you'll be with (e.g., your "ex"), what sort of food you're in the mood for (let's say, Asian cuisine), where you'll go after dinner (a place with good scotch), and so on. It reacts to an individual's specific needs. Choices unfold through interchangeable sentence fragments, revealing information in a personalized manner.

The Next Move targets six cities: New York, Los Angeles, San Francisco, Las Vegas, Chicago, and Miami. It detects the time and uses GPS sensors to pinpoint location, providing an array of selections that are nearby, open for business, and suitable to one's

needs. Once an establishment is selected, a map, phone number, and description are a click away. There's also a randomized option that lets the occasion unfold as it may.

One challenge the agency faced during the engagement was incorporating a paid automobile sponsorship into the application. They did so by building the vehicle (a new model convertible) into a lifestyle-oriented brand association, enhancing the sense of adventure inherent to UrbanDaddy. They also replicated the experience in a Web site that allows you to plan ahead, choosing up to four "moves" or locations to later visit. So whether you prefer to make arrangements in advance or make up your mind along the way, you've got practical, easy-to-access options.

—Big Spaceship

> *Relevant to the target audience*

> *Engaging to the audience (and definitely does not annoy them)*

> *Not disruptive and does not creep where it really shouldn't*

> *Ethical*

> *Interesting enough for the press to want to cover it*

> *Entertaining or interesting enough for people to share mobile photos, blog, and talk about it*

> *Engaging and flexible enough to be extended into other media or brand experiences*

Figure 15-5

UNCONVENTIONAL MEDIA:"WIEN IN MODE"

STUDIO: SAGMEISTER INC. / NEW YORK

Concept and Design: Stefan Sagmeister

Client: Museum of Modern Art, Vienna, Austria

> Relevant to the target audience

> Engaging to the audience (and definitely does not annoy them)

> Not disruptive and does not creep where it really shouldn't

> Ethical

> Interesting enough for the press to want to cover it

> Entertaining or interesting enough for people to share mobile photos, blog, and talk about it

> Engaging and flexible enough to be extended into other media or brand experiences

Figure 15-5

UNCONVENTIONAL MEDIA:"WIEN IN MODE"

STUDIO: SAGMEISTER INC. / NEW YORK

Concept and Design:
Stefan Sagmeister

Client: Museum of Modern Art, Vienna, Austria

We've been listening closely to what our customers have been telling us since 1984. We listen in person, by phone and, in 1995, we started Dell.com, realizing the long-term importance of the Internet for our direct business model. About 1.6 million customers visit us every day online and our teams do their best to understand what's on our customer's minds at all times.

[In 2005 and 2006]...The marketplace changed, global markets expanded and there was tremendous growth in the blogosphere. What's most important, in the long run, is how we learn from any situation and improve the customer experience. The reality is that my response to finding out about a customer's problem with our equipment is the same today as it was then—let's resolve our customer's issues as quickly as possible and let's learn from each opportunity and get better every time. . . . When you look at the world and see that the number of people online will double from 1 to 2 billion in a few years, it makes a compelling case for understanding where this growth is occurring and what it means. Our goal is to join the conversation and speak directly and candidly with our customers. The more we engage, the more we learn and the better we can do for our customers."*

Q: Tell your Dell story: How you use social media, technology, and advertising to connect and share your story.

At Dell social media is becoming part of how we do business and contributes to continuously making us better at it in ways that go beyond just sharing the Dell story. We believe the interactivity, using the social Web to connect with customers, is what we are all about as a company—direct relationships. Therefore, we hope by joining conversations and sharing more information about Dell in various forms (Slideshare, YouTube, Flickr, blogs, Twitter, Friendfeed, etc.), our customers can find and access the information they want from us...when and where they want. While that is partly about sharing the Dell story, it is also about various other aspects of the business, such as:

> *Understanding issues and changing business processes based on information and conversations in social media;*

> *Including more customers in opportunities to connect and meet with Dell people, furthering the relationship between customers and us;*

> *Identifying issues earlier than we would have previously, thanks to blog and social media commentary, and acting on them;*

> *Contributing to, and integrated into, Dell's product development. For example, the Ideastorm community where ideas have resulted in product changes.*

*. "SAP Global Survey: Michael Dell," *Global Neighbourhoods*, February 10, 2008, http://redcouch.typepad.com/weblog/2008/02/michael-dell-ph.html.

SHOWCASE

INTERVIEW WITH RICHARD BINHAMMER
SENIOR MANAGER AT DELL AND STRATEGIC CORPORATE COMMUNICATIONS, SOCIAL MEDIA AND CORPORATE REPUTATION MANAGEMENT

Richard Binhammer plans and implements strategic corporate communications to achieve business success and support/ build positive corporate reputations—currently helping lead Dell's digital media outreach and blog response. Richard has over twenty years of experience positioning diverse business sectors, senior corporate executives, government officials, and community leaders with key constituent groups, including extensive media relations and campaign/ issues management experience.

Q: What is Dell doing to connect the brand with people in what you call the "Connected Era"? Which media channels do you utilize and why?

Richard Binhammer: One billion people are now online—a figure that will double by 2011. In fact, every day 500,000 new users come online for the first time. Content is exploding. There was more content on YouTube in 2006 than on the Web in 2000. Facebook users alone have uploaded 15 billion photos. Rather than static Web sites that we view or read, the Internet has become the global information technology infrastructure that underpins a rich, interactive, and fully featured way to mash up video, text, and audio to communicate and connect.

This represents a significant shift in what we think of as media, or put another way, what [information people get] and how people get information. Taken together, we are experiencing changes to the dynamics of how people connect, interact, process information, and form opinions. People find information they want—when they want, as well as share that information and their own perspectives.

This change in, or addition to, how people connect and converse results in new communities, people's own communities, sharing information in ways they care about and in a manner that makes sense to them. Therefore, it is about something more than "media channels" per se. It's more about

understanding that these conversations are going on all around us and that any business can listen, learn, and participate in the conversation—wherever it is and wherever it may take you. Rather than think about a media channel, we think in terms of what are people talking about, where are they sharing information, and how can we listen, learn, and engage in a way that constantly makes Dell a better business, while also enhancing our direct customer connections.

As a result you will find Dell across the Web, often in different places doing different things. A few examples: on Facebook Dell offers small business tips for using social media as a business tool; on Twitter we offer customers ways to find special offers—they can subscribe to Dell information or interact with Dell people about all aspects of the business; Dell's techcenter is a place for information technology (IT) pros to interact and address complex data center solutions for their businesses; and blog posts around the Web will often get a response or follow up from us.

Q: How did you start the Dell conversation with its customers?

I think I will reference a Michael Dell interview to answer this, as it was Michael who said to the team, "our customers interact every day all around the Web, why are we not part of those conversations with our customers?"

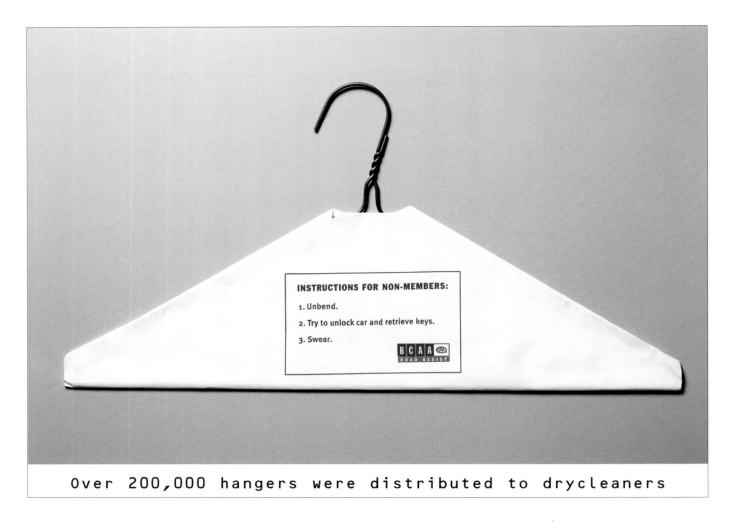

INSTRUCTIONS FOR NON-MEMBERS:

1. Unbend.

2. Try to unlock car and retrieve keys.

3. Swear.

BCAA
ROAD ASSIST

Over 200,000 hangers were distributed to drycleaners

to convey the benefit of belonging to the BCAA road assistance program (figure 15-4). Unconventional marketing is used in mostly unpaid media spaces. It can be anything from living and breathing actors, as street teams or stunt performers, to projections on walls.

Unconventional advertising can make people notice—that is, it can break through to consumers in ways that traditional ads don't or can't, and it might garner free publicity from the news media, as did "Wien in Mode" by Sagmeister Inc. for the Museum of Modern Art in Vienna (figure 15-5). Sagmeister comments: "'Wien in Mode' is a fashion show held yearly in the Museum of Modern Art in Vienna. The concept was to

dress up the regular Viennese advertising kiosks with actual fabric. The public relations company responsible for booking the kiosk space for the posters messed up, and eight weeks before the show we found ourselves with no outdoor advertising space . . . We simply built our own kiosks out of aluminum, polyester, and fabric; put them on wheels; and hired students to 'drive' them around the pedestrian zones."

Make sure the brand experience is:

> *In keeping with the brand or group's larger strategy and campaign*

> *In keeping with the brand or group's larger storytelling effort*

Figure 15-4

UNCONVENTIONAL MEDIA: "HANGER"

AGENCY:
RETHINK ADVERTISING
/ VANCOUVER, BRITISH
COLUMBIA

Art Directors:
Ian Grais and Martin Kann

Copywriter: Heather Vincent

Client: BCAA

> *There were more than 193 million site visits, and 123 million elves were created.*

> *More than 210 million elf dances were viewed.*

> *Sixty elves were created per second.*

> *Users spent a combined 2,600 years on the site.*

UNCONVENTIONAL ADVERTISING

Print, television commercials, radio, and out of home are considered traditional advertising because of how and where they are seen and heard. Since the public recognizes traditional advertising and expects advertising to interrupt television programming and to permeate magazine articles, many have learned to tune it out. With people watching less television, with more channels to watch splintering audiences while they hold remote controls, with digital video recorders (DVRs) allowing people to skip commercials, and with people spending more time gaming or online, television commercials are no longer the unfailing message carriers they once were.

Unconventional advertising "ambushes" the public, it appears in public or private environments—places and surfaces where advertising does not usually live, such as on the sidewalk or at the bottom of golf holes. This is also called guerrilla advertising or stealth, ambient, or nontraditional marketing.

Ambient Advertising

Using existing structures in public spaces—such as bus shelters, lampposts, fire hydrants, corners of buildings, parking spaces, or staircases—ambient advertising gets under people's ad radar to surprise them.

Effective unconventional solutions have been shown to successfully promote brands or groups in breakthrough ways that live beyond their media space; such as the use of a staircase in this ambient campaign by Forsman & Bodenfors (see figure 15-3).

CONSIDERATIONS FOR UNCONVENTIONAL ADVERTISING

There are basic questions to ask when you create unconventional advertising:

> *What is the goal? Why would you employ unconventional marketing rather than conventional or screen media?*

> *What will the audience get out of it? Something worthwhile?*

> *Since unconventional advertising intrudes into nonpaid media space, will it be more beneficial than annoying?*

Often, clients and agencies turn to unconventional marketing when the budget is too low for television or for rich Web solutions. The underpinning hope is that a terrific unconventional solution will garner free attention from the press.

What can you offer people? A variety of utilities have been branded and offered to people for free. For example, free charging stations in airport terminals (Samsung) or a free clean bathroom in Times Square (Charmin).

Context is important, as it is in all advertising and marketing. Playing off the hanger as a tool that people use to retrieve keys locked inside their cars, Rethink distributed over two hundred thousand British Columbia Automobile Association (BCAA) hangers to dry cleaners, using this novel approach

The content must hit us where we live. It must hit a nerve, prompting us to think: yeah, that's how I feel, that's what I think—my friend Joe or Aunt Jane might relate to this too.

The content could make us feel altruistic—we think our friends would benefit from what we find compelling.

Finally, and most critically, we must be able to personalize the content. If we can interact with it, put our own stamp on it, we are engaged. The Elf Yourself campaign (figure 4-2), for example, was personally engaging and the campaign results were impressive:

> *ElfYourself.com became a holiday destination in 2007 and from November 20, 2007 to January 2, 2008.*

Figure 15-3

AMBIENT: PAPERBOY RECRUITMENT CAMPAIGN

AGENCY: FORSMAN & BODENFORS / GOTHENBURG, SWEDEN

Art Directors: Staffan Forsman and Staffan Hœkanson

Copywriters: Björn Engström and Martin Ringqvist

Photographer: Henrik Ottosson

Client: Göteborgs-Posten

Want to work as a paperboy? This unconventional campaign allows you to try the job on for size.

Generated a record **6 million +** consumer engagements

3200 entries posted on over **8000 URLs**
including MySpace, Facebook, Xanga, LiveJournal and myYearbook

Winning design

Sample consumer designs

To view all entries go to www.brickfish.com/coachtote

Figure 15-2

SOCIAL MEDIA CAMPAIGN: "DESIGN A COACH TOTE" COMPETITION

AGENCY: BRICKFISH

Client: 2009 Coach, Inc.

© Coach, Inc.

Overview of Program: *As part of an ongoing initiative to target the youth demographic, Coach partnered with the award-winning social media–distribution platform, Brickfish, to launch an online social media campaign entitled "Design a Coach Tote." This campaign, with a focus on viral marketing and user-generated content, asked online users to put their artful stamp on their versions of the perfect Coach tote. The winning tote design was produced as a special edition item and sold in select Coach locations across the country. The campaign was promoted on the Brickfish.com site, through an iFrame on the Coach site, and through intensive public relations (PR) efforts targeting online fashion blogs.*

Results: In just six weeks, the Coach campaign generated over 3,200 entries and a record 6 million+ consumer engagements on over 8,000 URLs, including Facebook, MySpace, Xanga, LiveJournal, hi5, and more. Each campaign participant engaged over 20 times and spent an average of 8.5 minutes with the brand. The campaign also added over 7,000 e-mails to the Coach customer database. This unique campaign successfully encouraged younger consumers to interact with the brand, built awareness and buzz, and created endless viral sharing of branded content consumers had designed.

"The 'Design a Coach Tote' campaign was an exciting chance for us to both partner with Brickfish and connect with our younger customers across the Internet," said David Duplantis, senior vice president of Global Web & Digital Media for Coach. "The creativity and innovation of the entries was amazing and we were delighted to have inspired so many fans of the brand to participate. We have since partnered with Brickfish on yet another successful campaign tied to our new Poppy collection, and will continually support them as innovators in the social media marketing space."

—Coach

a party, to chocolate, or to anything that the audience would find pleasing.

Shareable: it enables sharing, sending, downloading, and linking, and uses standard protocols.

VIRAL INTENT

Online marketing goes viral when people are infected by it (like a viral infection), and they spread it to others. To become infected, people have to *like the content* enough to share it; they must be engaged by it and want to pass it on to friends and family. What type of content do people usually find engaging?

The content must be entertaining. If we find it humorous, uplifting, touching, zany, surprising—something that moves us—we will forward it to our friends.

▸ Figure 15-1

**INTERACTIVE PLATFORM:
"HAPPY IT'S HERE \ WHISPER"**

AGENCY: ARC WORLDWIDE
/ SINGAPORE

Creative Director:
Valerie Cheng

Art Director: Yeo Yenyen

Designers: Belinda Lu,
Celeste Ang, and Ivan Yeh

Copywriter: Lynn Chiam

Illustrator: Sokkuan

Account Directors:
Sue Mulhall and Jorida Ong

Account Manager:
Jacinta Francis

Managing Director:
Nick Handel

Project Manager: Justin Ong

Based on research showing that few women were able to identify the effects of changing hormones during a menstrual cycle on their minds and bodies, this campaign provides an educational yet cheery experience where women can learn and share.

The interactive platform is linked to Whisper's Facebook group and allows visitors to compliment their girl friends via the 'Happy Apps'. Wallpaper downloads and animated icons are also available to cheer up people everyday.

Source: "Whisper | Happy It's Here | Singapore," *Media.Asia*, August 21, 2009, http://www.media.asia/The-Workarticle/2009_08/Whisper--Happy-Its-Here--Singapore/36709 (accessed March 31 2010).

CONSIDERATIONS FOR SOCIAL MEDIA

Social media is most effective when it is relevant, authentic, valuable, enticing, and shareable (RAVES):

Relevant: it demonstrates an understanding of its target audience based on insights into the audience, brand, or group, and the product, service, or group category (figure 15-2).

Authentic: it lives up to its brand essence, claims, and values, and does not lie or offer half-truths.

Valuable: it offers something of value to the audience (a utility, information, entertainment, laughs, or knowledge), which in turn helps the brand or group grow.

Enticing: it offers something unique, sought after, or cool, something people cannot get elsewhere—an equivalent to

15 DESIGNING FOR SOCIAL MEDIA AND UNCONVENTIONAL MARKETING

Social media can be described, informally, as all the conversations people are having online. It offers brands and groups the opportunity to talk to people . . . as well as *listen!*

People go online for a reason, whether practical, social, or for diversion. When a brand or group hampers someone's pursuit, it is not good for anyone. When a brand enhances or helps someone's online experience, that is called smart marketing. To the surprise of many, people become brand fans when they can relate to what a brand or group is doing in *their* social space. People do not relate to a brand represented by just another ad interjected into their Web space. There has to be something engaging, something utilitarian, something fun. For example, the Wisk-It application for Facebook, from the makers of Wisk detergent, "lets you identify the pictures you'd like the friend to remove, and then send a request her way. When the friend installs Wisk-It, it

pulls up the offending photos and asks her to delete them."

"Currently, there's really no easy way or efficient way to remove pictures, so we're finding that we have cracked the efficient way to clean up your online profile," said Elisa Gurevich, brand manager for Wisk, owned by the Sun Products Corporation.

"We thought perhaps we could take our stain-fighting heritage, and take it online to Facebook," Ms. Gurevich said.[1]

How do you get people to spend their time with you? Offer them something of interest, as in figure 15-1. "Deep down, women are thankful each time their period arrives, as it's the sign of a healthy, functioning body," said Valerie Cheng, creative director of Arc Worldwide Singapore. "We hope to intrigue them, and initiate an open conversation and a new movement that will lead to a renewed sense of appreciation of their female cycle."

---

1. Stephanie Clifford, "An Application to Help Scrub Those Regrettable Photos from Facebook," *New York Times*, 2 November 2009.

CASE STUDY

UrbanDaddy | The Next Move iPhone Application

Web site: http://www.thenextmove.urbandaddy.com

Digital Agency: Big Spaceship / Brooklyn

The market is full of mobile apps designed to help you find the right bar, restaurant, or club. Most of these try to be everything to everyone. They're pragmatic. With The Next Move, Big Spaceship took a targeted, narrative-based approach. The application, created for UrbanDaddy (a lifestyle site for hip, upscale guys), is designed for guys who want to stay "in the know." In helping them forge the perfect plan, it tells the story of their day or evening to come.

The UrbanDaddy audience is hungry for this type of app. They want to keep up on all the latest hot spots, but they're also concerned with fashion and appearances. The agency addressed their desires with a tool that marries functionality with style, helping them decide on a destination and placing a premium on design. (Apple has even been featuring The Next Move in its television and print campaign.)

While developing their strategy, Big Spaceship adopted a holistic perspective, factoring in the *who, what,* and *where* of one's plans. The app considers whom you'll be with (e.g., your "ex"), what sort of food you're in the mood for (let's say, Asian cuisine), where you'll go after dinner (a place with good scotch), and so on. It reacts to an individual's specific needs. Choices unfold through interchangeable sentence fragments, revealing information in a personalized manner.

The Next Move targets six cities: New York, Los Angeles, San Francisco, Las Vegas, Chicago, and Miami. It detects the time and uses GPS sensors to pinpoint location, providing an array of selections that are nearby, open for business, and suitable to one's

needs. Once an establishment is selected, a map, phone number, and description are a click away. There's also a randomized option that lets the occasion unfold as it may.

One challenge the agency faced during the engagement was incorporating a paid automobile sponsorship into the application. They did so by building the vehicle (a new model convertible) into a lifestyle-oriented brand association, enhancing the sense of adventure inherent to UrbanDaddy. They also replicated the experience in a Web site that allows you to plan ahead, choosing up to four "moves" or locations to later visit. So whether you prefer to make arrangements in advance or make up your mind along the way, you've got practical, easy-to-access options.

—Big Spaceship

CASE STUDY

Panasonic "Share the Air" Campaign

Agency: Renegade / New York

The Challenge: Position Panasonic products as the perfect accompaniment to the action sports lifestyle.

Target Insight: Action sports fans are all about creative expression, social connectivity, and community experience.

The Program: Panasonic "Share the Air" is a fully immersive off-line and online experience that invites attendees to play with Panasonic and get inside Ryan Sheckler's head. Off-line, the Panasonic "Share the Air" Village provided multiple interactive experiences, like the 103-inch plasma TV room that lets you see and feel the eye-popping power of the world's largest plasma, and an interactive instant-win game where everyone was a winner. Panasonic also provided a camera loaner program, where fans could spend the day capturing the coolest Dew Tour tricks themselves. Participants were given the Secure Digital (SD) card inside the cameras so they could take their pics home and load them on Sharetheair.net to continue the experience. Ryan fans could also take a tour through a re-creation of Ryan's room, listening to his favorite playlists and taking the "Do You Know Ryan?" interactive test to find out just how much they know about the two-time Dew Tour skate champion.

Renegade extended Share the Air online, with Sharetheair.net, a destination site for the action sports community. Besides being a portal into all things Ryan, including his favorite musical artists, Sharetheair.net also allowed visitors to get involved through a photo blog featuring five of the best Dew Tour athletes, behind the scenes news from the skate community, and videos of the latest tricks. The site also let aspiring photographers and videographers share their photos and videos for

a chance to win amazing prizes, ranging from cameras to a $10,000 HD video package.

The Results: Now in its third year, Panasonic continues to engage thousands of consumers at each stop of the Dew Tour, driving retail and on-premise sales, and converting action sports enthusiasts into Panasonic evangelists.

—Renegade

Executive Creative Director:
Drew Neisser

Creative Director: Fanny Krivoy

Associate Creative Director:
Alan Irikura

© Renegade.com

GLOSSARY

abstraction: a simple or complex rearrangement, alteration, or distortion of the representation of natural appearance, used for stylistic distinction and/or communication purposes.

adoption: appropriating another form of visual art, such as fine art, or another form of artistic work, such as a children's book.

Ad Council: an organization that identifies "a select number of significant public issues and stimulates action on those issues through communications programs that make a measurable difference in our society. To that end, the Ad Council marshals volunteer talent from the advertising and communications industries, the facilities of the media, and the resources of the business and nonprofit communities to create awareness, foster understanding, and motivate action."—www.adcouncil.org

advertisement (ad): a specific message constructed to inform, persuade, promote, provoke, or motivate people on behalf of a brand or group.

advertising: the generation and creation of specific visual and verbal messages constructed to inform, persuade, promote, provoke, or motivate people on behalf of a brand or group.

advertising agency: a business that provides clients with creative, marketing, and other business services related to planning, creating, producing, and placing advertisements.

advertising campaign: a series of coordinated ads—in one or more media—that are based on a single, overarching strategy or theme, and each individual ad in the campaign can stand on its own.

advertising idea: the creative conceptual solution to an advertising problem—a strategic formulated thought that communicates a message, calling people to action.

airings: aired (deployed) advertising solutions in various media, such as broadcast, broadband, environmental, and mobile.

alignment: the positioning of visual elements relative to one another so that their edges or axes line up.

ambient: advertising that uses existing structures in the environment to create messages.

analysis: a phase in the design process, examining all information unearthed in the orientation phase to best understand, assess, strategize, and move forward with the assignment.

animation: a moving image consisting of a series of drawn, painted, or modeled scenes. In advertising, animation can be thought of as a method or technique of visualizing an idea.

application: an advertising format or vehicle, such as a TV commercial or print magazine consumer ad.

art director: the creative professional in an advertising agency responsible for ideation, art direction (overall look and feel, visual style, selection of photographer or illustrator), and design.

assemblage: a work created by combining and composing a collection of different objects.

asymmetry: an equal distribution of visual weights achieved through weight and counterweight, by balancing one element with the weight of a counterpointing element, without mirroring elements on either side of a central axis.

attribute: a defining property or characteristic.

attribute listing: a method for analyzing and separating data through observing and identifying various qualities that might have otherwise been overlooked; a diagrammed list of attributes.

audience: any individual or group on the receiving end of a graphic design or advertising solution; the target audience is a specific targeted group of people.

balance: stability or equilibrium created by an even distribution of visual weight on each side of a central axis, as well as by an even distribution of weight among all the elements of the composition.

benefit: the useful or emotional characteristics of a product or service.

billboard: a very large board, usually by the roadside or attached to a building, used for displaying advertising; also called outdoor board.

bleed or **full bleed**: a printing term referring to type or a visual that extends off the edges of the page, filling the page with an image.

body copy: narrative text that further explains, supplements, and supports the main advertising concept and message; type that is 14 points and less is used for setting text, also called text type.

borders: a graphic band that runs along the edge of an image, acting to separate the image from the background, by something as simple as a thin rule or as ornate as a Baroque frame.

brainstorming: a technique to generate ideas that could be solutions to advertising problems.

brand: the sum total of all functional (tangible) and emotional (intangible) assets that differentiate a product, company, or group from the competition.

brand icon: a recurring character used to represent a brand or group, which can be an actor, a proprietary illustrated character, or a cartoon or animation.

brand name: the main verbal identifier and differentiator for a product, service, or group.

brand strategy: the core tactical underpinning of branding, uniting all planning for every visual and verbal application.

branded entertainment: content-marketing, vehicles for brands for and across media, including broadcast TV and radio, motion pictures, broadband content, social networks, gaming, and mobile.

branded utility: a utility—a useful brand experience—in any form, from books to Web sites to mobile phone applications.

branding: the entire development process of creating a brand, brand name, and visual identity, among other applications.

broadband: transmission of mass media messages across broadband channels, such as the Internet.

broadcast: transmission of mass media messages on television and radio.

capitals: the larger set of letters, also called uppercase.

cartoon: a single panel pictorial sketch or a sequence of drawings that tells a very short story or comments on a topical event or theme.

cause advertising: advertising that raises funds for nonprofit organizations and runs in paid media sites. It is generally affiliated with a corporation and is used in part to promote a corporation's public persona or brand, unlike public service advertising where there is no commercial affiliation.

chronology: the order of events.

chunking: related to modularity in graphic design, content is split or information is grouped into chunks by combining units or capsules of content or information into a limited number of units or chunks.

closure: the mind's tendency to connect individual elements to produce a completed form, unit, or pattern.

collage: a visual created by cutting and pasting bits or pieces of paper, photographs, cloth, or any material to a two-dimensional surface, which can be combined with handmade visuals and colors.

column intervals: spaces between columns.

columns: vertical alignments or arrangements used to accommodate text and images.

commercial: a broadcast or broadband advertisement placed in paid media, such as television, radio, or the Web.

commercial advertising: advertising that promotes brands and commodities by informing consumers; also used to promote individuals and groups, including corporations and manufacturers.

common fate: the idea that elements are likely to be perceived as a unit if they move in the same direction.

comp or **comprehensive**: a detailed representation of a design concept thoughtfully visualized and composed.

comparison: a format compares and contrasts one brand either in relation to a competing brand (or two brands) or to the entire product or service category in order to discover the differences between them and ultimately claim that the brand being advertised is superior.

composition: the form, the whole spatial property and structure resulting from the intentional visualization and arrangement of graphic elements—type and visuals—in relation to one another and to the format, meant to visually communicate and to be compelling and expressive.

concept or **design concept**: the creative thinking underpinning the design solution. The concept is expressed through the integration and manipulation of visual and verbal elements; also called **idea**.

construct: a quality or position a brand "owns" against the composition.

consumer-generated content: content generated by consumers; handing over creation of content to consumers.

containment: the idea that separate elements are most easily perceived as a unit when placed in an enclosed area.

content: the body of information that is available to visitors on a Web site, mobile phone, public screen, and consumer electronic devices.

continuing line: the idea that lines are always perceived as following the simplest path. If two lines break, the viewer perceives the overall movement rather than the break; also called implied line.

continuity: the idea that elements that appear to be a continuation of previous elements are perceived as linked, creating an impression of movement. *Continuity* also means the handling of design elements, like line, shape, texture, and color, to create similarities of form; it is used to create family resemblance.

copywriter: the creative professional in an advertising agency responsible for ideation and writing.

correspondence: a visual connection established when an element, such as color, direction, value, shape, or texture, is repeated, or when style is utilized as a method of connecting visual elements, for example, a linear style.

creative approach: a master general structure, a mode or method of presentation, an underlying schema or framework.

creative brief: a written document outlining and strategizing an advertising or graphic design project; also called a design brief.

creative director: the top-level creative professional in an advertising agency (or design studio) with ultimate creative control over art direction and copy; usually the supervisor of the creative team who makes the final decisions about the idea, creative approach, art direction, and copywriting before the work is presented to the client.

creative team: in an advertising agency, a conventional creative team includes an art director and a copywriter. Interdiscinplinary creative teams may include an account manager, an information technology (IT) expert, an interactive designer, and a marketing expert, among others.

critique: an assessment or evaluation of work.

cropping: the act of cutting a visual, a photograph, or an illustration in order to use only part of it.

demographic: selected population characteristics.

demonstration: a display of how the product or service works or functions, usually providing evidence or proof to the brand's soundness.

differentiation: distinguishing a brand from others by how it is characterized in terms of its visual and verbal identity; by each media unit; and by the nature of every user experience. Simply stated, differentiation is what makes a brand different from the rest.

diffusion: characterized by blurred forms and boundaries, transparencies, muted color palettes, layering, open compositions, and painterliness.

documentary: in visual communication, a presentation of facts and information, usually about a social, historical, or political cause.

drama: in advertising, an ad, still or in motion in any media, intended to portray life or to tell a short story, usually involving conflicts and emotions.

economy: using visuals stripped to fundamental forms, using as little description and few details as possible for denotation.

emotional benefit: an asset based on feelings and responses, not on a functional characteristic of a product or service.

emphasis: the arrangement of visual elements, stressing or giving importance to some visual elements, thereby allowing two actions: information to be easily gleaned and the graphic design to be easily received.

endorsement: a public statement of approval for a product or service; it can include verbal statements or depictions of the name, signature, likeness or other identifying personal characteristics of an individual or the name or seal of an organization.

environmental branded utility: useful services that become part of people's daily lives, where a brand sponsors a handy service, such as a sponsored space.

execution: the fulfillment of the concept through physical processes that include the selection and manipulation of materials and/or software.

expressionistic: characterized by a highly stylized or subjective interpretation, with an emphasis on the psychological or spiritual meaning; expressionism has no strict adherence to things as they appear in nature, as opposed to naturalism.

figure: a definite shape; also called a positive shape.

figure/ground: a basic principle of visual perception that refers to the relationship of shapes—of figure to ground—on a two-dimensional surface: also called **positive and negative** space.

flow: elements arranged in a design so that the viewer's eyes are led from one element to another, through the design; also called movement.

focal point: the part of a design that is most emphasized.

formal elements: fundamental elements of two-dimensional design: line, shape, color, value, and texture.

format: the defined perimeter as well as the field it encloses—the outer edges or boundaries of a design; in actuality, it is the field or substrate (piece of paper, mobile phone screen, outdoor board, etc.) for the graphic or advertising design.

fractured space: multiple viewpoints seen simultaneously, as in cubist style of fine art.

frame: a single static image, one of many composed together to create motion graphics; the illusion of motion is created when we see a series of frames in rapid succession.

framing: conceptual structures that characterize meaning, the meaning of an argument, the meaning of a situation.

full-service agencies: businesses that offer a full range of business and creative services related to the advertising process, including planning, creative ideation and design, production, implementation, and placement.

functional benefit: the practical or useful characteristic of a product or service that aids in distinguishing a brand from its competition.

graphic design: a form of visual communication used to convey a message or information to an audience; a visual representation of an idea relying on the creation, selection, and organization of visual elements.

graphic interpretation: an elemental visualization of an object or subject, almost resembling a sign, pictogram, or symbol in its reductive representation.

graphic organizer: a visual aid used to illustrate the relationships among facts or ideas, similar in purpose to a mind map; it is a visual way to picture information, which facilitates seeing previously unrealized significant connections.

grid: a modular compositional structure made up of verticals and horizontals that divide a format into columns and margins. It may be used for single-page or multipage formats.

ground: shapes or areas created between and among figures; also called negative space.

grouping: perceiving visual units by location, orientation, likeness, shape, and color.

gutter: the blank space formed by the inner margins of two facing pages in a publication.

harmony: agreement within a composition, where elements are constructed, arranged, and function in relation to one another to an agreeable effect.

headline: the main verbal message in an advertisement (although it literally refers to the main line of copy that appears at the head of the page); also called the line.

high contrast: a wide range of values.

home page: the primary entrance to a Web site that contains the central navigation system.

icon: a generally accepted (pictorial or symbolic) visual to represent objects, actions, and concepts; an icon resembles the thing it represents or at minimum shares a quality with it—it can be a photograph, a pictorial representation, an elemental visual (think magnifying glass desktop icon), arbitrary (think radioactive sign), or symbolic (think lightning bolt to represent electricity).

idea: the creative thinking underpinning the design solution. The idea is expressed through the integration and manipulation of visual and verbal elements; also called **concept or design concept**.

ideas: phase 3 in the design process, conceptual development.

illusion of spatial depth: the appearance of three-dimensional space on a two-dimensional surface.

illustration: a visual rendering that accompanies or complements printed, digital, or spoken text to clarify, enhance, illuminate, or demonstrate the message of the text.

implementation: phase 6 of the design process, where solutions are deployed, aired, and put into effect.

independent agencies: privately owned ad agencies, usually small; they often attract clients who prefer to work directly with the principals of an agency. Sometimes referred to as boutique agencies.

index: a visual that directs the attention of the interpreter (viewer) without describing or resembling the thing signified due to its neighboring relationship to it.

information architecture: the careful organization of Web site content into hierarchical (or sequential) order.

in-game advertising: ads embedded into games, such as product placement or live billboard feeds.

in-house agencies: companies that own and create their own advertising

integrated branding program: a comprehensive, strategic, unified, integrated, and unique program for a brand, with an eye and mind toward how people experience—interact and use—the brand or group.

interactive: graphic design and advertising for screen-based media; also called experience design.

interactive agencies: ad agencies that focus on screen media; also called digital agencies.

intricacy: complexity; using many component parts and/or details to describe and visually communicate.

kiosk: in advertising, a small structure used to post an advertisement or interactive brand experience.

leading: in metal type, strips of lead of varying thickness (measured in points) used to increase the space between lines of type; also known as **line spacing**.

lecture: in advertising, a product or service is featured by discussing it; a brand is presented for your consideration, typified with a presentation.

letterspacing: spatial interval between letters.

light and shadow: employed to describe form; most closely simulates how we perceive forms in nature.

line spacing: the spatial interval between two lines of type; also known as **leading**.

line type: refers to the way a line moves from its beginning to its end; a line attribute.

linear: using line as the predominant element to unify a composition or to describe shapes or forms in a design.

link: on a Web page, a connection from one location to another location or from one Web site to another Web site; also called a hyperlink.

logo: a unique identifying symbol that represents and embodies everything a brand or company signifies. It provides immediate recognition; also called a brand mark, mark, identifier, logotype, or trademark.

margins: the blank space on the left, right, top, or bottom edge of any printed or digital page.

media: various means of mass communication, such as television, newspapers, World Wide Web, mobile.

microsite: a sub–Web site, usually thematic.

mind map: a visual representation, diagram, or presentation of the various ways words, terms, images, thoughts, or ideas can be related to one another.

misdirection: a technique in which an ad starts out one way and then suddenly changes direction. Thinking the TV commercial is about one thing, viewers are surprised by the real message.

mixed media: a visual resulting from the use of different media, for example, photography combined with illustration.

mobile: transmission of mass media messages across cellular networks.

mobile apps: packaged software suitable for use on portable media, usually cellular.

mockumentary: a spoof created or shot in the style of a documentary; from *mock* + (doc)*umentary*.

modularity: a structural principle used to manage content using modules.

module: any single fixed element within a bigger system or structure, for example, a unit on graph paper, a pixel in a digital image, a rectangular unit in a grid system, or a fixed encapsulated chunk of a composition.

montage: the assembling of various pieces of short clips or images into a sequence, usually married by look and feel or theme, music, or voice-over narration.

morphological method: an analysis of a problem by defining all of the important factors, or parameters, as well as options. Then you synthesize—combine the factors and options to produce a matrix containing possible solutions.

motion aesthetics: the process and consideration of how form creates impact over time in a design.

motion graphics: time-based visual communication that integrates visuals, typography, and audio; created using film, video, and computer software; includes animation, television commercials, film titles, promotional, and informational applications for broadcast media, broadband and mobile media, or any screen.

musical: in advertising, a narrative or play that is music-based and where music, singing, and/or dancing are the main vehicles for telling the story.

naturalistic: in visual communication, characterized by full-color or tone using light and shadow that attempts to replicate an object or subject as it is perceived in nature; also called realistic.

navigation system: the visual design of information architecture on a Web site.

nonobjective: characterized by purely invented visuals, not derived from anything visually perceived; it does not relate to any object in nature and does not literally represent a person, place, or thing; also called nonrepresentational.

notation: a linear, reductive visual that captures the essence of its subject, characterized by its minimalism.

opaque: dense, solid seeming, not see-through.

out-of-home: advertising that is placed outdoors in paid media, such as digital outdoor screens, billboards, bus shelters, buses and taxis, and in malls, airports, subways, and at sports stadiums and arenas; also called OOH or outdoor media.

overview: phase 1 in the design process, an orientation—the process of becoming familiar with an assignment, the advertising or graphic design problem, and the client's business or organization, product, service, or group.

ownership: differentiates a brand or group by "owning" a selling point, benefit, attitude, or any characteristic that contributes to a distinct construct.

parity products: products that are equivalent in value.

participation: in advertising, when the audience takes an active role in the marketing message.

photography: a visual created using a camera to capture or record an image.

photomontage: a composite visual made up of a number of photographs or parts of photographs to form a unique image.

pictograph: an elemental, universal picture denoting an object, activity, place, or person, captured through shape; for example, the images denoting gender on bathroom doors.

picture plane: the blank, flat surface of a page.

plane: a two-dimensional surface bound by lines that define the outside of a form; it has length and breadth, position and direction, but no thickness.

platform: a branded proprietary utility, owned media.

pod busters: very short-form content—called bitcoms, minisodes, microseries, and customized spots—created to complement the TV program *and* commercials; they contain sponsor messages, and they interrupt the commercials that interrupt shows.

portfolio: a body of work used by the visual communication profession as the measure of one's professional ability.

positive and negative: a basic principle of visual perception that refers to the relationship of shapes—of figure to ground—on a two-dimensional surface; also called **figure/ground**.

problem finding: the process of sketching or making marks that allows visual thinking and discovery as well as opening the mind to possibilities during the visual-making process; this is also called problem seeking.

problem / solution: in advertising, the product, service, or group successfully solves an actual problem.

product placement: embedding brands into television or Web programs in order to bank on the program's cachet, hoping the viewer will associate the brand with the characters in the show. Brands are also embedded into games and novels.

production: phase 5 in the design process, producing advertising solutions for various media.

proportion: the comparative size relationships of parts to one another and to the whole.

proximity: closeness; elements near each other, in spatial proximity, are perceived as belonging together.

public service advertising (PSA): advertising that serves the public interest.

repetition: occurs when one or a few visual elements are repeated a number times or with great or total consistency.

rhythm: a pattern that is created by repeating or varying elements, with consideration to the space between them, and by establishing a sense of movement from one element to another.

rhythmic relationships: connections that can be created in screen-based media through the duration of each shot, and in print or screen-based media through the interaction of visuals with contrast and variation.

roughs: sketches that are larger and more refined than thumbnail sketches and show the basic graphic components in a design.

scale: the size of an element or form seen in relation to other elements or forms within the format.

shape: the general outline of something.

sharpness: characterized by clarity of form, detail, clean and clear edges and boundaries, saturated color, readable and legible typography, proximate vision, hyperrealism, photorealism, closed compositions, and limited type alignment.

sign: a visual mark or a part of language that denotes another thing.

sign-off: material at the bottom of an ad that includes the brand's or group's logo, a photograph or illustration of the brand, or both.

silhouette: the articulated shape of an object or subject taking its specificity into account (as opposed to the universal visual language of a pictograph).

similarity: likeness; like elements—those that share characteristics—are perceived as belonging together. Elements can share likeness in shape, texture, color, and direction. Dissimilar elements tend to separate from like elements.

slice-of-life format: in advertising, a drama showing a realistic portrayal of life, featuring everyday situations to which average people can readily relate.

social media: media channels that allow people to connect and converse online in communities

spatial relationships: the distance between the thing seen in relation to the viewer, how far/how close, and the shifts between near and far.

spatial zones: regions formed by grouping several grid modules in order to organize the placement of various graphic components.

splash page: the first screen a visitor sees on a Web site; it serves as an introduction to the site and usually features animation or an engaging visual.

spokes-character: a recurring character used to represent a brand or group; can be an actor, a proprietary illustrated character, or a cartoon or animation; also referred to as a **brand icon**.

spokesperson: an individual—an average person, actor, model, or other celebrity who positively represents the product, service, or group; becomes the face and voice of that brand or group.

sponsorship: a deal in which a company (or brand) subsidizes radio, television, broadband, or mobile programming.

storyboard: a chart that illustrates and narrates key frames of a television advertising concept.

strategy: the core tactical underpinning of any visual communication, unifying all planning for every visual and verbal application within a program of applications.

strategic brand alliances: deals between companies to create a unique branded utility or branded experience.

storytelling: a narrative format where a tale is told to an audience using voice, gesture, and/or imagery; used in advertising to create a brand personality or a narrative in a commercial.

style: the qualities or characteristics that make something distinctive.

symbol: a visual having an arbitrary or conventional relationship between the signifier and the thing signified.

symmetry: mirroring of equivalent elements, an equal distribution of visual weights, on either side of a central axis; also called reflection symmetry.

tagline: a catchphrase that conveys the brand benefit or spirit and generally acts as an umbrella theme or strategy for a campaign or a series of campaigns; also called a claim, end line, strap line, or slogan.

target audience: a specific targeted group of people.

taxi topper: print advertising messages on top of taxis.

template: a compositional structure with designated positions for the visual elements.

temporal relationship: in screen-based media, the relationship or interplay between two separate events or images; this involves chronology.

testimonial: a favorable message delivered by an expert, the gal or guy next door, or a celebrity (purportedly) reflecting his or her opinions, beliefs, findings, or experiences in support of the sponsoring advertiser.

thumbnail sketches: preliminary, small, quick, unrefined drawings of ideas in black and white or color.

transparent: see-through from one image to another, from one letterform to another, from one texture to another.

trompe l'oeil: literally, "to fool the eye"; a visual effect on a two-dimensional surface where the viewer is in doubt as to whether the object depicted is real or a representation.

TV spot: a broadcast advertisement placed on television; also called a TV commercial.

type alignment: the style or arrangement of setting text type.

type family: several font designs contributing a range of style variations based upon a single typeface design.

type font: a complete set of letterforms, numerals, and signs—in a particular face, size, and style—that is required for written communication.

type style: the modifications in a typeface that create design variety while retaining the essential visual character of the face. These include variations in weight (light, medium, bold), width (condensed, regular, extended), and angle (Roman or upright, and italic), as well as elaborations on the basic form (outline, shaded, decorated).

typeface: the design of a single set of letterforms, numerals, and signs unified by consistent visual properties. These properties create the essential character, which remains recognizable even if the face is modified by design.

typography: the design and arrangement of letterforms in two-dimensional space (for print and screen-based media) and in space and time (for motion and interactive media).

unconventional advertising: advertising that "ambushes" the viewer; often it appears or is placed in unpaid media in the public environment—places and surfaces where advertising does not typically appear, such as the sidewalk or on wooden construction site walls; also called guerrilla advertising, stealth marketing, and nontraditional marketing.

unity: when all the graphic elements in a design are so interrelated that they form a greater whole; all the graphic elements look as though they belong together.

variation: a quality established by a break or modification in the pattern or by changing elements, such as the color, size, shape, spacing, position, and visual weight.

viral marketing: the use of a self-perpetuation mechanism, such as a Web site, to grow a user base in a manner similar to the spread of a virus; it also means a marketing phenomenon that facilitates and encourages people to pass along a marketing message.

visual: a broad term encompassing many kinds of representational, abstract, or nonobjective depictions—photographs, illustrations, drawings, paintings, prints, graphic elements and marks, and elemental images such as pictograms, signs, or symbols; also called images.

visual hierarchy: an arrangement of graphic elements according to emphasis.

visual identity: the visual and verbal articulation of a brand or group, including all pertinent design applications, such as letterhead, business cards, and packaging, among many other possible applications; also called brand identity and corporate identity.

visual weight: the illusion of physical weight on a two-dimensional surface.

Webisode: in advertising, a short audio or video presentation on the Web used to promote a brand or group, preview music, and present any type of information or entertainment.

Web site: a collection of "pages" or files linked together and made available on the World Wide Web; Web sites are authored and owned by companies, organizations, and individuals.

watchdog groups: public groups comprised of citizens (consumers) who protect the public against fraudulent or harmful advertising.

widget: a branded utility, essentially a microapplication, typically built on top of a Web service.

word spacing: the space between words.

BIBLIOGRAPHY

Advertising

Aitchison, Jim. *Cutting Edge Advertising: How to Create the World's Best Print for Brands in the 21st Century.* 2nd ed. Singapore and New York: Pearson Prentice Hall, 2004.

Berger, Warren. *Advertising Today.* London: Phaidon, 2001.

Bernstein, David, Beau Fraser, and Bill Schwab. *Death to All Sacred Cows: How Successful Business People Put the Old Rules Out to Pasture.* New York: Hyperion, 2008.

Fallon, Pat, and Fred Senn. *Juicing the Orange: How to Turn Creativity into a Powerful Business Advantage.* Boston: Harvard Business Press, 2006.

Fortini-Campbell, Lisa. *Hitting the Sweet Spot: How Consumer Insights Can Inspire Better Marketing and Advertising.* 3rd ed. London: Copy Workshop, 2001.

Goodrum, Charles, and Helen Dalrymple. *Advertising in America.* New York: Abrams, 1990.

Higgins, Denis. *The Art of Writing Advertising: Conversations with Masters of the Craft.* New York: McGraw-Hill, 2003.

Hopkins, Claude. *Scientific Advertising.* London: Waking Lion Press, 2008.

Lois, George. *$ellebrity: My Angling and Tangling with Famous People.* London and New York: Phaidon, 2003.

———. *George Lois: On His Creation of the Big Idea.* New York: Assouline, 2008.

Lucas, Gavin, and Michael Dorrian. *Guerrilla Advertising: Unconventional Brand Communication.* London: Laurence King Publishers, 2006.

McDonough, John, and Karen Egolf, eds. *The Advertising Age Encyclopedia of Advertising.* 3 vols. New York: Fitzroy Dearborn, 2003.

Ogilvy, David. *Confessions of an Advertising Man.* London: Southbank Publishing, 2004.

———. *Ogilvy on Advertising.* New York: Vintage, 1985.

Pincas, Stéphane, and Marc Loiseau. *History of Advertising.* Translated by Liz Attawell, Kim Sanderson, and Kelly Pennhaligon. Cologne and London: Taschen, 2008.

Ries, Al, and Jack Trout. *The 22 Immutable Laws of Marketing: Violate Them at Your Own Risk!* New York: HarperBusiness, 1994.

Robbs, Brett, and Deborah Morrison. *Idea Industry: How to Crack the Advertising Career Code.* New York: One Club Publishing, 2008.

Sullivan, Luke. *Hey, Whipple, Squeeze This: A Guide to Creating Great Ads.* 3rd ed. Hoboken, N.J.: John Wiley & Sons, 2008.

Vonk, Nancy, and Janet Kestin. *Pick Me: Breaking into Advertising and Staying There.* Hoboken, N.J.: John Wiley & Sons, 2005.

Wallas, Graham. *The Art of Thought.* London: Jonathan Cape, 1926.

Young, James W. *A Technique for Producing Ideas.* New York: McGraw Hill, 2003; Chicago: Advertising Publications, 1944.

Branding

Gobe, Marc. *Emotional Branding: The New Paradigm for Connecting Brands to People.* New York: Allworth Press, 2001.

Landa, Robin. *Designing Brand Experiences.* Clifton Park, N.Y.: Cengage Learning, 2006.

Neumeier, Marty. *The Brand Gap: How to Bridge the Distance Between Business Strategy and Design.* Berkeley, Calif.: Peachpit Press, 2003.

Roberts, Kevin. *Lovemarks: The Future Beyond Brands.* New York: PowerHouse Books, 2004.

———. *The Lovemarks Effect: Winning in the Consumer Revolution.* New York: PowerHouse Books, 2006.

Wheeler, Alina. *Designing Brand Identity: An Essential Guide for the Whole Branding Team.* 3rd ed. Hoboken, N.J.: John Wiley & Sons, 2009.

Composition and Design Principles

Arnheim, Rudolf. *Art and Visual Perception: A Psychology of the Creative Eye.* Berkeley: University of California Press, 2004.

Dondis, Donis A. *A Primer of Visual Literacy.* Cambridge, Masso: MIT Press, 1973.

Hofmann, Armin. *Graphic Design Manual: Principles and Practice.* Sulgen, Switzerland: A. Niggli, 1965.

Kandinsky, Wassily. *Point, Line, and Plane.* 2nd ed. New York: Museum of Non-Objective Painting, 1947.

Kepes, Gyorgy. *Language of Vision.* Chicago: Paul Theobald, 1961.

Landa, Robin. *Graphic Design Solutions.* 4th ed. Boston: Wadsworth, 2010.

Landa, Robin, Rose Gonnella, and Steven Brower. *2D: Visual Basics for Designers.* Boston: Cengage Learning, 2008.

Lidwell, William, Kritina Holden, and Jill Butler. *Universal Principles of Design*. Gloucester, Mass.: Rockport Publishers, 2003.

Wong, Wucius. *Principles of Form and Design*. New York: Van Nostrand Reinhold, 1993.

History

Drucker, Johanna, and Emily McVarish. *Graphic Design History: A Critical Guide*. Englewood Cliffs, N.J.: Prentice Hall, 2008.

Eskilson, Stephen J. *Graphic Design: A New History*. New Haven, Conn.: Yale University Press, 2007.

Fiell, Charlotte, and Peter Fiell. *Graphic Design for the 21st Century*. Cologne, Germany: Taschen, 2005.

"Graphic Design and Advertising Timeline." *Communication Arts* 41, 1 (1999): 80–95.

Heller, Steven, and Seymour Chwast. *Graphic Style: From Victorian to Digital*. New York: Harry N. Abrams, 2001.

————. *Illustration: A Visual History*. New York: Abrams, 2008.

Heller, Steven, and Elinor Pettit. *Graphic Design Timeline*. New York: Allworth Press, 2000.

Heller, Steven, and Mirko Ilic. *Icons of Graphic Design*. 2nd ed. London: Thames & Hudson, 2008.

Hollis, Richard. *Graphic Design: A Concise History*. London: Thames & Hudson Ltd, 2001.

————. *Swiss Graphic Design: The Origins and Growth of an International Style, 1920–1965*. New Haven, Conn.: Yale University Press, 2006.

Johnson, J. Stewart. *The Modern American Poster*. New York: The National Museum of Modern Art, Kyoto, and The Museum of Modern Art, New York, 1983.

Livingston, Alan, and Isabella Livingston. *Graphic Design and Designers*. New York: Thames & Hudson, Inc., 1992.

McDonough, John, and Karen Egolf, eds. *The Advertising Age Encyclopedia of Advertising*. 3 vols. New York: Fitzroy Dearborn, 2003.

Meggs, Philip B. *Meggs' History of Graphic Design*. 4th ed. Hoboken, N.J.: John Wiley & Sons, 2005.

Müller-Brockmann, Josef, and Shizuko Müller-Brockmann. *History of the Poster*. London and New York: Phaidon, 2004.

Poynor, Rick. *No More Rules: Graphic Design and Postmodernism*. New Haven, Conn.: Yale University Press, 2003.

Weill, Alain. *Graphic Design: A History*. New York: Harry N. Abrams, 2004.

Theory

Arnheim, Rudolf. *Visual Thinking*. Berkeley: University of California Press, 2004.

Bentham, Jeremy. *Bentham's Theory of Fictions*. Edited by C. K. Ogden. London: K. Paul, Trench, Trubner & Co., 1932.

Gombrich, E. H. *Art and Illusion*. Princeton, N.J.: Princeton University Press, 2000.

Kelly, George. *The Psychology of Personal Constructs*. New York: Norton, 1955.

Kubler, George. *The Shape of Time: Remarks on the History of Things*. Rev. ed. New Haven, Conn.: Yale University Press, 2008.

Ortega y Gasset, José. *Dehumanization of Art and Other Essays on Art, Culture and Literature*. Princeton, N.J.: Princeton University Press, 1968.

Panofsky, Erwin. *Meaning in the Visual Arts*. Chicago: University of Chicago Press, 1983.

Wolfflin, Heinrich. *Principles of Art History*. New York: Dover Publications, 1950.

Typography

Burke, Christopher. *Active Literature: Jan Tschichold and New Typography*. London: Hyphen Press, 2008.

Carter, Rob. *American Typography Today*. New York: Van Nostrand Reinhold, 1989.

Carter, Rob, Ben Day, and Philip B. Meggs. *Typographic Design: Form and Communication*. 3rd ed. New York: John Wiley & Sons, 2002.

Craig, James. *Basic Typography: A Design Manual*. New York: Watson-Guptill Publications, 1990.

————. *Designing with Type*. New York: Watson-Guptill Publications, 1992.

Dodd, Robin. *From Gutenberg to OpenType: An Illustrated History of Type from the Earliest Letterforms to the Latest Digital Fonts*. Dublin: Hartley and Marks Publishers, 2006.

Lupton, Ellen. *Thinking with Type: A Critical Guide for Designers, Writers, Editors, and Students*. New York: Princeton Architectural Press, 2004.

Meggs, Philip B. *Type and Image: The Language of Graphic Design*. New York: Van Nostrand Reinhold, 1989.

Müller, Lars. *Helvetica: Homage to a Typeface*. Baden, Switzerland: Lars Müller, 2002.

Perry, Michael. *Hand Job: A Catalog of Type*. New York: Princeton Architectural Press, 2007.

Ruder, Emil. *Typography*. New York: Hastings House, 1981 [1967].

Rüegg, Ruedi. *Basic Typography: Design with Letters*. New York: Van Nostrand Reinhold, 1989.

Solomon, Martin. *The Art of Typography: An Introduction to Typo.Icon.Ography*. New York: Watson-Guptill, 1986.

Spencer, Herbert. *Pioneers of Modern Typography*. Rev. ed. Cambridge, Mass.: MIT Press, 2004.

Spencer, Herbert, ed. *The Liberated Page: An Anthology of Major Typographic Experiments of This Century as Recorded in* Typographica *Magazine*. London: Lund Humphries, 1987.

Spiekermann, Erik, and E. M. Ginger. *Stop Stealing Sheep and Find Out How Type Works*. 2nd ed. Berkeley, Calif.: Adobe Press, 2002.

Tschichold, Jan. *The New Typography: A Handbook for Modern Designers*. Translated by Ruari McLean. Berkeley: University of California Press, 1995.

Weingart, Wolfgang. *My Way to Typography*. Baden, Switzerland: Lars Müller, 2000.

Zapf, Hermann. *Hermann Zapf and His Design Philosophy*. Chicago: Society of Typographic Arts, 1987.

Visualization

Berger, John. *Ways of Seeing*. New York: Penguin, 1990.

Chen Design Associates. *Fingerprint: The Art of Using Hand-Made Elements in Graphic Design*. Cincinnati, Ohio: HOW Design Books, 2006.

Gonnella, Rose, and Christopher Navetta. *Comp It Up*. Clifton Park, N.Y.: Delmar Cengage Learning, 2010.

Landa, Robin, and Rose Gonnella. *Visual Workout: A Creativity Workbook*. Clifton Park, N.Y.: Delmar Cengage Learning, 2004.

Miscellaneous

Gladwell, Malcolm. *The Tipping Point*. New York: Back Bay Books, 2007.

———. *What the Dog Saw: and Other Adventures*. New York: Little, Brown and Company, 2009.

Goffman, Erving. *Frame Analysis: An Essay on the Organization of Experience*. Cambridge, Mass.: Harvard University Press, 1974.

Miller, Geoffrey F. *Spent: Sex, Evolution, and Consumer Behavior*. New York: Viking, 2009.

Ropaille, Clotaire. *The Culture Code: An Ingenious Way to Understand Why People around the World Live and Buy as They Do*. New York: Broadway Books, 2007.

Smoke, Trudy, and Alan Robbins, eds. *The World of the Image: A Longman Topics Reader*. New York: Pearson Longman, 2006.

Tharp, Twyla, and Mark Reiter. *The Creative Habit: Learn It and Use It for Life*. New York: Simon & Schuster, 2006.

Vaihinger, Hans. *The Philosophy of "As If," a System of the Theoretical, Practical and Religious Fictions of Mankind*. Translated by C. K. Ogden. London: K. Paul, Trench, Trubner & Co., Ltd.; New York: Harcourt, Brace & Company, Inc., 1924.

Woodbridge, Homer E. *Essentials of English Composition*. New York: Harcourt, Brace and Howe, 1920.

Online Sources

PROFESSIONAL ORGANIZATIONS

American Advertising Federation: www.aaf.org
American Association of Advertising Agencies: www.aaaa.org
Art Directors Club of New York: www.adcglobal.org
The Advertising Council: www.adcouncil.org
American Institute of Graphic Arts (AIGA): www.aiga.org
AIGA Design Archives: http://designarchives.aiga.org
D&AD: www.dandad.org
Icograda: www.icograda.org
International Typographic Organization: www.atypi.org
The One Club: www.oneclub.org
Society of Illustrators: www.societyillustrators.org
The Type Directors Club: www.tdc.org

PUBLICATIONS

Ad Age: www.adage.com
Ad Age Advertising Century Report: www.adage.com/century
Adweek: www.adweek.com
Brandweek: www.brandweek.com
CMYK magazine: www.cmykmag.com
Communication Arts: www.commarts.com
Contagious Magazine: www.contagious.com
Creativity magazine: www.creativity-online.com
HOW magazine: www.howdesign.com
Lurzuers Archive: www.lurzuersarchive.com
Print: www.printmag.com
Step Inside Design: www.stepinsidedesign.com

BLOGS

Ad Freak: adweek.blogs.com/adfreak
Ads of the World: http://adsoftheworld.com
Design Blog Cooper-Hewitt: blog.cooperhewitt.org
Design Observer: www.designobserver.com
Marketing as Service: http://thedrewblog.com
Media Decoder: http://mediadecoder.blogs.nytimes.com
Seth's Blog: http://sethgodin.typepad.com
Under Consideration: www.underconsideration.com
WSJ Blogs: http://blogs.wsj.com

INDEX